THE RISE OF THE UNITED ASSOCIATION

THE RISE

OF THE UNITED ASSOCIATION:

National Unionism in the Pipe Trades, 1884-1924

MARTIN SEGAL

PUBLISHED BY THE WERTHEIM COMMITTEE, HARVARD UNIVERSITY

Distributed by Harvard University Press, Cambridge, Massachusetts

1970

196063

*Distributed in Great Britain by Oxford University Press, **London***

Library of Congress Catalog Card Number 79-101012
SBN-674-77300-4

Printed in the United States of America

FOREWORD

For its national and local officers, and for its present three hundred thousand members, the Rise of the United Association constitutes a definitive account of the struggle to organize and the successful establishment of national unionism in the pipe trades. The leaders of the United Association today are appropriately concerned that present officers and members have a deeper appreciation and dispassionate view of the problems and choices, the conflicts and obstacles, and the ideals and resolution which characterized the founding fathers of the union and those who helped to shape the persistent policies of the organization. Citizenship in a union should require no less an understanding of its history than citizenship in our country should draw upon the heritage of national institutions and values.

The history of the United Association has been grossly neglected. No detailed account exists of the rise of this significant national union. The present volume treats the period from the early efforts in the 1880's to form national unions of plumbers and steamfitters to the divide of the Great Depression. The neglected events of this early period are so decisive and significant to the institutions, policies and character of the United Association — and to the labor movement as well — that they warrent a detailed account. The subsequent events, from the 1930's on, would result in an inordinately long single volume if they were to be included with this careful review of the formative years.

For scholars and students of the labor movement and collective bargaining, Professor Martin Segal of Dartmouth College has helped us to enrich our analysis of the rise of national unions in local market industries, at least in the case of the United Association, by pointing to a number of factors often neglected. The contribution of the Knights of Labor in promoting organization among craft workers is better understood. The regulation of apprenticeship is particularly significant. The persistent ideal of a national union and the impact of dedicated union leaders and administrators was of independent consequence. The role of Gompers and the Federation in patiently insisting upon merger and accommodation among competing pipe trade organizations was a factor of considerable importance.

As concerns labor organizations and collective bargaining, this volume should help one to recognize how significant a keener perception of the formative years is to current and future problems and decisions. The options in private and public policy, as well as procedures to confront new challenges and opportunities, are shaped very deeply by the historical forms, administrative policies and leadership styles of a national union.

John T. Dunlop

CONTENTS

TABLES

ILLUSTRATIONS

(following page 98)

Title page of the 1886 constitution of the International Association of Journeymen Plumbers, Steam Fitters and Gas Fitters — one of the predecessors of the United Association

Letter written on April 25, 1889 by Patrick J. Quinlan to Richard O'Brien

Title page of UA constitution printed in 1891 — the earliest printed constitution available

Patrick J. Quinlan, one of the founders and first president of the UA

Richard A. O'Brien, one of the founders and first secretary-treasurer of the UA

W. J. Spencer, first national organizer of the UA

John Alpine, president of the UA, 1906–1919

Thomas Burke, secretary-treasurer of the UA, 1909–1941

John Mangan, one of the founders of LU 597 and vice-president of the UA, 1921–1930

John Coefield, president of the UA, 1919–1940

Power Laboratory in the Washburn Training School where the steam fitters' apprentices of LU 597 received their training

AUTHOR'S PREFACE

THIS VOLUME is a history of the national union of plumbers, steam fitters, gas fitters, and other workers in the pipe trades — the union known today as the United Association of Journeymen and Apprentices of the Plumbing and Pipe Fitting Industry of the United States and Canada. As indicated in the first chapter, the volume concentrates on the rise and development of the national organization rather than on the history of the local UA unions. Indeed, the main theme of the volume is the process through which the United Association, originally a loose federation of locals composed largely of plumbers, developed into a strong national union of all the pipe trades — plumbers, steam fitters, gas fitters, sprinkler fitters, and others.

This study could not have been written without the generous cooperation of the officials of the United Association. I am indebted to General President Peter T. Schoemann, former Secretary-Treasurer William C. O'Neill, and Assistant General President Martin J. Ward for making available to me the documents and publications in the U.A. library, and to Assistant Research Director Joseph Cribben for assistance in the processing of these documents and publications. I am also indebted to Joseph P. Corcoran, Director of the UA.'s Training Department for Apprentices and Journeymen, and to Norman F. Piron, Assistant Director of that department for providing me with valuable information concerning the technical aspects of the pipe crafts.

I also wish to acknowledge the help from librarians in several libraries which house important documents pertaining to the history of the United Association. In particular I am indebted to Miss Margaret Lough, History Library, Johns Hopkins University; Mrs. Claire Brown, Industrial Relations Library, Harvard University; Miss Virginia Close, Baker Library, Dartmouth College; and the librarians at the Detroit Public Library, Wayne State University, the New York State Department of Labor Library and the library of the U.S. Department of Labor.

My greatest debt is to John T. Dunlop who originally suggested the undertaking of this study and who, throughout the period of research and writing, provided both encouragement and valuable critique of the manuscript.

Martin Segal

Geneva, 1969.

THE RISE OF THE UNITED ASSOCIATION

Chapter 1

Introduction

A WELL-KNOWN economist who read an earlier version of this study referred to the United Association as "this successful 'nuts and bolts union.'" In a sense, this is a correct description, for the organization of the pipe trades has always concentrated its main efforts on the "nuts and bolts" of trade unionism — wages, benefits, apprenticeship, and jurisdiction. Yet the phrase does not adequately convey the quality that has perhaps always been the dominant characteristic of the United Association — its highly pragmatic approach to the problems it faced. The pragmatism of the UA — its flexibility and ability to seek new solutions where old ones had failed — was an important factor during the critical decades of its development into the national union of plumbers, steam fitters, gas fitters, and other pipe crafts. And it is perhaps this attribute that explains why many of the UA leaders — brought up as they were in the institutional tradition of their union — have played a major role in the national and local bodies of the building trades and in the governing councils of the AFL.

This volume is an historical study of the United Association — or to use its official name during the first decades of its existence — The United Association of Journeymen Plumbers, Gas Fitters, Steam Fitters and Steam Fitters' Helpers.* A study of a complex institution must inevitably select the themes that it will develop. The present volume gives only limited attention to the history of United Association locals and concentrates on the involved process of the rise and development of the national organization. The study covers a span of forty years that represent a crucial period in the history of national

* The official name of the union has been modified a few times. Its present name is United Association of Journeymen and Apprentices, of the Plumbing and Pipe Fitting Industry. The term "pipe fitting trades" or "pipe fitting crafts" was used historically to denote the basic crafts of plumbers, gas fitters, and steam fitters. In this volume, the term "pipe trades" or "pipe crafts" will be used to identify these crafts as a group.

unionism in the pipe trades. At the beginning of this period — in the early 1880's — local unions of plumbers, steam fitters, and gas fitters were making their first attempts to form national organizations; by the mid 1920's — the end of the period — the United Association had been in existence for three and a half decades, was unchallenged in its position as the national union of the pipe trades, and was one of the strongest organizations in the biulding trades and in the AFL.

The development of the United Association — the problems that it had to face and the policies that it evolved — may be best understood in the context of the changing technological and economic environment in which the pipe trades have operated. Accordingly, the following two sections of the chapter will deal with this environment.* The final section will outline briefly the content of the study.

The Pipe Crafts

By the mid 1880's — the time of the founding of their first national unions — the journeymen employed in the plumbing and heating industries could be classified without any serious ambiguity into three basic crafts: plumbers, steam and hot-water fitters, and gas fitters. Of the three crafts, the plumbers were the most numerous and remained so throughout the period covered by the study. The U.S. Census does not provide us with data on the number of journeymen in each of the crafts,[1] but an idea of their relative numerical strength in the 1880's may be gained from the data on union membership in the New York region. A rather conservative estimate would indicate that in the mid-1880's the plumbers constituted about 70 per cent of the journeymen. The same data suggest that the steam fitters comprised about 20 per cent, and the gas fitters about 10 per cent.[2] In the following decade, the relative position of the steam fitters appears to have increased somewhat — perhaps reaching the level of 25 per cent of the combined number of journeymen in the three crafts.[3]

The plumbers represented not only the most numerous but also, by far, the oldest of the three crafts.[4] As the name implies (from *plumbum* — Latin for lead) the plumbers were traditionally workers in lead.[5] Lead is highly malleable and has a relatively low melting

---

* The following two sections deal primarily with the technological and technical environment of the pipe trades as it existed and developed in the years 1880–1910. Economic and technological changes that were of special importance to the course of United Association history after 1910 will be considered in later chapters.

point. The metal could thus be shaped fairly easily into pipes which could be then soldered together. As a result from the pre-Roman period on lead was widely used for making pipes for the conveyance of water and drainage.

During the early decades of the nineteenth century the plumbers in America used lead for a variety of purposes. They lined troughs, made lead pipe for rain leaders or conveyance of water from outside sources, beat out pantry sinks or basins, and made and installed lead linings in wooden bathtubs. They also made their own solder and soldering irons and fashioned crude fire pots. The early American plumbers both made articles out of lead and installed them in households and buildings.

During the decade of the 1840's American cities generally installed municipal systems of pressurized water supply, and of sanitary drainage connected with public sewerage systems. These developments made possible a general installation of plumbing fixtures in private and public buildings joined to outside water and drainage systems. The result was a basic change in the nature of the plumber's work. Instead of a general worker in lead he became a craftsman concerned primarily with the means of safe removal of waste and sewage matter to public sewers or other accepted places of deposit; with the exclusion of sewage air and gas from buildings; and with the introduction of proper water supply to private and public buildings.

The changes in the plumber's functions did not eliminate the need for his basic skill in shaping articles of lead and of joining lead pipes. Indeed this skill now found a wide application. To be sure, by the time of the 1840's lead pipe was already manufactured in special plants and sold commercially. But where there was a need for special connections and pipe shapes near the installed fixtures, the plumber had to fashion his own pipe formations and pipe fittings.[6] More importantly, whether he worked with pipe manufactured by others, or with hand-made pipe, the plumber had to employ constantly his very special skill of wiping joints — that is joining lead pipe, after shaping and fitting it, by means of melted solder, and wiping the connection with special cloth to achieve a smooth surface. The plumber also fashioned traps from lead sheets to be installed in the drains of individuals fixtures. (The traps were an essential part of plumbing installations because they prevented the escape of noxious odors and sewer gases through the openings of the plumbing fixtures.) And, finally, during the 1850's and 1860's, the plumber still made by hand parts of fixtures — service boxes for closet tanks, linings for bathtubs and sinks, and water hydrants.

During the decades following the Civil War there were many important improvements in the design of plumbing systems and of plumbing fixtures. Thus a major development was the introduction of vent pipes connected to the drains at the trap outlets. This improvement, which came into wide use in the late 1870's, provided an effective way of preventing fixture trap seals (water in the traps) from being lost because of siphonage or back pressure conditions in the drains, and thus proved to be an effective means of eliminating the problem of ordors and sewer gas escaping through fixture outlets. The result was that the installation of water closets and other fixtures connected with the sewage system within the buildings and dwellings became generally accepted. Other developments were initiated by manufacturers of plumbing fixtures. In the 1880's and 1890's sinks and bathtubs made of enameled cast iron were put on the market; at the same time vitreous china water closets with improved flush action and built-in traps were introduced. These fixtures not only provided new high standards of sanitation but were reasonably priced and could be widely distributed and installed.

While these improvements increased the demand for the services of the plumber, they largely put an end to his role as a maker of fixtures. Also, another set of technological changes greatly affected other aspects of his work.

1) During the first half of the nineteenth century there were important improvements in the methods of manufacturing cast iron pipe and of reducing its resistance to corrosion. By the 1870's cast iron pipe was generally used, instead of lead pipe, in the installation of soil and waste piping (that is, piping that drained human and nonhuman waste to sewer connections). Cast iron pipe was cheaper than lead and easier to install. A major reason was that, unlike the lead equivalent, cast iron pipe was joined by the process of caulking rather than "wiping joints" or soldering. (The operation of caulking is performed by stopping the joint with tow, oakum, or other filling material, and then "ramming it home.")

2) In the post Civil War decades manufacturers began to put a variety of ready-made plumbing traps on the market. These were made of cast iron or cast lead, and were generally superior to those

fashioned by the plumbers. By that time solder was already also manufactured outside plumbers' shops and sold commercially.

3) In the late 1880's and 1890's galvanized wrought iron pipe was widely introduced as a means of carrying water supply in buildings. The wrought iron pipe was joined either by screwing threaded pieces of pipe or by means of several pipe fitting devices developed to facilitate connecting threaded pipes.

4) During the 1880's and 1890's there appeared a variety of special devices for joining pipes — cast iron fittings of many shapes, wrought iron couplings, ferrules attached to lead pipes or pipe bends, and flanges. All of these facilitated and speeded up the process.

5) The changes in plumbing supplies continued during the first decades of the twentieth century. Thus during that period manufacturers introduced ready-made brass joints; nickel-plated brass pipe that could be screwed tight by the means of screw nuts and rubber washers; and brass tubing that was meant to supplant lead pipe joints in basins and sinks.

The above technological changes had important effects on the nature of the plumbers' work. One was to reduce his opportunity to utilize his traditionally unique skill — that is, working with lead and joining lead pipes. Another effect was to change the relative allocation of working time between the shop and the job site. To a much greater degree than in any previous period the plumber now became a mechanic concerned with installation rather than with making or processing articles used in the plumbing system.

After all these changes, the craft still required many special skills. Indeed, during the 1890's and the following years plumbing was viewed by informed contemporaries as "one of the most difficult of trades." [7] Thus lead piping — involving a considerable amount of wiping joints — was generally used until the 1920's in the waste and vent pipe adjacent to the installed fixtures, in connecting fixtures with the main piping, and in the more intricate runs of waste pipes. The improvements and greater complexity of plumbing installation — particularly in the very large commercial and industrial buildings — called for an increasing practical knowledge of some aspects of hydraulics and pneumatics; the availability of many types of pipe fittings, connections, and the like required more knowledge of the characteristics of various metals and plumbing materials; and the new types of pipe called for a greater variety of manipulative skills. Finally, as urban communities began to introduce codes and ordinances pertaining to plumbing, the knowledge of these regulations became necessary to the practice of the craft.

The second of the pipe crafts — the steam and hot water fitters — is of much more recent origin.[8] Some steam heating was apparently installed in industrial plants as early as 1817, and some hot water heating in the 1840's. But neither system appears to have been widely used until the 1870's.[9] Indeed, the Bureau of the Census did not include the steam fitters in its list of occupations until the 1890 Census. (In 1880 most of the steam fitters were probably included in a group called "plumbers and gas fitters." By 1890 this group was called "plumbers, gas fitters and steam fitters.")

The work of the steam fitters consisted originally of installing and connecting pipes, valves, pipe fittings, traps, radiators, and boilers that constituted the heating system of industrial plants and of public and private buildings. As improvements were made in the design and equipment (in the use of pumps to return water obtained from condensation to the boiler, in the utilization of exhaust steam for heating in industrial plants, and in the type of radiators to be installed), the work of steam fitters became more complex. However, neither these improvements nor other technological changes introduced in the years 1880–1910 drastically affected the installation of the steam and hot water heating system.

Until about the early 1870's the pipe used in steam and hot water heating installations was made of cast iron. In the early 1870's wrought iron pipe was introduced, and by the time of the 1880's it largely supplanted the cast iron product. Thus, in the 1880's and in the following decades the basic skills of the steam fitters involved, in addition to measuring and cutting of iron pipes, both the process of caulking and the process of connecting threaded pipe, pipe fittings, and valves. In working with wrought iron pipe, the steam fitters used many of the materials (various types of pipe fittings) and tools (taps and dies for threading) that were also used by the plumbers.

Although installation of heating systems provided by far most of the work for the steam fitters, by the 1880's and 1890's the fitters were also employed on other types of installations. The most important proved to be refrigerating equipment.[10] In the northern part of the country mechanical refrigeration was being widely introduced in breweries and meat packing plants; in the south refrigeration machines were used in the manufacture of ice. Extensive piping was required not only for the conveyance of the refrigerant (ammonia) but also for circulation of liquids to be chilled (salt brine in meat packing plants). The growth of refrigeration was thus reflected in a rising demand for the service of craftsmen skilled in the installation of iron pipe.

The relatively early employment of steam fitters in installing refrigeration equipment foreshadowed, in effect, the way in which technological changes influenced their work from 1890 on. These changes influenced the nature of the work not so much by modifying the techniques of hot water and steam heating systems as by the spread of piping installations — requiring their service — to other types of construction projects.

The third of the pipe fitting crafts, the gas fitters, traced its origin to 1820–1850, the period during which gas lighting was introduced, spreading rapidly to the major urban areas.[11] During the early years the installation of gas piping within the building was done by journeymen plumbers, and tinners, and apparently lead pipe was used. Gas fitting involved a more limited range of duties (for example, there was no need to fashion traps), and, as a result, some journeymen began to specialize in this particular installation.

By the 1880's the functions of the gas fitters were well defined. They consisted of cutting, fitting, and installing piping that distributed gas inside the building; installing gas fixtures; testing of the system for leakage by means of a special pump and spring or mercury gauge; and of connecting tubes in gas fixtures with the gas pipes. In some cases gas fitters who worked for plumbing and gas fitting contractors also installed the service pipes that connected the street gas main with the piping inside the building; more commonly this was done by workers employed by the gas company.

The service pipe was made either of cast or wrought iron. But the piping system that distributed gas throughout the building was made by the 1880's — and in the following three decades — of wrought iron. (In some cases where the piping was exposed — for example, in offices — copper or polished brass pipe was used.) The gas pipes were usually connected with threaded (screw) joints and threaded pipe fitting. The gas companies normally prescribed the sizes of pipes required to convey gas to a given number of outlets; however, the gas fitters exercised considerable discretion in determining many aspects of the installation of the piping system inside the particular buildings.

The preceding discussion makes apparent that one of the effects of the technical changes in plumbing — that is, of the substitution of iron pipe for lead pipe, and of the increased emphasis on installation at job site rather than shop work — was to reduce the difference between the work of the plumbers and that of the other two pipe crafts. This was clearly recognized by leaders of the early unions.

The more we study the time we live in, and the agencies at work . . . the sooner we will recognize the transformation going on — especially in the plumbing branch, which tends to make us all pipers . . . In some places, plumbers work at the three branches. Again gas fitters in many cases work more on plumbing work than at gas fitting, while very many steam fitters take a turn at gas fitting and plumbing in the shape of galvanized iron and brass pipe. . . . Our interests and other branches are interwoven; we are one; we cannot separate ourselves if we would and we should not if we could.[12]

These statements, made in 1886 by Patrick Coyle, the dominant figure of the period in the unionism of the pipe crafts, exaggerated the long-run effects of the technical change in the plumbing craft. The three crafts retained their separate identities and did not become "all pipers." Nevertheless, Coyle's statement illustrates the deep awareness, on the part of the early unionists, of the impact of technological changes. This awarness influenced union policies concerned with such important matters as the issue of bringing all pipe crafts into one national organization and the problem of drawing strict lines between the jurisdictions of these crafts.

In addition to journeymen the work force of the pipe industry also consisted of helpers and apprentices. The relative position of these workers in the particular crafts requires a brief description.

The job of helper was firmly established in steam and hot water fitting. Because journeymen fitters had to lift, work with, and install heavy pipes, coils, and fixtures, they were normally assisted by less-skilled workers — the so-called steam fitters' helpers. In later years, after 1900, formal provisions were made in union constitutions whereby the helpers' could eventually become journeymen. Basically, however, during the 1880–1910 period and even in later decades the job of steam fitter's helper was not viewed as preparing one for a journeyman's status. Neither the employers nor the unions imposed any age restrictions on the helpers, and being a steam fitter's helper could, and very frequently did, become a lifetime occupation.

The steam and hot water fitters did not have any tradition of apprenticeship training and, in fact, never used the term "apprentice" in connection with their work. The same was true of the gas fitters. The latter craft normally worked without any assistance; however, some of the work that required less skill (for instance, connecting tubes in the fixtures with the gas pipes) was sometimes performed by a group of workers whose skills were more limited — the so-called "fixture hangers."

The position of apprentices and helpers in the plumbing craft was more complicated. The plumbers had a tradition of indentured apprenticeship dating back to the English guilds. When plumbers still fashioned articles or pieces of pipe out of lead and made plumbing traps, much of an apprentice's time was spent in the master's shop. While the apprentices were primarily learners, they also assisted in the shops where they worked. During the process of installation, however (at the job site), the plumbers also relied on the assistance of "helpers." These workers carried the tools and assisted in tasks requiring considerable physical effort; as a rule they had little opportunity to become journeymen plumbers, and were presumably clearly distinguished from the apprentices. As the amount of work in the shop diminished and the work performed at the site increased both in amount and in complexity, the distinction between apprentices and helpers became blurred. The apprentices were learning most of the skills by observing, helping, and performing their tasks during the work on the site; the helpers, while assisting the journeymen, could now observe virtually the whole range of the plumbers' work.[13]

The blurring of the distinction between the two types of workers was reflected in the common usage of the terms "apprentice" and "helper." In the 1880's and 1890's many plumbers considered the term "helper" as synonymous with "apprentice."[14] This practice was so widespread that in 1897 the leaders of the United Association considered it advisable to insert a special provision in the constitution dealing with the matter. The provision stated that "the term helper shall not be used in connection with term apprentice by the United Association."[15]

The actual conditions of plumbing apprentices and helpers in the 1880–1910 period varied considerably in different areas. In some cases the journeymen considered their assistants as apprentices in the traditional sense; in other cases the boys were viewed as helpers whose main duty was to assist the journeyman but who would presumably learn the craft through a process of observation and eventual increase in the scope of assigned tasks. In still other situations there were some boys who were apprenticed to the master plumber, and others who were hired on a more temporary basis to carry the tools and assist the plumber in difficult tasks. Yet even in the latter case it was recognized that, if employed for any length of time, these workers could pick up at least some aspects of the craft.

The Plumbing and Heating Industry

The majority of the pipe trades have always worked for so-called specialty contractors — plumbing and heating firms which acted as sub-contractors to general building contractors or as separate prime contractors to the owners of buildings or architects.[16] These firms represented a wide range of types and specializations. Some employed only plumbers and did only plumbing work; others combined plumbing with some gas fitting and also employed gas fitters. Some firms did plumbing, gas fitting, and steam and hot water fitting work, and employed all three crafts. And, finally, many firms specialized only in heating work and employed only steam fitters and steam fitters' helpers. In addition, within each group some shops could handle large projects, both residential and nonresidential, while others worked on smaller projects or primarily did remodeling and repairs.[17]

Although at any point of time the firms specialized in a particular kind of work, for many of them the boundaries were not rigid. Depending on circumstances, a plumbing shop could add gas fitting or steam fitting; a steam fitting firm could branch out into gas fitting or even plumbing; and a repair shop could, under favorable conditions, expand into work on additions to building or small residential construction.

The plumbing industry and the steam heating industry had many common characteristics, and in many respects no hard and fast line could be drawn between them (gas fitting was usually combined either with plumbing or steam heating). But, as the data in Table 1 indicate, there have also been some notable differences.

The data come from the only really complete Census of Construction — that of 1939. By that time hot water and other types of mechanical heating had become much more widespread in smaller dwellings (one-or two-family houses) than they were in the last decades of the nineteenth and the first decade of the twentieth centuries. This explains the relatively large number of establishments that performed both plumbing and heating work. But in the present context the more interesting aspect of the data is the contrast in the number and size of establishments that did only heating and piping and those that performed only plumbing work. As can be seen, the plumbing establishments were much more numerous than the heating firms; a much smaller proportion of them did work whose annual value equalled or exceeded $25,000; and the average value of work per establishment was less than one-third that of the heating industry.

TABLE 1. Establishments in the Pipe Trades,[a] 1939.

Type of establishment	Number of establishments	Per cent of establishments with value of work performed $25,000 and over	Value of work performed per establishment (annual)
Heating and piping	2,882	25.7	$26,214
Heating, piping, and plumbing	13,166	16.5	$19,070
Plumbing	16,609	5.5	$ 8,509

[a] Excluding 4455 establishments which in addition to "Heating and Piping and Plumbing" did "Sheet Metal Work" and 1322 establishments in plumbing whose annual value of work was less than $500.

Source: Computed from data in Bureau of the Census, Census of Business 1939, Volume IV, Construction 1939 (Washington, 1943), Table 1a.

In the absence of contemporary statistics we cannot be certain that the differences between heating and plumbing businesses shown in Table 1 were equally pronounced during the earlier decades. The data are, however, supported by the more aggregate statistics pertaining to 1929, and are consistent with such descriptions of the two industries as are available in earlier writings.[18] Thus an economist who examined plumbing and steam heating in connection with a study of helpers and apprentices drew the following contrast between the conditions of the two industries at the beginning of the present century:

Plumbing is predominantly an industry of small shops. There are, of course, large jobs requiring contractors of considerable capital and responsibility; but a great part of plumbing of a city consists of small jobs, putting in a single closet, sink or bathtub. These small jobs, together with a large amount of repair work, afford a means of livelihood for the master plumber with little capital, and offer a field of work for the low-grade mechanic . . . In steam fitting there is not the same likelihood that so many small shops will be established. Steam fitting jobs are usually the installations of large plants, work upon which is done as a unit. The contractor must possess some capital and must be a man of considerable responsibility.[19]

The differences in the economic characteristics of plumbing and steam heating industries were also reflected in the statements and writings of the unionists. Throughout the first decades of UA history union leaders and members made numerous references to the fact that the plumbing industry was characterized by the presence of very small enterprises — some of them "one man shops" and some consisting of only a few partners.[20] In contrast, no such references were made with respect to the steam heating industry.

The preceding discussion should not suggest that steam and hot water heating enterprises represented in any sense a highly concentrated or monopolistic industry. During the first decades of national unionism in the pipe trades, steam and hot water heating was, in fact, done mainly in relatively large structures such as public or office buildings; and also the pipe fitting performed in connection with refrigeration, or with hydraulically operated elevators, involved establishments that would be considered large in the pipe industry. But in every major city there were several steam heating establishments and a general contractor could also, at times, subcontract the work to a firm from another city. Moreover, as compared with much of manufacturing, the entry into the heating business was not difficult, and the costs of starting business relatively low.[21] For example, in 1929 the average value of equipment in the reporting establishments of heating and piping — all of them doing annual business of $25,000 or more — was only $4248, hardly a sum that could provide an important barrier to entry into the industry.[22]

The entry into the plumbing industry was actually easier than into steam heating. Indeed, in order to operate as a "one-man shop" all one needed, in addition to a license (if such was required), was a kit of tools and some access to a supplier who would sell the necessary materials at a discount. Frequently, such access was easily obtained, since many dealers of plumbing supplies — eager to obtain new customers — would offer both credit and discounts to journeymen who planned to establish their own shops.[23] Once a small shop was established it usually did work on maintenance and repairs. But, in addition, many small shops had opportunities to do work on remodeling of residences or even on plumbing installations in small new houses.

Since the owners of small shops lacked working capital and were frequently unable to obtain large credit with suppliers, and, since they also lacked experience in estimating costs or in managing large crews, small plumbing enterprises would not normally perform any work on such large construction projects as commercial or industrial buildings, or schools and apartment houses. Nevertheless, the ease of entry into the industry clearly had an important effect on the extent of competition prevailing among the larger plumbing firms. For one thing, smaller firms competed with some larger ones for work on repairs and single-family houses. Secondly, and more importantly, with relatively free entry there was always the opportunity for new firms to expand, accumulate working capital, secure longer lines of credit, and thus threaten the position of the established shops in bidding for work on larger projects. The result was that a high degree of interfirm competition existed throughout the entire range of establishments in the plumbing industry.[24]

The competitive pressures that existed in the plumbing industry— and to a large extent also in the steam heating industry — led at various times to attempts to reduce competition among the shops that did business in a particular city or locality. Thus in some areas contractors resorted to collective action designed to "control competition" in bidding on contracts; in other areas associations of contractors made attempts to limit the number of plumbing or steam heating firms that would operate in the local market.[25]

Another problem which frequently elicited collective action among employers — action that also involved occasional cooperation of the local unions — was that of distribution of materials and supplies. While this problem appeared to be particularly acute in the plumbing industry, it was also, at least in 1880–1910, a major concern of the master steam fitters.

The cost of materials and supplies has always represented a very important share of the total cost of plumbing and steam fitting installations. This share has varied depending on the nature of work, being generally relatively low in the repair work performed by the small shops. Yet even in the case of the very smallest plumbing shops whose annual business in 1939 was less than $5000 it represented 37.6 per cent of the value of work performed. In installations performed by large plumbing firms the share of materials in 1939 was about 55 per cent. Very similar variations among the firms — between 40 and 54 per cent — are indicated also in the case of heating contractors. Both in 1929 and 1939 the average share of the cost of materials in the total cost of plumbing and heating installations was about 52 per cent.[26]

Since costs of materials have constituted such a large share of the total costs of installations, it has always been important to the plumbing and steam heating contractors that they should act as the final distributors or retailers of plumbing and heating supplies, that is, that they should be both sellers and installers of plumbing and heating equipment. The profit on the sales of plumbing and heating materials to the general contractor, to the owner-builder or to any house owner contracting for repairs would become a very substantial part of overall returns from business, determining in many cases whether a particular shop could survive.[27] However, the plumbing and steam heating contractors could successfully act as retailers only if the jobbers or wholesalers who dealt with and represented the manufacturers of materials would refuse to sell directly to general contractors, to owners of buildings, and to the public in general. Accordingly, the plumbing and heating contractors resorted, at various times, to collective action, such as boycotts of certain dealers, to compel the jobbers and the manufacturers to observe "the regular channels of trade," that is manufacturer to jobber to specialty contractor, in the flow of materials.[28]

The problem of the channels of distribution of plumbing materials has been an important issue in the industry ever since the period of its rapid growth, 1880–1900. Indeed the contractors' desire to protect themselves "against the dealers and manufacturers who treat buyers of material (whether plumbers or not) alike" was one of the important factors that led to the founding, in June 1883, of the National Association of Master Plumbers — essentially an association of local bodies of plumbing contractors already in existence in many cities.[29] Similarly, the problem of obtaining discounts from dealers and manufacturers of heating apparatus and supplies, and of barring sales of such materials to customers outside the trade became a major concern of the National Association of Master Steam and Hot Water Fitters which was founded in Chicago in 1889. From the very beginning of its existence, this association — a federation of local associations of steam heating contractors — carried on a vigorous campaign to obtain for its members the sole right of acting as retailers of heating supplies.[30]

During the years 1880–1900 most American cities passed local ordinances that dealt with construction of buildings, and with the standards of their sanitation, ventilation, and fire protection.[31] These ordinances instituted regulation of a whole range of construction activities, and particularly of plumbing. Indeed, the new plumbing codes were frequently quite detailed, specifying in some cases not only the requirements concerning drainage, venting, or trapping but also the size and type of pipe to be installed and even the methods of pipe fitting.[32]

The plumbing contractors have always shown a very strong interest in the substantive contents of the codes pertaining to their industry, and in the personnel who would administer them — the plumbing inspectors.[33] In many cases the local master plumbers were instrumental either in establishing such codes or in partly determining their content.[34] To some extent this interest undoubtedly reflected the concern of those most familiar with the actual or potential hazards of faulty plumbing installations. But there were also purely economic motivations. Plumbing codes impose minimum standards of plumbing installations on builders and home owners. If such standards are relatively high — for example, if they require a great deal of venting of individual fixtures — they may, given favorable demand conditions, increase the total volume of business available to the local contractors.[35]

In addition to the restrictions imposed by building ordinances the plumbing industry (though not steam fitting) has also been generally regulated by state and municipal licensing. Occupational licensing of plumbers appears to have started in the early 1890's.[36] In the following years it was introduced in several states and in numerous municipalities.

As in the case of building codes, the licensing laws of individual communities and states varied considerably. In some cases the laws required that only master plumbers be licensed; in other cases the requirements extended to journeymen. Significant differences also existed in the provisions pertaining to requirements for the licensees, methods of administration, fees, and other factors.

Licensing was strongly supported by local associations of contractors and local unions. Indeed, these organizations played an important role in lobbying for and, at times, in formulating such legislation.[37] As a result of their experience in the industry, both contractors and union leaders were keenly aware of the fact that the licensing of plumbers could make a contribution to the protection of the public. However, licensing could also bring benefits to the organized contractors and journeymen of particular areas.

1) Since many laws required examinations of prospective licensees, they could be expected to bar from the industry some of the less-experienced and less-skilled contractors and workers. But it was precisely the relatively inexperienced shop owners and the workers who could not qualify as first-class mechanics who posed the threat of price cutting and "unfair competition" among the contractors, and of undermining union rates among the journeymen.[38]

2) Licensing legislation would hardly pass if it were to bar those who had been working as plumbers prior to the enactment of the laws. Thus in actual practice the regulation of entry into plumbing resulting from licensing would apply in the main to the newcomers rather than to those who were already operating as contractors or working as journeymen at the time the laws were passed.[39]

3) Some licensing laws favored the local master plumbers because they required that licensed contractors have an established business within the limits of the particular municipalities. The effect was that local contractors were protected from competition from other towns.[40]

Licensing naturally made entry into the industry more difficult, and, as a result, it probably reduced the number of master plumbers in certain areas and also affected the supply journeymen. But its importance should not be exaggerated. Licensing laws have obviously not transformed the structure of the industry. As indicated by the statistics cited previously, plumbing has been, since its early days, a competitive industry characterized by relatively easy entry and large numbers of firms.

Outline of the Study

The span of forty years of unionism in the pipe trades covered in this study may be divided roughly into four periods: the years 1884–1889 which witnessed the beginning of the first national organization of the pipe trades and ended with the founding of the United Association; the period of 1889–1897, the early years of the newly founded UA; the crucial years 1898–1914 during which the UA was transformed into an important national union and absorbed thousands of steam fitters previously organized in another national union; and the decade of 1914–1924, a period during which the UA solidified its position as the national union of all the pipe trades and one of the influential organizations in the building trades. The chapters of the study follow in their basic order this chronological outline of the rise and development of national unionism in the pipe trades.

Chapter 2 describes the experience of the first national organizations of plumbers, steam fitters, and gas fitters, and deals with the founding of the United Association. As will be seen, some of the reasons for its founding were essentially the same as those that underlay the organization of other national unions — for instance, a desire on the part of the local unions to institute a strike fund. A unique aspect of the founding of the UA was the issue of apprenticeship. The United Association has been long known for its deep interest and success in establishing apprenticeship programs. It is thus significant that a desire to institute apprenticeship regulation on a national scale was an important factor motivating the local unions to band together to organize the UA.

Chapter 3 deals with the second period in the development of national unionism among the pipe trades — the early years of the United Association (1889–1897). As described in the chapter, during that period the UA essentially constituted a loose federation of autonomous local unions. The weaknesses of the national organization — revealed in the experiences of that period — provided a strong incentive for the reforms that followed in the subsequent years.

Chapters 4, 5, and 6 deal with the crucial years 1898–1914 during which the UA established itself as a true national union of all the pipe trades. Chapter 4 deals with the complex trial-and-error process of internal reforms pertaining to the government, finances, and the benefit system of the UA. These reforms eventually shifted the locus of power from the local unions to the organs of the national organization —the convention, the executive board, and the general officers. Chapter 5 describes the bitter and prolonged jurisdictional conflict between the UA and a national organization of steam fitters. As a result of its victory, the UA could, in fact, become a national organization of all the pipe fitters. In spite of its preoccupation with the problems of internal reforms and the jurisdictional conflict, during 1898– 1914, the UA also had to confront a number of issues relating to employers, to apprenticeship, and to organizing activities among newer branches of pipe fitting. The policies followed by the UA with respect to these problems are described in Chapter 6.

Chapters 7 and 8 describe UA experiences between 1914 and 1924 — the fourth and final period of the forty-year span covered in the study. Chapter 7 deals with the developments concerning the government and finances of the union, while Chapter 8 describes policies which were pursued to deal with crucial issues confronting the organization — the question of jurisdictional disputes among the pipe trades, the organization of the sprinkler fitters, and the establishment of apprenticeship programs. As these two chapters indicate, the UA which emerged from the 1898–1914 period of reforms and jurisdictional conflict was a strong national union — an organization that could solve many difficult problems and further solidify its position in plumbing and steam fitting, and in the labor movement.

Chapter 9 — the final chapter — provides a brief summary of the basic achievements of the United Association from the time of its founding to the middle 1920's when the union reached a plateau in its development, and indicates the key factors explaining these achievements.

Chapter 2

The Rise of National Unionism
In the Pipe Trades, 1884 - 1889

HISTORIANS and economists concerned with the rise of national unions have paid virtually no attention to the organizations of plumbers and steam fitters. This neglect is unjustified. The early unions of plumbers and fitters were directly involved in the conflict between the Knights of Labor and what the contemporaries referred to as "open unionism" (labor organizations that were trade unions rather than secret or semisecret societies); one of the predecessors of the United Association was deeply involved in a costly attempt to establish cooperative shops in the plumbing trade; and the newly formed United Association experienced all the problems of a national organization with local unions anxious to preserve their autonomy. What emerges thus from the sometimes fragmentary materials pertaining to the history of national organizations of plumbers and fitters is a story that provides major insights into the formative period of national unionism in America.

PREDECESSORS OF THE UNITED ASSOCIATION

Unionism in the pipe trades dates back at least to 1835. In that year a local union of journeymen plumbers participated in a "ten-hour day" strike of the Philadelphia building trades.[1] In the 1850's unions of plumbers were organized in New York City and Chicago, and unions of gas fitters in New York City.[2] However, none of these organizations appears to have been long-lived.

The plumbers and gas fitters also participated in the general revival of union activity that began in 1863. New organizations were established in New York, St. Louis, and San Francisco.[3] These and other local unions, founded during the early 1870's, had only a limited existence. Nevertheless, they provided valuable trade union experience to the craftsmen who were later involved in the first attempts to form a national organization.[4]

The first local unions responsible for the formation of national organizations of plumbers, gas fitters, and steam fitters arose in the late 1870's and early 1880's. The year 1879 marked the beginning of a decade of high prosperity in the building trades.[5] In the favorable climate of expanding construction activities and increasing demand for labor, local unions were re-established in cities where they had previously existed — New York, St. Louis, Chicago, San Francisco — and new organizations were formed in Providence, Cincinnati, Washington, Milwaukee and other urban centers.[6] Unlike their predecessors, many of the locals founded in the early 1880's turned out to be highly viable organizations — ones that could survive not only fluctuations in business activity but also defeats in strikes. Indeed several of them — like those in Brooklyn and Manhattan or Chicago — may be viewed as direct ancestors of the present local unions of the United Association in these areas.

As might be expected, most of the local unions organized in the early 1880's were plumbers' locals. However, some also included gas fitters and steam fitters. In addition, in New York City, Chicago and Cincinnati gas fitters organized their own locals.[7] Equally important in the context of future growth of unionism, this period also witnessed the organization of separate local unions of steam fitters. Thus the New York City steam fitters' local — the Enterprise Association which eventually became Local Union 638 of the UA — was organized in April 1884; the Chicago steam fitters' local — now Local Union 597 — was founded in June 1885.[8] About the same time, other steam fitters' unions were organized in Boston, Baltimore, and Toronto.

The early part of the 1880's saw the rising influence of the Knights of Labor. Between 1881 and 1886 the Knights grew from 19,000 to over 700,000 members.[9] Moreover, the figures of actual membership at any given point of time understated the importance of the Knights. The organization was characterized by a high turnover, and its impact affected many workers who, for a variety of reasons, may have joined for only a short time.[10]

The organization of the Knights played an important role in the early history of modern unionism in the pipe trades. Virtually all the important local unions that were re-established or newly organized during that time were affiliated, at one time or another, with the Knights of Labor. Indeed, the first real attempt to create a national body of plumbers, gas fitters, and steam fitters was made within the framework of that organization.

While the conditions in which the various local unions become affiliated with the Knights varied from city to city the general reasons for such affiliations were essentially similar. To the individual unions of plumbers and steam fitters — unions without any tradition, experience or support of a national body of their own trades — joining the Knights represented affiliation with a legitimate and recognized labor organization, a promise of general support from the working community of the area and sometimes immediate and tangible help from local labor leaders of other trades.

Thus, the New York City plumbers joined the Knights and became Local Assembly 1992 after a defeat in the 1882 strike for higher wages; the affiliation apparently contributed greatly to the recovery of the local.[11] The Brooklyn plumbers, in turn, were organized with the help of Local Assembly 1992 and were therefore affiliated with the Knights from the very beginning. In other cities, like Rochester and San Francisco, the plumbers' unions joined the Knights during a general upsurge of the movement that included thousands of the cities' workers.[12] The New York City steam fitters were organized as Local Assembly 3189, while the Chicago steam fitters were invited shortly after the formation of their union and joined what was, as their leader John Mangan put it, "The prevailing organization of those days." [13] These and other unions were all functioning as trade assemblies of the pipe crafts. In addition, some plumbers and steam fitters were also in the so-called "mixed assemblies" — composed of workers of many trades.

In September 1884 the leaders of several local trade assemblies of the Knights organized a conference in New York. The purpose was to consider formation of a national body of plumbers, gas fitters, and steam fitters. No direct record of the proceedings of the conference is available. Nevertheless, from the contents of certain contemporary documents, it is possible to glean some of the reasons leading to the meeting, and of its main results.

One of the factors that motivated the leaders appears to have been a desire to gain more autonomy within the organizational structure of the Knights of Labor. By 1884, there were in the New York City area five local assemblies composed solely of pipe craftsmen. These assemblies were attached to District Assembly 49, the powerful New York City organization of the Knights of Labor, which comprised many crafts and mixed assemblies.[14] Under the provisions of the Knights' constitution, it was possible, however, to organize district and even national assemblies composed of one particular craft, or of workers of one particular industry.[15] In the New York City situation, the formation of a trade assembly would save the local unions of plumbers and steam fitters considerable amounts of money which, instead of being sent to District Assembly 49, could be used for the furthering of the interests of the journeymen in the pipe trades. Perhaps equally important, a separate assembly would also free the pipe unions from the interference of the leaders of District Assembly 49.[16]

The purpose indicated above could presumably be accomplished merely by forming a district trade assembly in New York. But judging from the content of some of the available documents, as well as from the subsequent history of the local unions in New York, the leaders of the local assemblies of plumbers and pipe fitters must have been also vitally concerned about the problem of apprentices and helpers, and about the possibilities of mutual strike help among the local unions of the pipe fitters.[17] These two problems played a critical role in the founding of the United Association, and they will be considered at length later. But it is fairly obvious that as long as the journeymen could travel from one city to another — and particularly in the thickly populated eastern part of the country — no local or district assembly alone could hope to solve the problem of what was viewed as oversupply of labor created by chaotic apprenticeship conditions. Similarly the question of help to the striking locals would be dealt with most satisfactorily within the framework of an organization extending beyond a particular city.

The result of the New York conference was the formation of a national body * to be called National Association of Plumbers, Steam Fitters and Gas Fitters.[18] The National Association was to function within the framework of the Knights of Labor, presumably as a national trade assembly. This meant that each local union of the organization would be at the same time a local assembly of the Knights.

Since, in order to function as a national trade assembly, it was first necessary to obtain a special charter from the General Assembly of the Knights of Labor, the National Association actually had no official standing within the framework of the Knights. However, the delegates seemed confident that such a charter could be obtained. The

* This organization should not be confused with the National Association of Steam and Hot Water Fitters, organized in 1888.

New York conference made no provisions for a constitution or other laws to guide the new organization, but the delegates elected a president — Patrick Coyle, a prominent member of the New York City plumbers' union. They also provided him with funds to enable him personally to contact local unions not affiliated with the Knights, or not represented at the New York conference.

Following the conference — or First Annual Convention as it was later called — newly elected President Coyle began his organizing activity. Many of his visits to various cities were successful in bringing unions into the new organization. In particular, the plumbers' and the gas fitters' unions in Chicago and the plumbers' union in Milwaukee joined both the Knights and the National Association. Yet Coyle also learned, as he later explained, that in many cities there was either dissatisfaction with the Knights of Labor, or considerable reluctance to join it.

Two other developments of some importance took place in 1885, prior to the second convention of the new national body of plumbers and fitters. First, the local unions in New York City and Brooklyn received, as a result of a much earlier application to the General Assembly of Knights of Labor, a charter for District Assembly 85. This meant the formal creation of a Knights of Labor body composed of several unions of plumbers, steam fitters, and gas fitters. Secondly, in April 1885 a plumbers' strike began in Milwaukee. The striking journeymen were helped financially by the New York union and others, and with this help established a cooperative shop in the city. The original purpose of the shop was largely local — simply to provide employment to strikers, and to put pressure on employers. But the affairs of this enterprise were to play a critical role in the future course of national unionism in the pipe trades.

By the time of the second convention of the National Association — in Cincinnati, on September 8, 1885 — the new organization consisted of nineteen local unions or assemblies, with a total membership of 2000 to 2500. The affiliated unions were, in addition to New York, in such major cities as Chicago, Boston, Cincinnati, St. Louis, St. Paul, Milwaukee, and others. Nine of the local unions were composed only of plumbers; four, of plumbers and gas fitters; three, of plumbers, gas fitters and steam fitters; two of only gas fitters; and one (in New York), of only steam fitters.[19]

The crucial problem facing the Cincinnati convention was the ultimate organizational form of the National Association. More specifically, the question was whether to continue within the Knights of Labor and try to obtain a national trade district charter, or to withdraw and establish either an independent trade union (an "open union") or an independent organization modeled after a Knights' assembly.

Some of the unions, as already stated, were very critical of the Knights. The nature of these criticisms is well exemplified in the speech delivered by the delegate from Boston.

> Mr. President, allow me to say for my Association that I think it would be better for us to withdraw from the K. of L. We certainly have not received any benefits from them . . . For the first three or four months we met with considerable success, then assessments came in, and the brothers objected to paying out money all the time for outsiders who are always in trouble — shoemakers, tailors, etc. fighting all the time, to say nothing of appeals for aid for strikes in other parts of the country. Summing it all up, I am in favor of withdrawing from the K. of L. and having an open organization of our own.[20]

Other delegates made similar complaints. The assemblies were assessed for the benefit of others; they had to obey men and laws "entirely outside of their own trade"; in smaller towns plumbers and fitters were told to join mixed assemblies. In spite of these complaints, it appeared that the majority of delegates preferred an affiliation with the Knights, provided their organization could function as a national trade assembly.

The decision of the convention was critically influenced by a document produced by President Coyle who apparently made up his mind beforehand to change the status of the National Association. The document was a letter from the general secretary-treasurer of the Knights, in which he replied to Coyle's inquiry concerning the possibility of obtaining a charter for a national trade assembly. The brief letter suggested, in effect, that the plumbers and fitters postpone any application for a national trade assembly charter. The reason was that great pressure was being then put on the General Assembly to abolish the constitutional provision permitting the formation of national assemblies within the Knights of Labor.

Both the delegates whose unions joined the Knights primarily to participate in the National Association, and those whose locals had already had troublesome experiences during the affiliation were aware of the opposition of an influential faction within the Knights to any trade basis of organization. The letter produced by Coyle appeared to indicate that the antitrade elements were gaining the upper hand in the General Assembly, and it also suggested that it might take a long time before any national trade assembly charter would be granted. Under these conditions, the delegates decided that "the National Association be no longer governed by the rules, and usages, and laws of the Knights of Labor as an organization."

The form of this important resolution was suggested by Coyle. It presumably permitted both individuals and local organizations to remain in the Knights of Labor, if they so desired. But the National Association as a body was taken out of the Knights.

Following this crucial decision, the name of the organization was changed to International Association of Journeymen Plumbers, Steam Fitters, and Gas Fitters. (Referred to hereafter as IAPSG).[21] The delegates also made provisions for a constitution for the union, and re-elected Patrick Coyle as president. Thus, the net result of the 1885 convention was the formation of a national union as one would understand the term today — an essentially open and independent national organization of the pipe crafts.

The second term of Coyle's presidency was in many ways very successful. Between September 1885 and September 1886, seventeen additional local unions — including steam fitters' organizations in Chicago, Detroit and Cincinnati, and plumbers' unions in Detroit, Cleveland, and Minneapolis — affiliated with the IAPSG. Moreover, the cooperative shop in Milwaukee appeared to function satisfactorily, increasing the prestige of the new organization. However, the IAPSG suffered a major setback — the withdrawal of the New York City and Brooklyn locals.

The reason for this apparently was that the membership of the New York City and Brooklyn assemblies — all of them in the District Assembly 85 — refused to be affiliated with an organization that was to function outside the Knights of Labor. Some of the New York leaders were among the most vocal advocates of withdrawal at the Cincinnati convention. But under the impact of the membership sentiment, and perhaps also of other local influences in New York, they now changed their minds. Moreover, newer leaders — who were not present in Cincinnati — apparently came to the fore. The result was a decision on the part of the original member assemblies of District Assembly 85 — and of some newly organized unions in the New York City area —

to remain in the Knights, and to apply for a national trade assembly charter.

President Coyle made several attempts to thwart the formation of what he conceived to be a rival body. He tried direct persuasion on both the leaders and the members of the New York unions. When these efforts failed, he turned to Terrence Powderly, the general master workman of the Knights. In a formal letter Coyle called Powderly's attention to the fact that there was already in existence "a strong and rapidly increasing and distinct International Association of the . . . craft in existence," and that the formation of a national trade assembly would mean "splitting the trade in two." The letter ended with an appeal:

For this reason I am impelled as President of the International Association, as a member of the Order of K. of L. and as a friend of unity among all toilers, to respectfully but earnestly protest against granting said charter, and ask you and the K. of L. in the name of Industrial Humanity to refuse becoming a party to an attempt of a few assemblies, who failing to rule, would now disrupt one of the great Trade Organizations of the country.

This effort was unsuccessful. In his reply, Powderly indicated that the New York City and Brooklyn assemblies had a perfect right to a trade charter and, indeed, suggested that the Knights' (and his own) position on this matter was purposely misinterpreted during the Cincinnati convention.

As might be expected from the tenor of Powderly's letter, the General Assembly responded favorably to the application of District Assembly 85. In June 1886 New York City and Brooklyn received a charter for a national trade assembly. Following this event — and some ensuing correspondence with locals in other cities — a preliminary convention took place in Brooklyn, and a new organization, officially called United Progressive Plumbers, Steam- and Gas-Fitters, National Trade Assembly No. 85 was founded. (Referred to hereafter as NTA 85.)

The leaders of NTA 85 were apparently hopeful that they could induce the locals affiliated with the IAPSG to join the new union. Thus, even prior to the preliminary convention they wrote Coyle and suggested a joint and open convention of NTA 85 and the IAPSG. This correspondence continued while the preliminary convention of NTA 85 was taking place, and the result was an agreement to hold a joint meeting in Chicago.

The joint NTA 85–IAPSG convention, which took place in September 1886, represented what was up to that time — and indeed for years to come — the most impressive meeting of unionized plumbers, steam fitters, and gas fitters. But as a device to bring unity to the labor movement in the pipe crafts, the convention was a complete failure.

There were undoubtedly many contributing factors — the absence of extensive negotiations between the leaders prior to the open meeting; the fact that individual NTA 85 delegates were "instructed" — that is, could only vote for their own side; the suspicion that unionists from the "East" wanted to dominate the crafts; personal antagonism between NTA 85 leaders and Coyle. But the main reason seemed to reflect the difference between the advocates of independent trade unionism and the followers of the Knights.

Most of the delegates from the IAPSG had high praise for the ideals of the Knights of Labor; and several of them professed to be members of the organization. Analogously, NTA 85 or the "Eastern" delegates — as they were called — expressed a strong belief in the need for an autonomy of the trade organization of the pipe crafts. But agreement ended at this point. Most of the IAPSG delegates, under Coyle's leadership, emphasized the negative aspects of functioning within the larger framework of the Knights of Labor — the potential interference of the leaders in the affairs of the trade; continuous assessments for the benefit of other crafts or industries; the reluctance of many workers, perhaps for religious reasons, to join an organization affiliated with the Knights; the calls for participating in sympathetic strikes to support other crafts; the unfortunate experiences of the Knights of Labor in the famous telegrapher strikes and in the strike in the southwest.[22] The NTA 85 delegates, in turn, argued that under the new organizational arrangement the pipe unionists would have complete autonomy and freedom to pursue their trade interests; that the affiliation made possible successful boycotts against recalcitrant employers; and that only since joining the Knights and using the prestige of that body had they been able to build a really viable organization. As one of them put it: "The idea of leaving an army of a million and joining an army of forty thousand men is too ridiculous for me." [23]

The open debate did not produce any significant changes in the views of individual delegates. The fact was that, under the impact of general prosperity and vigorous organizing, *both* organizations were doing well. The IAPSG expanded its sphere of activity and added several new locals; NTA 85 locals were increasing their membership, while the Knights of Labor was still at the peak of its strength and thus could be viewed as an important source of support. The individual delegates therefore saw little reason to change the organizational form of their unions. In a nonbinding ballot — taken merely as an expression of opinion — the 35 NTA 85 members were joined by only three IAPSG delegates in voting for an organization to be affiliated with the Knights. The other 21 delegates sent by the IAPSG locals voted for an independent organization. And in a separate session of only the IAPSG delegates, it was decided not to join NTA 85 and to continue as an independent national union. The end result was thus a reaffirmation of the split within the union movement of the pipe crafts.

The time of the joint convention represented the peak in the fortunes of NTA 85. The decline of the organization began after this fateful meeting. The IAPSG actually expanded its membership during the year after the joint convention but declined rapidly after 1887. By 1889 neither one of the organizations had any potential for becoming an effective national trade union of the crafts. Nevertheless, their experiences played an important role in the course of events leading to the founding of the United Association and deserve a brief description.

NTA 85 never really became a truly national organization. When it was founded, it consisted of nine assemblies in the New York metropolitan area (New York City, Brooklyn, and New Jersey) and of three additional assemblies in Boston, Baltimore and Toronto.[24] Somewhat later, the Washington assembly of plumbers joined in. In 1888 the NTA acquired its only midwestern local — an assembly of plumbers in Minneapolis.[25] By that time, however, the organization was very much weakened, both by the defection of several assemblies of steam fitters and a decline in the numerical strength of the New York plumbers' organization.

Two reasons seem to explain the relative failure of NTA 85 to develop as a national organization. The first was the rapid decline of the importance and prestige of the Knights of Labor after 1886. The possible advantage over the IAPSG that NTA 85 might have had through its affiliation with the Knights thus rapidly weakened. The second — and perhaps more important — was the fact that the fortunes of NTA 85 depended so heavily on the strength and activities of the New York City craftsmen — particularly on the conditions of the New York City plumbers organized in Local Assembly 1992. The members of that one assembly accounted for over 40 per cent of the entire NTA 85 membership; Local Assembly 1992 helped organize plumbers and steam fitters outside New York City — in Brooklyn and New Jersey; it sent thousands of dollars to the striking locals in Milwaukee and Washington. When this union suffered a crushing defeat in a contest with the New York City employers, NTA 85 potential as a national organization was virtually destroyed.

The strike of New York City plumbers started in September 1886 about the time of the joint NTA 85–IAPSG convention.[26] A contemporary source termed the conflict "a very peculiar strike" because the only issue was that of apprenticeship rules, and there was no disagreement on other matters.[27] The employers wanted to retain complete control over the apprenticeship system. The union insisted on a ratio of one apprentice to four journeymen; on union voice in accepting individual apprentices; and on union examinations for apprentices.

The strike dragged on for several months and ended in a complete union defeat. In spite of financial help and sympathetic strikes, the powerful organization of September 1886, claiming 95 per cent of the New York City craftsmen, was almost entirely destroyed.

In January 1887 some of the former Local Assembly 1992 members organized a local of the IAPSG. This led to what many termed "scabbing," and eventually to internal warfare and suppressive action within the body of unionized plumbers.[28] The local of the IASPG in New York City was short-lived, and, by the fall of 1888 Local Assembly 1992 appeared to recover some of its strength.[29] But its weak condition throughout the 1887–1889 period adversely affected NTA 85. Deprived of funds from its largest member, and with New York City leaders either defeated or engaged in a fight for survival, the national assembly could not effectively carry on its task of becoming a national body.

NTA 85 was also weakened by the defections of some member assemblies, following the decline of Local Assembly 1992. The most important was the secession of Enterprise Assembly No. 3189 — one of the two unions of the New York City steam fitters. In June 1888 the leaders of former Local Assembly 3189 met with representatives of steam fitters from Boston (also originally in NTA 85) and Philadelphia and organized a National Association of Steam and Hot Water Fitters. The Enterprise Assembly became Local No. 1 of the new organization, and William Walling, former master workman, became its first national president.[30] (In 1905 the new national organization changed its name to International Association of Steam and Hot Water Fitters and Helpers, and it is under this title that it became best known during its conflict with the United Association. Hereafter the steam fitters' union will be referred to as IA or International Association.)

By late 1889 — the time of the founding of the United Association (UA) — NTA 85 had, outside of New York City and Brooklyn, affiliated assemblies only in Washington, Baltimore, Jersey City, and Minneapolis. The major locals of steam fitters left the organization. And the New York City plumbers underwent another split when some of the most active unionists — including John H. Hamill, John Lee, and William Watson — decided that only a new organization could bring recovery to the trade in New York and, accordingly, founded a new local union — the "59th Street Society." [31] Only the Washington assembly — under the leadership of Richard O'Brien — appeared to have been functioning in a highly satisfactory manner.

The story of the decline of the International Association of Journeymen Plumbers, Steam Fitters, and Gas Fitters — the other predecessor of the UA — is more unusual. The IAPSG was in effect a relatively loose federation of local unions. Its president and secretary-treasurer — both elected annually — had little contact with the other officers and the executive board, and exerted minor influence on the policies of the affiliated locals; [32] the only national benefit was strike help; there were no constitutional provisions for a permanent transfer of membership from one local union to another. [33] At the same time, the IAPSG had in the 1885–1887 period a relatively wide and expanding geographical base. After the secession of the New York City–Brooklyn locals, the IAPSG still had fourteen locals in several midwestern and eastern cities. While there was some turnover, in the following two years about thirty other unions — in the midwest, the northeast, and also in Denver and Los Angeles — became affiliated. In the prosperous economic climate of the period, these unions made fairly regular payments to the IAPSG treasury, and sometimes gave generous donations to help striking affiliates.

Between 1885 and 1887, the IAPSG was thus experiencing growth both in the number of locals and in total membership, and appeared to be becoming an effective national union of the pipe crafts. This development (and, indeed, the very existence of the IAPSG) came, however, to a rapid end as a result of one factor — the deep involvement of the organization in the cooperative shops of Milwaukee.

There was nothing unusual in the IAPSG's founding a cooperative plumbing shop to increase the bargaining power of the striking craftsmen of Milwaukee. Cooperation was one of the main goals in the program of the Knights, and in the 1884–1887 period there were numerous attempts to set up producers' cooperatives.[34] The constitution of the IAPSG, reflecting the spirit of the time, stated in its preamble that one of the objects of the organization was to "establish cooperation, so as to abolish wage slavery."[35] An attempt to set up a cooperative shop was also made by the plumbers of New York City during the 1886 strike. The unusual aspect, and especially in an independent trade union, was that the various IAPSG leaders persisted in supporting the Milwaukee cooperative despite the fact that the venture was paralyzing the organization's other activties, and bringing it to financial ruin.

As already mentioned, the cooperative shops in Milwaukee were founded during the strike that began in April 1885. The original funds were supplied by the plumbers' unions in New York City and Chicago. Edward Farrell, one of the leaders of LA 1992 (New York), brought these funds to Milwaukee, and arranged for the shipment of the necessary supplies. At the same time, Patrick Coyle moved his headquarters to Milwaukee to become, in his capacity as president of the national union, the manager of the cooperative enterprise. In June 1885 the union opened four shops, with a total employment of 35 journeymen and 7 helpers.[36]

The Association of Master Plumbers tried to deprive the cooperative shops of sources of materials by putting pressure on the jobbers. These efforts, as well as attempts to intimidate prospective customers, failed. The cooperative shops cut prices and were able to underbid other shops. As a result, the business of the cooperatives expanded. In March 1886 the employers were willing to settle the strike on original union terms if cooperative shops were disbanded. Coyle however refused to liquidate these shops.[37]

When Coyle reported on the shops to the 1886 convention of the IAPSG, it appeared that the cooperatives were successful. After fifteen months of operation, total employment (including 25 laborers) comprised 74 workers. The excess of liabilities over assets was, according to Coyle, only $648. While there was need for additional working capital, business prospects looked promising.

In spite of his apparent success, both as president of the IAPSG and as manager of the shops, Coyle decided to resign. The reason he gave was his intention to start a plumbing business. The delegates then elected James P. Donnelly of Cincinnati as president. Donnelly was also supposed to act as manager of the shops. In view of the burden of the job, the delegates also chose an assistant manager — William Halsey of Milwaukee.

Under Donnelly's management, at first the shops appeared to prosper. As late as March 1887, a contemporary economist wrote a glowing description of the venture and termed it "a brilliantly successful experiment," But difficulties were soon apparent. Although the cooperative shops were doing a larger volume of business than the rest of the local plumbing shops, the cooperative was deeply in debt to its main supplier — the Thomas and Wentworth Company of Milwaukee. The supplier insisted on (at least) partial payment of the debt, and urged Donnelly to collect funds from the local unions. Donnelly tried, but, when these efforts were unsuccessful, he decided to submit the whole matter to the national convention. The 1887 convention of the IAPSG was planned for Cleveland, but, in view of the difficulties, the delegates met in Milwaukee.

Virtually the entire agenda of the 1887 convention was devoted to the cooperative shops. The accounts indicated that the liabilities of the cooperative exceeded its assets by $9,700.[38] Almost all liabilities consisted of a debt of $25,000, owed to the supply house of Thomas and Wentworth. Faced with this fact, the convention turned itself, in effect, into an investigative body.

Although the inquiry by the delegates had to be brief, it did reveal the factors underlying the plight of the cooperative enterprise. The main reason was clearly a lack of management and financial control over the operation of the shops. The shops were able to secure many contracts, but the bids were usually so low that the shops frequently incurred losses. In many cases, additional work — not included in the original cost estimates — was done without revising bid prices. Little control was exercised over the requisitions made by individual shop foremen and general purchase of supplies. The conduct of the cooperative shops was, in effect, subsidized by the supplier who kept extending the credit line.

Mismanagement apparently dated back to the time of Coyle's presidency. As it turned out, the financial account given by Coyle to the 1886 convention understated the excess of liabilities over assets by $1300. But the situation worsened under Donnelly who seemed unable to cope with the responsibilities.

In spite of evidence of gross mismanagement, the convention voted to continue the cooperative venture. To be sure, a few voices declared that it would be better "to ruin the shops than the Association." But the majority clearly believed that the prestige of the IAPSG was vitally dependent on the success of the shops. The delegates elected a new president — Francis Graham of New York — and a new manager of the shops. To restore the cooperative to a sound financial position and re-establish its line of credit, the delegates decided to collect $20,000 through a special assessment of 80 cents per week — to last for twelve weeks.

The solution did not work. The locals, most of which did not send delegates to Milwaukee, did not collect the required amount. Some funds must have been forwarded, however, because the shops continued for another year, and the line of credit was further extended. But by the time of the convention of 1888, the monies of the IAPSG were not even sufficient to pay the expenses incurred by President Graham.[39] The convention elected Edward D. Connor of Chicago as president — a dedicated advocate of cooperation. Again, despite mounting debts, it was decided to continue the shops. The cooperative was to be incorporated with a capital of $50,000; individual members of locals — both in the International Association and the NTA 85 — were asked to buy $10.00 shares.[40] As might be expected, the subscription quota was not filled. By the fall of 1899, the cooperative shops were still in existence, but the International Association was approximately $32,000 in debt.[41] The locals which still maintained contact with the national union were either unwilling or unable to contribute further funds.

Over a period of three years, the journeymen affiliated with the IAPSG — and also the local assemblies of NTA 85 — invested thousands of dollars in the Milwaukee enterprise. During the same time, every president of the IAPSG was forced to devote virtually all his time (along with duties as organizer) to the affairs of the shops. By 1889, it was clear that the cooperation venture was the undoing of the union.[42]

Although both NTA 85 and the IAPSG had only brief existence, their functioning must be viewed as a significant step in the development of national unionism in the pipe trades.

1) Both the IAPSG and NTA 85 established an important precedent in that they were national organizations of *all* craftsmen in the pipe trades — plumbers, steam and hot water fitters, and gas fitters. In the mid-1880's the problem of intercraft jurisdiction had not become as acute as it was to be in later years. Moreover, both the IAPSG and NTA 85 preceded the founding of most of the local unions of steam fitters, and also preceded the creation of the separate national union of the craft. Although convention proceedings of both the IAPSG and NTA 85 revealed the existence of the jurisdictional problem, there was never any questioning of the fact that all the crafts should be in one national organization. The precedent established by the two organizations was almost automatically followed by the new national union which claimed their heritage and their jurisdiction — the United Association.

2) The predecessors of the UA constituted the first important means of contact among the local organizations of plumbers and fitters. By the time of the founding of the United Association, the leaders of local unions in New York City, Boston, or Washington knew the names and addresses of the leaders of almost all the existing locals in other cities; they also knew many of them personally.[43] The inter-local contacts made through participation in the IAPSG and NTA 85 played an important part in the formation of the new national union.

3) Above all, the existence of the two unions demonstrated the feasibility of a national organization in the pipe trades. To be sure, neither one turned out to be a success. But their failure, and particularly that of the IAPSG, was clearly the result of special circumstances and of what with the benefit of hindsight appeared to the contemporaries as culmination of mistakes. At the same time, past experience indicated that local unions throughout the country could be interested in participating in a national organization and that they would indeed contribute substantial funds to support such a body. In this sense then the brief period of IAPSG and NTA 85 activity broke the ground for a new national union.

THE FOUNDING OF THE UNITED ASSOCIATION

The pressures for a strong national organization in the pipe trades were never a result of only economic factors. Such advocates of strong national unionism as Richard A. O'Brien or, later, William J. Spencer, were motivated by many other reasons — commitment to the idea of a national organization *per se*, general faith in a united trade union movement, and perhaps also an expectation of personal reknown in a countrywide body of their craft. Nevertheless, there is little question that (as in the case of other national unions) the founding and development of the United Association had its roots in the economic conditions of the pipe trades. In 1889 the various local unions of plumbers and fitters faced several problems whose potential solution appeared to call for a renewed attempt to form a national union.

One of these problems was that of the traveling workers. As in the case of other building trades, the pipe crafts had a large number of journeymen who traveled about the country in order to secure work. Much of this involved relatively short distances. But the records of the unions suggest that it was by no means unusual to find journeymen traveling as far as from Cleveland to Georgia.[44]

These journeymen created difficulties in any local attempts to control entry into trade. Moreover, they constituted a particular threat to the local unions during strikes. Whether they arrived without any knowledge of job opportunities or were attracted by advertisements, the newcomers constituted an important source of strikebreakers.[45]

As contemporary records indicate, the local leaders of plumbers and fitters well understood that the problem of the traveling journeymen could not be solved without an effective national organization.[46] Without one, the local organizations were unable to inform the workers about conditions and strikes in their areas. They also had no means for organizing areas which were sources for potential strikebreakers, or to attempt to instill in the craftsmen of other cities the principles of unionism.

The problem of traveling journeymen had another aspect. For those unionists who had to leave their home locals and seek jobs elsewhere, finding employment was frequently difficult because of the chaotic conditions of unionism in the pipe trades. After the joint IAPSG–NTA 85 convention, the two national organizations signed an agreement providing for the exchange of membership cards and temporary work permits for traveling members. A joint committee of the two unions was also supposed to issue traveling cards.[47] The agreement was never carried out. After the attempt to establish an IAPSG local in New York City, the relations between the two organizations completely deteriorated. In addition to the active struggle in New York, NTA 85 also interfered in the organizing efforts of the IAPSG in Philadelphia.[48] As a result, there were no arrangements for the traveling members of one organization who might find themselves in a city organized by an affiliate of the other union.

Quite apart from the IAPSG–NTA 85 conflict, the traveling members of local unions undoubtedly encountered other difficulties. For one thing, by 1889 there were independent unions in several cities with no travel card arrangements with any other organization. Also, as the locals of the IAPSG were severing their affiliation (or, at least, loosening their actual contacts) with the national union, they were at the same time doing away with the modest system of traveling card acceptance assured by the IAPSG constitution.

Related to the problem of traveling workers was the question of regulating the conditions and numbers of apprentices and helpers. This question, always of vital interest to all the pipe crafts, constituted one of the most critical issues facing the plumbers' unions throughout the country in the late 1880's.

The unionists' concern with the problem of apprentices and helpers reflected the conditions of the plumbing trade described in the previous chapter: the technical changes in the plumbers' craft and the spread of plumbing installations; the disappearance of traditional apprenticeship and the blurring in distinction between apprentices and helpers; the easy entry and highly competitive conditions of the trade.

In spite of technical changes, the plumbers still remained highly skilled craftsmen. Nevertheless, the introduction of these changes provided job opportunities for men who could perform only limited work — joining iron pipes by means of couplings or flanges, installing and connecting some of the more common manufactured fixtures or traps, repairing installed plumbing equipment. With the spread of plumbing installations to smaller dwellings, work opportunities were thus presented to former helpers who, during a year or two, acquired some working knowledge of certain aspects of the job, or to former apprentices who did not serve their full term.[49]

The breakdown of formal apprenticeship made it possible for these novices — both apprentices and helpers — to seek employment after only limited experience in a plumbing shop. More important, such employment was encouraged and stimulated by the highly competitive conditions of the trade. Former helpers and apprentices could find work in many small shops which performed only a limited range of installations, or which specialized in repairs. And by leaving the cities in which they were first known as apprentices or helpers, they could also find jobs — at relatively low wages — as full-fledged journeymen, acquiring further experience as they went along. Under the impact of competition and with easy entry into the trade, employers were frequently eager to secure such help — help, which, in turn, increased competition among the journeymen plumbers. Indeed, it was claimed by the craftsmen that during slack times even many larger and unionized employers would lay off the more skilled and more highly paid journeymen, and retain the boys who had acquired practical experience.[50]

The men who acquired training as helpers or who did not finish their apprenticeship represented another danger to the organized craftsmen. Some of the former novices who could not be admitted to the union became self-employed. By forming one-man shops, they provided competition for unionized establishments, and contributed to the downward pressure on union wages. Other novices worked as "bumpers" (that is, on a contract according to which they were paid a specified sum for the whole job rather than on an hourly or daily basis). This, too, undermined union standards of wages and hours.

In the view of the unions, this situation thus presented three dangers: 1) an "oversupply" of journeymen, 2) increased competition from one-man shops and small nonunion establishments; 3) the threat of splintering the craft into narrow specializations and undermining the union-negotiated wage rates.

The early records of union activity among the plumbers (convention proceedings and union journals) are filled with reports from various local union leaders who cited the large numbers of apprentices and helpers working in the respective areas.[51] These reports undoubtedly exaggerated, at times, the dimension of the problem. But the data available for New York indicate that in that well-unionized city the ratio was two journeymen to one apprentice or helper — much higher than the unions considered appropriate.[52]

From the viewpoint of the unions of the 1880's the problem could not be solved satisfactorily without some national organization. The main reason was the geographic mobility of former helpers and apprentices. In many areas — whether unionized or not — there were no restrictions on the number of learners, and no regulations for a minimum training period. The pressures for keeping relatively large numbers of boys in the shops frequently originated not only from employers but also from journeymen who wanted to be relieved of the more strenuous work.[53] Since former helpers and apprentices frequently moved to other areas, the only effective way of controlling the situation was to introduce apprenticeship regulations in the already unionized cities, and to organize the other areas. However these tasks could be accomplished only through a national organization.

Another problem that could be solved by a national organization was that of strike help. Throughout the 1880's, the various locals of the pipe crafts sent considerable sums of money to help striking unionists in other cities. The ability of local unions to provide such help reflected the prosperous conditions in the building trades and their unions. But strike aid did not work between the groups of local attached to the two separate national organizations. And as many locals, including Chicago, severed their connections with the IAPSG, there was no organization that could effectively mobilize the funds necessary to help striking unions.

The steps that led to the founding of the new national union apparently began with an exchange of letters between Patrick Quinlan, a leader of the independent plumbers' union in Boston, and Richard A. O'Brien, a leader of the Washington union and secretary-treasurer of NTA 85.[54] As he considered the experience of the past few years, Quinlan concluded that there was no hope of unity between the two existing national unions. There was bitter antagonism between the leaders of NTA 85 and the IAPSG; Connor, president of the IAPSG, was committed to the continuation of cooperative shops; the Knights of Labor members would never agree to many demands of the IAPSG. Under these circumstances, Quinlan suggested a formation of "a new and distinct organization where all may join issues for the benefit of the whole craft, adopting the good points of both organizations as a basis to work on." [55]

As a result of further correspondence — involving other officers of NTA 85 — a meeting of delegates representing unions affiliated with both NTA 85 and the IAPSG and independent local unions was called. A circular signed by O'Brien promised that "questions of vital importance to our Trade will be formulated, with a view of having one Grand Association, comprising all the Journeymen Plumbers, Gas and Steam Fitters and Steam Fitter's Helpers, now, or that may hereafter be, organized in the United States and Canada." [56] This circular was sent to all the local unions of plumbers and fitters known to the officers of NTA 85.

The response was favorable. The meeting, which took place in Brooklyn, July 29 through 31, 1889, was attended by about a hundred delegates. Although the general sentiment appeared to favor the founding of a new national union, many delegates had no instructions from their locals, and did not feel free to commit their unions. However, the delegates did elect an executive committee and empowered it to call a general convention in Washington "to the end that a single organization may be formed." The committee was instructed to issue such a call if a majority of the delegates reported that their unions favored "unification." [57]

The executive committee elected by the Brooklyn meeting was composed of Richard O'Brien as representative of NTA 85; Edward Connor, president of the IAPSG; and of Philip Connealy, president of the Boston plumbers, who represented the independent unions. Shortly after the meeting, the committee issued a circular which invited the various local unions to attend a general convention scheduled to take place in Washington on October 7, 1889. In accordance with the instructions given during the Brooklyn meeting, each organization was entitled to send one delegate for one hundred members or less, and one additional delegate for "each majority fraction of one hundred members."

The general convention, or the first annual convention of the United Association (as it was later called) was attended by 40 delegates from 23 local unions. Most of the unions represented were either affiliated with NTA 85 or were independent. The 8 locals belonging to the IAPSG were represented by 12 delegates. In addition, Edward Connor represented the executive branch of his organization.[58]

This makeup of the convention determined its decision on the major issue of cooperative shops. Connor and the other IAPSG delegates wanted the new union to assume the debts of the Milwaukee shops and to continue the cooperative enterprise. After a bitter debate, NTA 85 and the independent delegates — acting as a bloc — defeated Connor's resolution, and passed one to the effect that "the cooperative shops and their debts cannot be assumed by this new organization." However, the decision of the majority was not accepted by most of the IAPSG delegates. Shortly after the vote on the cooperative issue, Connor and eight delegates of the IAPSG locals withdrew from the Washington convention.

The remaining work was devoted almost entirely to the actual founding of the new union. The delegates approved and signed the preamble to the constitution; adopted the constitution as prepared by a special committee; and approved the title of the new union. During its final day, the convention elected the officers and the executive board. Patrick J. Quinlan of Boston became the first president of the United Association, and Richard A. O'Brien of Washington its first secretary-treasurer.

When the UA was founded, it therefore consisted almost entirely of former NTA 85 locals and of previously independent unions. Only two former IAPSG locals — in Denver and Kansas City — joined the new organization during its first convention. The founders of the UA were convinced, however, that once the new organization was formed many IAPSG locals would soon join, and this turned out to be the case. Within a few months after the convention, several former IAPSG unions responded to the circular sent out by O'Brien, and joined the United Association. By the time of its second convention, in July 1890, the UA had 41 local unions and several applications for new charters.[59]

However, the new organization had little success with local unions of steam fitters. The major New York City union — former Enterprise Assembly 3189 — sent no delegates to Washington. Five other steam fitters' unions did, but two of them (Chicago and Pittsburgh) left the convention with Connor. The delegates of three other steam fitters' unions (an NTA 85 local in New York, a Boston independent union, and a New York City local of steam fitters' helpers) took active part in the proceedings, and signed the preamble to the constitution. But their organizations never ratified the action of the delegates and, as a result, the unions did not affiliate with the UA. By the time of its second convention, the UA had actually only one affiliated local composed solely of steam fitters — the Pittsburgh union, which had left the first convention but early in 1890 decided to join and became Local Union 23. Other steam fitters who belonged to the UA were in locals whose members were mostly plumbers.

The generally negative reaction of most steam fitters' locals to the new national organization would seem to reflect the growing problem of internal jurisdiction within the pipe crafts.[60] As the conflicts between plumbers and fitters multiplied, most of the steam fitters' locals preferred to stay away from an organization in which the plumbers constituted a large majority.

Chapter 3

The Beginning Years
Of the United Association, 1889 - 1897

DURING the first years of its existence, the United Association essentially represented a federation of local unions rather than an actual national union of the pipe crafts. The early constitutions of the UA specifically stated that "this Association shall consist of organized Unions of Journeymen Plumbers, Gas Fitters, Steam Fitters, and Steam Fitters Helpers." [1] This phrase was eliminated in 1906, but its inclusion in the early constitutions was not fortuitous. Representing, as it were, an explicit acknowledgement of the relative importance of the locals in the national organization, the description correctly reflected the balance of power in the early UA. "The present construction of the constitution," stated the 1897 report of the secretary-treasurer, "makes the association subordinate . . . to the local unions. Nothing that is created can rise superior to the creator when the latter restricts its powers." [2]

The development of a stronger national organization was impeded by changes in business conditions in the country. The 1889–1892 period was relatively prosperous. However a sharp economic decline occurred early in 1893. From that time until mid-1897, the country experienced the "depression of the nineties." [3]

Changing business conditions naturally affected the membership of the new organization. Until 1893, it grew rapidly but, after that year, declined significantly. As unemployment spread, many journeymen started their own businesses and withdrew from the unions; other journeymen, unable to pay dues, were suspended by the locals; still others went on the road, leaving their locals, or tried to change occupations. The total effect on the local unions was frequently very dramatic. For instance, the Brooklyn local declined from 334 members in 1892 to about 50 in 1897.[4] Total UA membership changed as follows: [5]

1890	2850
1891	4600
1892	4806
1893	6667
1894	5000–5500
1896	4742
1897	4438

Declining membership and unemployment reduced the income of the locals and of the UA — thus greatly affecting the course of government in the national organization. Attendance at conventions fell off sharply; there were no funds for organizing or for striking locals; there was no possibility of instituting a system of national benefits. The result was that most of the affiliated locals had only a tenuous contact with the national organization, and the national organization had no means of extending its authority.

The greatest achievement of the UA in these years was perhaps that, though very new, it managed to survive the severe period of economic crisis. While membership was fluctuating, the number of new locals officially affiliating with the union was actually increasing throughout the 1889–1897 period. During the depression, many of these locals existed in name only; and, by 1896–1897, only a few made actual contributions to the national treasury. Nevertheless, formal contacts between local leadership and the national organization were established. By 1897, the UA had on its official rolls 151 local unions, each of them presumably with an elected secretary. These unions were in most of the major urban areas in all sections of the country, with a few in Canada. This organizational framework proved to be of great importance during the period of economic recovery. In late 1897 — at the end of the depression — the UA may indeed have been the "bag of wind" William J. Spencer, one of the advocates of strong national unionism, termed it.[6] But there is no question that, in spite of its obvious weaknesses, the union had laid the groundwork for future growth.

PROBLEMS OF UNION GOVERNMENT

Conventions and officers. The early constitutions of the UA provided for annual conventions. Accordingly (with the exception of 1895), it held conventions every year from 1889 till 1902, when the provision was changed. The cost of sending delegates was borne by the local unions. As the depression deepened, the number of delegates sent by the locals fell off. In 1897, for instance, only 22 delegates attended, and they were sent by 15 locals (or only 10 per cent of all the local unions officially affiliated). During the early period, when there were no traveling representatives, the convention was an important means of creating ties between the locals and the national union. The poor attendance thus represented a weakening of internal cohesion.

Under its constitution, the officers and the executive board of the UA were elected by annual convention.[7] A number of changes in provisions pertaining to the officers were made in 1889–1897 — the basic framework remaining the same. By the end of this period, the elected officers were: president, secretary-treasurer, auxiliary secretary, and eight vice-presidents who constituted the executive board. The country was divided into four regions — north, south, east and west — and each of these was represented by two vice-presidents. There was, however, no clause that provided for the representation of particular crafts (for instance, steam fitters) among the officers or on the executive board.[8]

The secretary-treasurer was the only officer receiving a salary from the UA. Until 1892, it ($500 at first and then $600) was to compensate for part-time work. In 1892, when the convention voted to establish a journal, the secretary was made its editor, and his salary was raised to $1200. In addition, he had a small monthly allowance for room rent — a room which actually was used as headquarters for the union — and was paid for extra expenses (attending the convention, for instance). The other officers were expected to work at the trade, receiving reimbursement only for special expenses and for attending the convention. (The UA also paid for the convention expenses of one member of the executive board.[9])

During the early period, there was considerable turnover among the officers of the UA. For example, during its first eight years, the organization had six different presidents. (The main officers are listed in the Appendix to this chapter.) To some extent, the changes in officers reflected the fear of some local unions that the national organization could be taken over by a "ruling clique." [10] The first constitutions specifically prohibited re-election of members of the executive board.[11] In 1893, an attempt was made to bar anybody who was not a local union delegate from election. Such a provision would have made it more difficult for the re-election of the president or secretary.[12]

Another reason for the turnover was the presence of alternative economic opportunities. While most of the UA offices offered no salary, many plumbers who displayed leadership qualities had a good chance of advancing economically and socially by entering the plumbing business or becoming city inspectors. Some of the most active leaders in the early days of the UA — men like former President Patrick H. Gleason, former Auxiliary Secretary J. Foy, or former member of the executive board and business agent of Local 2, E. Farrell — opened plumbing establishments; others, like former Secretary-Treasurer Richard A. O'Brien, became plumbing inspectors and refrained from active union participation.

As might be expected, the paid office of secretary-treasurer experienced the least turnover. In particular, the office was held by one man, M. J. Counahan, from 1892 to 1897. Counahan represents the major example of slowly developing professional leadership in the UA.

A former president of the Pittsburgh local of the old IAPSG, Counahan represented his union at the second convention of the UA and was then elected to the executive board.[13] Elected secretary in 1892, he also became, ex officio, the editor of the newly founded journal. In 1893, the offices of secretary and treasurer, separated in 1890–1892, merged, and Counahan was re-elected to this combined office. He held the position until the 1897 convention. At that time, he withdrew from the union to enter the plumbing business. In later years, Counahan became an active member of the Master Plumbers' Association.

Counahan held office throughout the entire period of the severe depression. During his tenure, there were five presidents and a complete change in vice-presidents. In spite of the most discouraging circumstances — the sharp drop in income, resignations of other officers, and weakening contacts with the locals — Counahan managed to keep the UA functioning. His tenure provided the much needed stability for national office in the UA.

Organizing. Until 1896, the UA had no national organizer. The early constitutions provided for appointments of organizers either by state associations of the locals, or by the secretary of the UA. The organizers [14] were paid for time spent, and were usually chosen by recommendation of the local unions where organizing was to be performed. The constitution also provided that no charter to a new local could be issued without the approval of the nearest union affiliated with the UA.[15] Decisions pertaining to the establishment of new unions were thus significantly influenced by the policies of particular locals.

In 1896, the UA convention established the office of general organizer, with a salary of $1200. He was to be elected annually and to function under the supervision of the president and the executive board. The first man elected was William J. Spencer, a former leader of the Buffalo local of plumbers and an energetic and devoted advocate of a strong national organization.

Spencer's organizing activity was, however, restricted by the usual lack of funds.[16] And, in 1897, financial difficulties compelled the convention to combine the office of organizer and president — making it, for all practical purposes, temporarily inactive. Spencer then became the new secretary-treasurer, succeeding Counahan.

Revenue and strike aid. The UA derived its income from a quarterly per capita tax. In 1889–1897 the tax varied — from 15 cents to 25 cents. In 1896, the convention introduced a national initiation fee of $1.00 per member. In addition, the national organization was selling supplies like charters, seals, constitutions, and so forth, to the locals.

In the early period, the only national benefit provided for by the constitution was help for striking locals. In order to receive assistance, the strike had to be approved by the executive board (and there would be no assistance unless the strike lasted at least three weeks). In 1891, a provision establishing a defense fund was added. The fund was to be maintained by setting aside 5 cents from each per capita payment. Its only purpose was to provide assistance to striking locals.

The defense fund was actually never used because no money was set aside.[17] Throughout the 1889–1897 period the UA's financial position was consistently precarious. At times the union had to borrow from various locals. The balance, at the end of its accounting period, never exceeded a few hundred dollars and, in 1896, was actually less than $50.00. Under these conditions the Fund provisions were disregarded.

The result was that any form of help given to the striking locals was extremely limited. Actual aid came from individual locals which would send funds directly to the union. This ineffectiveness was demonstrated dramatically in the 1895 strike of the Buffalo plumbers — led by Spencer. Although the strike was sanctioned by the executive board, the UA did not provide any funds. An appeal was made to the locals, but only 34 responded. The total received amounted only to $1465. After 16 weeks, the union admitted defeat, and the strike was called off.[18]

As already indicated, these financial problems partly reflected the depressed economic conditions of the trade. But, as Counahan, Spencer, and others recognized, another reason was that the quarterly per capita payments were simply not sufficient to maintain an effective national organization — and the conventions refused to raise the payments.

To advocates of strong national unionism, it was obvious that the system of payments perpetuated dominance of the locals over the national body. As these people reasoned, the remedy was to "nationalize" the funds of the locals — that is, to institute a system whereby local treasuries could be used effectively to aid striking locals, to finance nationwide organizing, to pay convention expenses of delegates, and thus make the annual meeting truly national. The term "nationalization" — originally referring to the reform of the financial system of the UA — became a watchword to the men whose aim was to increase the importance of the UA, and to reduce the independence of the local unions. No real steps were taken in this direction until after 1897. But future action grew out of the experiences and debates of the mid-nineties.

Traveling members. As we have already indicated, the problems of traveling journeymen contributed to the rise of the UA. In its early circulars, which urged journeymen to form locals of the UA, particular stress was put on advantages which would accrue to traveling workers from the intra-UA transfer of membership, and the UA working card.[19] In actuality, however, it took time before effective arrangements were developed. The early system of transferring members and regulating jurisdiction over those "on the road" reflected the strongly autonomous position of the locals, and as a result a number of difficulties arose.

The second convention of the UA (1890) introduced a national working card which was to serve as a kind of pass book. However, possession of this card did not entitle one to a transfer to another local. Such a transfer was supposed to be accomplished by means of a special card.[20]

These transfer cards (after 1900 they were called "clearance cards") were to be issued by the home locals to those who wished to travel. The cards were valid for three months, and the dues for this time had to be paid in advance. In addition, the local issuing the card had the right to demand from the prospective traveler "such additional sum for the cost of the card as the local Association may determine." [21] The early constitutions did not indicate that the traveling member *had* to be admitted by the union in the new locality. Nor did they specify which local — member's local or the new one — was to claim dues for time spent in travel in excess of three months.

Originally, a traveling member was supposed to carry his transfer card with him. But after 1892, apparently in order to prevent falsification, the card was to be sent by the secretary of the home local to the new local when the traveling journeyman had reported his arrival.

This system led to many difficulties. In addition to the conflicting claims of locals over dues, correspondence between the secretaries of the locals frequently took a long time; and many secretaries were negligent in answering letters about transfers.[22] By the time a transfer card would arrive — assuming that one was actually issued — many a traveling journeyman would have left for another location and would thus lose the "faith money" which he had paid to the local union where he had held the temporary job.

An important step toward nationalization of UA membership was taken in 1896. Under a completely rewritten constitutional provision, the transferring of members was to be done by the secretary-treasurer of the UA. The local union to which the traveling member reported was to collect all dues and fines owed by the journeyman. These dues were sent to the national office which sent part of them back to the collecting local. The secretary-treasurer then issued a transfer card. The amended constitution specifically stated that, upon the receipt of the transfer card, the local was obliged to admit the traveling journeymen.[23]

The new system had some obvious limitations. Membership acquired through transfer did not carry with it the right to vote, and a great deal of correspondence was still necessary in making the transfer. Nevertheless, the 1896 changes established two principles: 1) that all dues were to be collected by the receiving local, and 2) that the locals were under obligation to accept traveling members whose financial status was in good order. These rules formed the basis for the later system of "clearance cards."

New York and Chicago locals. Because, in its early days, the UA could not provide any real help for its affiliates, or could not solve the apprentice problem, it was viewed with disappointment by many journeymen. Under such circumstances, it was inevitable that some locals considered that it would be more advantageous to carry on independently. The most outstanding example of this separatist tendency was the action of the New York City union of plumbers and gas fitters — Local 2 of the UA.

Local 2 was a direct descendant of the LA 1992, of the Knights, the mainstay of NTA 85. Its leaders played a crucial role in the founding of the UA. Its former president, John Lee, filled in as vice-president of the UA, took over the unexpired term of Patrick Quinlan's presidency in 1891, and in 1893 was elected president of the national union.

By the early nineties, the New York City union recovered fully from its disastrous defeat of 1886, and, with a membership of over 1000, constituted the largest local in the UA. Local 2 had a detailed and (in comparison with other locals) a highly favorable agreement with the New York Master Plumbers' Association.[24] It provided, among other things, for a closed shop; in return the union agreed that its members would work "for none but members in good standing of the Association of Master Plumbers of the City of New York." Wage rates for journeymen in New York were among the highest in the country. Secure in its strong position in the local market, Local 2 instituted high dues; its initiation fee was $50.00 — an amount equal to more than two and one-half weeks' wages paid to New York plumbers.[25]

In May 1895, after a series of preliminary moves, the New York journeymen, acting as a body, left the UA and instituted themselves as the Amalgamated Society of Journeymen Plumbers and Gas Fitters of the City of New York. The new union signed a contract with the New York employers which, except for minor improvements, was principally the same as Local 2's old agreement.[26]

The main reason for the secession of the New York City local was its unwillingness to accept traveling members who came to New York in search of jobs. Another was the cost of belonging to the UA.[27] The usual initiation fees in locals outside New York were $10.00 or even less. Accordingly, the New York plumbers felt that the local membership, and thus the supply of union craftsmen, would be unduly increased by incoming journeymen who could join the UA for much less than the New York plumbers or gas fitters. And, since it could not expect any financial help from the national union, the New York local also felt that its quarterly contributions to the UA were a waste of funds.

The "exclusive agreement" between the New York employers and the Amalgamated, and the refusal of the latter to exchange membership cards with other unions, created a difficult situation for the UA locals in such areas as Brooklyn, Newark, and Jersey City. These locals urged the UA to found another union in New York City. The national officers tried conciliation and even invited the Amalgamated to send delegates to the 1896 convention. These efforts were unsuccessful.[28] By late 1897, it became obvious that, given its strong position in the important New York market, the Amalgamated presented a real threat to the existence of the UA in the whole New York metropolitan area. "If the Amalgamated Union are permitted to remain an independent body . . . our locals in the vicinity of New York will be eventually absorbed by the Amalgamated" stated Spencer who, in his capacity as general organizer, tried to induce the New York leaders to rejoin the UA.[29] In 1897, however, the UA — at low ebb in membership and in poor financial condition — had no immediate means to deal with the situation.

The secession of Local 2 meant a loss of about a quarter of the membership. This was to a large extent offset, however, by the affiliation of the Chicago union of plumbers. In December 1895 — only a few months after the New York defection — the Chicago union joined and was granted a charter as Local 130.[30]

The Chicago union — a former member of the old IAPSG — was at the time of the founding of the UA in a weak condition and sent no delegates to the Washington conference. Partly because of the bad experience in the IAPSG, the union resisted repeated attempts to induce it to affiliate with the new national union.[31] As in the case of other building trades in Chicago, the union gained strength during the local boom caused by the 1893 World's Fair, and, by the middle 1890's, it constituted a strong organization with the second largest local membership in the country. Its affiliation therefore represented an important gain for the UA.

One of the reasons for its affiliation appeared to be its desire to achieve greater control over local employers. Many of the Chicago building firms did considerable business in other midwestern cities. The bargaining strength of the Chicago union could be increased if, in addition to control over the local labor supply, it also had jurisdiction over the plumbers working for Chicago contractors in other cities. At the insistence of the Chicago delegates, the 1897 convention thus added to the constitution a clause which specified that any local which ordered a strike in a shop in its jurisdiction "shall be empowered to order out and otherwise control any member of the United Association, who may be employed by said shop in any other locality."

Another reason might have been the belief of the Chicago leaders that, by affiliating with the UA while the organization was in a weakened position, they could become dominant in the national union. Whether this was true or not, the Chicago leaders did, in fact, begin to play an important role. In 1896, only a few months after the affiliation, the convention elected as a president William P. Redmond, one of the Chicago leaders. Redmond resigned — apparently for personal reasons — after a few months, and his unexpired term was filled by the first vice-president, Thomas H. O'Brien from Denver. But at the 1897 convention, the Chicago influence was clearly predominant. Of the 23 delegates who came to Nashville, nine were from Chicago. The convention elected John S. Kelley from the Chicago local as president of the UA. At the urging of delegates from Local 130, the convention also voted to establish UA headquarters in Chicago — to be located in the building used by the Chicago union.

These moves formally marked the geographic shift of the administrative and power center of the UA. The organization was founded and first guided mainly by the leaders of the northeastern locals — Boston, Brooklyn, New York. By the middle and late nineties, however, the dominant influence, was that of local unions in the midwest.

RELATIONS AMONG THE PIPE CRAFTS

The technological changes in the functions of the plumbers and the expansion of the work of the steam fitters inevitably led to problems of intercraft jurisdiction. With the change in the nature of pipe and in the methods of joining it, the plumbers were performing a great deal of work that was very much like gas and steam fitting; by the same token, the other two crafts had skills that were applicable to many aspects of plumbing installation. In some installations, moreover, it was not easy to tell whether certain pipes were part of plumbing or heating. For example, discharge pipes for steam-driven pumps were sometimes also connected to plumbing fixtures.

Many shops employed both plumbers and gas fitters, and some, in addition, also employed steam fitters. It was unavoidable that in rush jobs (or jobs with particularly large installations), employers might assign plumbers to do gas fitting, or they might let gas fitters put in galvanized iron pipes used in plumbing. Such assignments, while frequently accepted by the craftsmen, created problems and conflicts.

Throughout the 1889–1897 period these situations were handled at the local level. In some areas the problems were solved, as they came up, through the decisions of the local leaders. In other cases, formal agreements between the locals of plumbers and steam fitters, or contracts with employers, spelled out the duties of particular crafts.[32] In spite of occasional demands to pass national laws dealing with inter-craft jurisdiction, until 1897 the leaders of the UA and the convention refused to take any action. The UA was considered too weak to handle a potentially explosive issue — an issue which, moreover, appeared to be dealt with satisfactorily through local action. Another reason was that many representatives of the local unions — in most cases the plumbers' majority — felt that any rigid rules pertaining to craft jurisdiction would deprive the journeymen plumbers of work opportunities in gas fitting.[33] In 1897, in spite of some opposition, the convention decided to bar the plumbers from working at gas fitting and to bar gas fitters from plumbing. But the constitutional provision that incorporated this law also stated that, if a local were unable to enforce the decision, a dispensation could be granted by the executive board of the UA.[34]

By 1897, there were signs that the problem between plumbers and steam fitters was taking on a new character. The International Association of Steam and Hot Water Fitters (IA) was expanding its organizing activity, and, in this process, came into conflict with a local of the UA.

Throughout most of the 1889–1897 period the UA had paid little or no attention to the existence of the IA. The basis of the latter organizations were the strong locals in New York City and Chicago. Neither of them joined the UA; however, they both worked out jurisdictional arrangements with the plumbers' unions in the two cities. By the mid-1890's the IA also had local organizations in Boston, Milwaukee, Cleveland, Pittsburgh, and several other cities. At first, however, the existence of these locals was not considered incompatible with the national jurisdiction of the UA.

In 1897, the IA organized a local of steam fitters in Toledo. The new union came into direct conflict with the local union of the UA — a "mixed" local containing both plumbers and steam fitters. When the matter was brought up before the UA convention, the leaders recognized that, as an organization claiming jurisdiction over all the pipe crafts, it was essentially confronted with a "dual union." [35]

The decision of the convention was that the executive board of the UA approach the IA to arrange affiliation. Some delegates feared that this might mean increased power of the fitters over the plumbers. But most of the convention, including Counahan, Spencer, and the future president, John S. Kelley, thought that, in view of the interdependence of the plumbers and steam fitters and the prospects of fights between the UA and the IA steam fitters, affiliation was highly desirable. The decision of the convention thus constituted the initial step on what turned out to be a rocky road to the eventual merger of the two organizations.

RELATIONS WITH EMPLOYERS

Perhaps the most outstanding characteristic of the relations between unions and employers in the pipe trades in the 1889–1897 years was the relatively wide acceptance of unionism by master plumbers and steam fitters. There were, of course, many cases in which non-union employers refused to deal with the labor organizations, and there were also conflicts and strikes in shops that did bargain with the unions. But in the large urban areas, most of the employers dealt with the locals; moreover, the conflicts with the employers were, by and large, over specific economic issues — wages, hours, and apprenticeship regulation — rather than over the principle of union recognition.

One reason for the policies of the employers was the relatively weak bargaining position of an individual shop. In areas where the union was established, and where other building crafts were organized, a shop frequently had little choice in union recognition. But there were also other factors. The organization of the journeymen was not viewed generally as an alien force in the trade. Since most shops were small, the contacts between bosses and journeymen were close. Employers frequently started out in the trade as journeymen, and were often former union members. In many cases the social and economic position of the master plumber was not markedly different from that of the highly skilled journeyman he employed; the employers and the unionists frequently shared common values and a similar view of society at large.[36] Also, in many ways, union activity was helpful to employers. For example, unions supported employers on such matters as changes in building codes, licensing of plumbers, and bans on the use of clay pipes. The establishment and enforcement of union rates in an area limited, to an extent, the degree of intershop competition in bidding for contracts. And in many areas, union agreements limited the number of shops, and helped employers secure positions as retailers of plumbing and heating supplies.

As in the case of other building trades, collective bargaining in plumbing and steam fitting was conducted by the local unions. The terms of collective bargaining agreements thus reflected the economic conditions and the policies of the locals and the employers in particular areas. But even in this early period, the leaders of the UA (and its conventions) believed that the national union had a role to play in influencing, and even determining, some aspects of agreements with employers.

One of the UA's first attempts was publicizing and (by implication at least) urging the unions to negotiate the so-called "conference board agreement." In 1891, a committee of the UA formulated a model agreement, which was to serve as a prototype of contracts to be made by the affiliated locals. However, the locals were under no compulsion or even special pressure to negotiate this agreement.[37]

The basic features of the model conference board agreement incorporated the "exclusive" features that were present (as already explained) in the contract of the New York plumbers' union. The agreement formulated by the UA thus provided for: 1) a closed shop; 2) an obligation on the part of the union to ban its members from working for any firm not belonging to the local Master Plumbers' Association; 3) an obligation on the part of journeymen not to work on any material not owned or purchased by the employer; 4) a joint union–employers' committee — the "conference board" — whose function was to settle grievances arising in administering the contract. The agreement also provided for an eight-hour day, and contained a clause which essentially called for the boycott of any manufacturer or dealer who "does not properly protect the trade" (one who presumably sold plumbing supplies directly to owners or general contractors).

During the 1890's, several locals negotiated agreements that incorporated the basic features of the conference board agreement. But it is doubtful that this was, in the main, a result of UA action. The provisions of these "exclusive agreements," as they are more generally termed, reflected the economic conditions of the plumbing trade — local product market, high degree of competition, and the importance of supplies in the total cost of installations. The provisions of the contracts attempted to cope with these conditions in a way that appeared advantageous to both established employers and unionized journeymen. In areas where there were strong employers' associations, and where the unions organized a large percentage of journeymen, there was a strong tendency to negotiate "exclusive agreements." In other areas where the conditions were not favorable — where the employers were not well organized — the conference board agreements were not negotiated.

The UA (or rather its annual conventions) made a more direct attempt to influence local agreement provisions pertaining to wage scales, hours, and technological changes in the plumbing trade. In 1891, a constitutional clause was added requiring a fixed scale of wages for each local; this clause was later changed so that the union scale was limited to only two wage rates in any area. In 1896, the convention voted to introduce an eight-hour day nationally. The same convention recommended that "united steps" should be taken to stop the use of various ready-made pipe connections (for instance, lead pipe with attached ferrules).

None of the laws was actually enforced on a national scale.[38] To be sure, in many areas the contract called for an eight-hour day and a standard rate; and, in some areas, the union also negotiated clauses that restricted the use of prefabricated piping. But in other places, journeymen worked nine hours per day, there were several wage rates, and there were no restrictions on the use of supplies. This diversity reflected the differences in the economic characteristics of the local markets — in their rate of growth, their supply of skilled labor, the strength of the employer and of labor organizations. Even a strong national union would encounter serious difficulties in enforcing general laws pertaining to contracts in diverse labor and product markets. A weak organization, such as the UA was at that time, could not be expected to exert any significant influence on the contents of the contracts.

APPRENTICES AND HELPERS

Regulation of apprentices and helpers in plumbing has been always viewed by the UA as essentially a national issue — one that properly belonged within the jurisdiction of the national organization.[39] One reason, as we have discussed, was the geographic mobility of young men with some plumbing skill as apprentices or helpers. For example, the Minneapolis union introduced very rigid controls on number of apprentices. But these controls were undermined by migration of men from St. Paul and Duluth where the local unions had no regulations. Another was that apprenticeship regulation constituted one of the major concerns of the National Association of Master Plumbers. As many employers realized, under the conditions of relatively easy entry into the trade, increasing the supply of journeymen also meant a growth in the number of potential master plumbers; other employers were concerned with the necessity of maintaining high skills.[40] The UA was obviously the only proper body to maintain contacts and make agreements with the national association of employers. Finally, many local leaders, unable to mobilize their own unions to fight for apprenticeship regulations, wanted to use the authority of the UA to establish control over apprentices and helpers in their own areas.

However during this early period any attempt to institute a national regulation was confronted with virtually insurmountable difficulties. One factor, of course, was that the UA had little control over the policies of the affiliated locals. But there were other obstacles.

(a) As we have pointed out, journeymen frequently demanded that they be assisted on a job by helpers and apprentices. In many areas, the institution of a plumber's assistant — were he an apprentice or merely a helper — became by the 1890's part of the established practice of the trade, and journeymen were reluctant to give it up.[41]

(b) The economic effects of the unregulated system of apprentices and helpers were not immediately apparent to individual journeymen. In contrast to an attempt to pay less than union rates, keeping one or two more boys around the shop (particularly during a busy period) did not appear as a threat to the security of the trained plumbers. As a result of this it was frequently difficult for local union leaders to press vigorously for control of apprentices and helpers.

(c) The presence of boys — whether apprentices or helpers — provided the employers with some degree of flexibility in managing labor costs. Accordingly, many of them were reluctant to submit to rigid regulation. The use of helpers and apprentices could at times provide a means to evade the relatively rigid area wage scale, and to gain competitive advantage on particular jobs.

(d) Many apprentices or helpers were being "trained" in shops in which the owner was the only journeyman. The local unions had little or no control over such establishments, since the owner-journeyman was, normally, not a member of the local union.

(e) Regulation of apprenticeship involved much more than setting the ratios of journeymen to novices. It also meant uniform length of training, providing for shifts of apprentices among the shops, determining the various phases of apprenticeship training, and so forth. These regulations called for the cooperation of local employer associations which could evolve and administer the programs. In addition, a national program required that the national association have control over the policies of its local affiliates. However, in many areas, employer associations had only limited degree of control over its members. And the National Association of Master Plumbers, which also included nonunion employers, was essentially a loose federation of local bodies.

Many of the problems were, of course, recognized by the leaders of the UA. Indeed, a special committee advised the second convention that it was not feasible to inaugurate a national apprenticeship system at the time (1890). But the issue was pressing, and each of the subsequent conventions took it up again.

The UA attempted to deal with the problem through negotiations with the National Association of Master Plumbers (NMPA); by urging local unions to adopt apprenticeship regulations; and through changes in constitutional provisions. But none of these methods proved successful.

The negotiations with the NMPA did not produce results partly because of lack of agreement on the type of apprenticeship program desired, and partly because the NMPA did not really have the authority to introduce a nationwide program. Thus, in 1892, the UA proposed the institution of a nationwide system of arbitration and apprenticeship. But the president of the NMPA answered that these matters should be handled on a local level.[42] Two years later, fulfilling the mandate of the 1894 convention, the UA proposed a rather detailed program of apprenticeship to be administered by a joint body of the UA and the NMPA. The representatives of the NMPA agreed to submit the program to the national convention of the employers' organization only after it was very substantially changed. The changes increased the ratio of apprentices to journeymen, and provided for considerable individual employer flexibility in administering the program. Moreover, it became apparent to the unionists that even if the amended programs were adopted by the NMPA convention (and this was very unlikely), the employer association had "no machinery which they (the masters) can employ in order to have the agreement acted upon in any of the several localities." Under these circumstances, the UA committee recommended that the apprenticeship program, as it emerged from the UA–NMPA conference, not be accepted by the national unions. According to the original decision of the 1894 convention, the program was to be submitted for approval to a general membership vote, and the membership rejected the amended apprenticeship program.

Each of the two failures in negotiations with the NMPA led to an attempt to introduce nationwide apprenticeship rules by influencing the policies of affiliated locals. In 1893, after the first unsuccessful contact with the NMPA, the UA convention recommended that the locals adopt the same apprenticeship regulations negotiated by Local 2, that were presumably being observed in the union shops of New York City. In 1896, a more drastic step was taken. The convention added to the UA constitution a special section dealing with the problem. This section permitted only one apprentice per shop, regardless of the number of journeymen; a term of training was set at six years, with the last two years spent at work with tools; and the institution of helper was abolished.[43]

As already suggested, neither the recommendations of the convention nor the constitution provision had any real effect on the status of apprentices and helpers. The actual conditions varied widely throughout the country. In cities like Chicago and New York, the locals negotiated agreements that restricted the numbers of learners, specified training periods, spelled out wage rates, and the like. But in 1897, most of the affiliated unions had no apprenticeship regulations, and did not draw any distinction between apprentices and helpers.[44] The constitutional provision of 1896 was simply disregarded; such regulations as existed in particular areas were a result of the local collective bargaining rather than of any influence exerted by the U.A.

AFFILIATION WITH THE AFL

The UA joined the American Federation of Labor as a result of the decision of the UA ninth convention which met in Nashville in 1897. From the viewpoint of future growth, this affiliation was one of the most important and salutary moves made by the UA in this early period. It is thus somewhat ironic that the motion to affiliate was at first defeated at the Nashville convention, and that in the final ballot on the issue it was passed by a narrow vote of twelve to ten.

The affiliation with the AFL followed repeated attempts by Samuel Gompers to induce the UA to join the federation.[45] In 1893, his efforts were ignored by the UA, but, in 1896, the convention considered a new request in the form of a letter, and decided to canvass the locals on the issue. The results showed a majority for affiliation; but since only 27 locals took part in the balloting, and, since the total vote was very small, the issue was taken up again at the 1897 convention. After a lengthy debate, the motion to affiliate was defeated by twelve to eight. However, the advocates of affiliation did not give up easily, and apparently continued discussing the problem with the delegates outside formal sessions. As a result, the convention voted to reconsider the question and, after another lengthly debate, the motion to affiliate was carried by the previously indicated margin of two votes.[46]

The reluctance to join the AFL is easily understandable. In the mid-1890's, the federation was a weak and struggling organization; many unionists saw in the affiliation additional costs and no benefits to the UA. Moreover, some of the UA unions (particularly the one in Chicago) were apparently in conflict with the local representatives of the AFL, and feared interference on the part of the federation in local affairs.

Characteristically, the strongest advocates were the leaders who were also the strongest proponents of the "nationalization" of the UA — Spencer, Counahan, and President Thomas O'Brien. To some degree, the views of these men were undoubtedly purely ideological — the desire to see a united labor movement in the United States. But there were also some practical reasons. The AFL had several organizers in various sections of the country; in a number of instances, they helped found local unions of plumbers which joined the UA. The advocates of affiliation believed that the resources of the federation — limited as they were — could still be used effectively to extend the organization of the pipe crafts. Equally important, they also felt that if the UA did not join the AFL, locals organized with the help of the AFL might not be transferred to the UA, but would join the federation directly. Also, as Spencer pointed out, there was a real possibility that the Amalgamated Society — the former New York City local of the UA — might join the AFL becoming a rival national union. These factors — combined with repeated assurances that the AFL guaranteed complete autonomy to its member unions — provided the basis for the final decision for affiliation.

Appendix to Chapter 3

A Record of the Principal Executive Officers
Of the United Association, 1889 - 1897

THE TWO main officers elected by the first convention of the UA were president and secretary-treasurer. Patrick J. Quinlan of Boston became president, and Richard A. O'Brien of Washington, D.C. was elected secretary-treasurer.

The second (1890) convention (in Pittsburgh) voted to separate the offices of secretary and treasurer. Quinlan was re-elected as president, and O'Brien was elected secretary. The office of treasurer was filled by Patrick H. Gleason of Brooklyn. All these officers were plumbers and represented plumbers' locals.

Quinlan was elected president for the third time during the 1891 convention in Denver. The other two offices were filled by new men. H. D. McGhan of Denver became secretary, and W. W. O'Keefe of New York, treasurer. Shortly after the Denver convention President Quinlan became ill and was unable to participate in union activities.[1] During the rest of his term (until the 1892 convention in Minneapolis), the presidential duties were performed by John A. Lee of New York. Lee's official position to which he was elected in Denver was that of first vice-president.

The 1892 convention (Minneapolis) elected a completely new slate of officers.[2] Patrick H. Gleason of Brooklyn was elected president, M. J. Counahan of Pittsburgh as secretary, and J. J. Foy of St. Louis as treasurer. As indicated in the text, Counahan also became the editor of the newly founded *United Association Journal*.

The 1893 convention which took place in New York introduced some changes in the offices of the UA. The offices of secretary and treasurer were combined, and a new position of auxiliary secretary was created. The results of the elections were: John A. Lee, president; M. J. Counahan, secretary-treasurer; and J. J. Foy, auxiliary secretary.

No changes either in the number or the nature of the main offices were made at the 1894 convention in St. Louis. M. J. Moran of St. Louis was elected president, and M. J. Counahan and J. J. Foy were re-elected. Foy resigned during the tenure of his office in order to enter private business and was replaced by Richard A. O'Brien. O'Brien also resigned before the next convention [3] and was, in turn, replaced by William J. Spencer of Buffalo who began a long and active career in building the national union.

The 1896 convention in Milwaukee elected William P. Redmond, one of the leaders of the Chicago plumbers' union, as president. Redmond resigned in March 1897, and the office was held until the next convention by Thomas H. O'Brien of Denver whose previous position was that of first vice-president. Counahan was re-elected to the office of secretary-treasurer, and James J. McKee of Allegheny, Pennsylvania was elected auxiliary secretary. The Milwaukee convention also created the office of national organizer, and Spencer was chosen for that post.

The 1897 convention witnessed important changes among the UA officers. Thomas H. O'Brien refused to run for the office of president, and the delegates elected John J. Kelley of Chicago. Since the office of organizer was combined with that of president, Kelley had to play a dual role. Counahan went into business and withdrew from the union. Spencer was then elected as secretary-treasurer. The third office — now called auxiliary secretary-treasurer — was filled by the incumbent, McKee.

Chapter 4

Nationalization of
The United Association, 1898 - 1914

THIS AND the following two chapters deal with a period of important achievements on the part of the United Association. For one thing, during the 1898–1914 period, the UA became a modern national union. What was in 1897 still a loose federation of autonomous local unions was transformed in a relatively short period into a national union that provided considerable benefits to member locals but also could, and at times did, exercise a great deal of control over them. "To the United Association of the United States and Canada is reserved the right to decide all matters pertaining to the jurisdiction of its affiliated Local Unions while to the Local Union is conceded the right to make all necessary laws and agreements for local government which do not conflict with the laws of the United Association." [1] This phrase, first introduced in the UA constitution in 1906, replaced the statement that the UA "shall consist of organized Unions of Journeymen Plumbers [etc]." The new wording clearly suggested the shift of power from the locals to the national body taking place at this time. By the end of the period, it was the organs of the national union — the convention, the executive board, and the salaried officers — rather than the locals that represented the dominant force in the UA. In the phrase used so frequently by its leaders during the period 1898–1914 the United Association became "nationalized."

The second important achievement of the period was the absorption by the UA of the membership of the International Association of Steam and Hot Water Fitters. After a conflict that lasted throughout the entire period the IA locals either affiliated with the United Association or merged with its local unions. The passing of the IA meant an elimination of what, from the UA's point of view, was essentially a dual union, and a constant threat to its jurisdictional claims. By the same token, it also meant that, for years to come, the

United Association was to be recognized by employers and unions alike as the only organization representing virtually all branches of the pipe trades — in construction and in many other industries.

TABLE 2. *Membership in the United Association, 1898–1913.*

Year	UA	AFL
1898	4,566	4,000
1899	8,590	4,000
1900	10,794	4,500
1901	11,816	8,700
1902	14,789	12,800
1904	17,944	16,500
1906	18,000 [a]	15,000
1908	23,000–24,000 [a]	18,000
1910	25,015	20,000
1913	35,768	29,000

Sources: UA figures from: *Proceedings, UA* (1898), p. 21; *Proceedings, UA* (1899), p. 19; *Proceedings, UA* (1900), p. 17; *Proceedings, UA* (1901), p. 20; *Proceedings, UA* (1902), p. 26; *Proceedings, UA* (1904), p. 43; *Proceedings, UA* (1906), p. 124; *Proceedings, UA* (1908), pp. 52, 117; *Proceedings, UA* (1910), pp. 58, 105; *Proceedings, UA* (1913), p. 80. AFL figures from L. Wolman, *The Growth of American Trade Unions, 1880–1923* (New York, 1924).

[a] The figures are estimates cited during convention debates. For 1906 the UA figures probably are too high; for 1908, the estimates are those of Burke and Alpine and probably close to the real figures.

These important developments were accompanied by — and closely related to — other changes in the United Association. As Table 2 shows, during the 1898–1913 years membership increased almost continuously; the percentage of increase over the entire period was significantly larger than that of the union movement as a whole.[2] The growth of the UA was also reflected in the number of local unions. During the fifteen years following the 1897 convention in Nashville, it gained over five hundred locals. Finally, a dramatic change took place in the UA's financial strength. The organization on the verge of bankruptcy in 1897 was able, sixteen years later, to finance a comprehensive system of strike, sickness, and death benefits; to pay full expenses incurred by the delegates to national conventions; and to pay the salaries of eleven general officers of the national union.

One can hardly overestimate the importance of the 1898–1914

developments in the future course of UA history. In early 1898 the UA was perhaps at its lowest. Membership had been declining for several years, and the organization had no funds for strike help or organizing. As president John S. Kelley later described it, in many local unions, "doubt seemed to be entertained that the United Association would survive another year." [3] The relatively rapid increase in membership and the improvement in its financial position put an end to these doubts, and facilitated both internal reforms and the continuation of the fight against the IA.

Internal changes and the elimination of the International Association provided the basis for further strengthening and developing the national union, and for continuous growth of membership during the decades that followed 1914. To be sure, in later years the UA introduced many modifications and changes in its constitution, in the actual conduct of union affairs, in its policies toward apprenticeship, and other issues. Nevertheless, most of the basic features of the organization shaped during this period remained largely unchanged for years to come. In this sense, the span of the UA's history covered in the following pages may be properly considered as constituting the formative period of the present-day United Association.

The years during which the UA was transformed into a modern national union were, by and large, a period of prosperity and expansion in the construction industry. Building construction revived sharply in 1898, reached a low point in 1900, and grew thereafter (except for a moderate drop in 1908) to a peak in 1909. After that year, activity was declining, but until 1916 the decline was fairly slow, with the volume of building staying on a level very much above that of the depressed 1890's. [4]

Expansion in activity and the prosperous conditions in construction had a highly favorable effect on the size of membership in the United Association. As employment in the industry kept growing, the affiliated locals increased their membership. In scores of areas where UA locals existed in the past, union activity was revived, and new charters were issued to lapsed unions. Equally important, expansion of employment led to the formation of unions in scores of communities that had never before had UA locals. [5]

During the period of the sharpest upswing in building activity — between 1900 and 1905 — most of the growth in membership came from local initiative and the desire of journeymen to form unions.

"Today we are witnessing the unusual spectacle of bodies of our fellow workers clamoring of their own volition to organize" Spencer reported at the 1901 convention. In 1904 the UA had, in addition to president and secretary, two full-time organizers in the field. But even in that year the first contacts between an overwhelming majority of the new locals and the national organization were by mail, with the unions organized by the local journeymen, with some help from UA members in neighboring communities. The fourfold increase in UA membership between 1898 and 1906 thus reflected to a large extent the impact of rising employment in construction rather than any direct organizing activity by the national union.

The prosperous conditions in construction favorably affected the finances of the United Association. The increases in the revenue of the national union closely followed the revival of building activity. In 1898 the yearly receipts were $4780 — about the same as the previous year. Three years later — 1901 — the UA receipts were $18,330, by far the highest amount collected until then. To be sure, even in these early years, some of the improvement in finances was the result of internal reform; but a relatively larger influence must be attributed to increasing membership, full employment among the pipe trades, and to rising wages — both money and real.[6]

The prosperous conditions in the building trades provided a highly favorable and suitable environment for internal changes in the United Association, and thus constituted an important factor contributing to the eventual success of the reforms of the national union. But the significance of the economic conditions should be viewed in proper perspective. While times were auspicious there was also need for initiative and persistence on the part of the officers of the union to inaugurate and carry out a program of "nationalization." In this respect the United Association was indeed fortunate to have had several able and determined leaders. These men, frequently aware of the problems encountered by the weak organization during the first years of its existence, took full advantage of the improvement in the economic position of the pipe trades, and carried out a program of changes that transformed the U.A. into a modern national union.

OFFICERS, CONVENTIONS, AND FINANCES

The changes during the 1898–1914 years affected virtually all aspects of the UA, and thus could be treated under several headings.

Nevertheless, those affecting officers and conventions and the financial system of the union were so intimately related that they may be considered as an integrated story. This story can be divided into three periods — the first under the presidency of John S. Kelley, the second under that of William M. Merrick, and the third covering the first eight years of the presidency of John R. Alpine.

Early attempts of reform: 1898–1901. During the four years of Kelley's presidency, UA leaders made a number of attempts to introduce changes in the financial system of the organization — changes that would, in their ultimate effect, strengthen the position of the national union in relation to that of the member locals. Most of these attempts were not successful. Nevertheless, the efforts of the UA leaders were not in vain: the events of the 1898–1901 period provided valuable experience for future reformers, and taught them a great deal about the problems of strengthening a national union. Accordingly, the 1898–1901 years may be properly considered as a period of necessary preparation for subsequent reforms.

The roles of two men — John S. Kelley and William J. Spencer — should be emphasized in connection with the events of this period. Kelley does not appear to have been either a particularly forceful president or an inaugurator of major reforms. But though serving without salary, he provided both stability and continuity of office during the critical years from the lowest ebb of the UA to its revival. Equally important was his part in selecting members of the "nationalization committees" for the 1898–1901 conventions. The task of the committees was to examine and formulate broad programs of financial and governmental change to be considered by the delegates. In appointing the committees, Kelley always selected men who were vitally interested in strengthening the UA, and, in his own speeches and personal contacts, he gave them his full support.

As mentioned earlier, Spencer was one of the earliest advocates of nationalization and a severe critic of the old financial system of the UA. Elected secretary-treasurer in 1897, he held that office until the 1900 convention when he became general organizer. As secretary-treasurer, Spencer was instrumental in introducing and administering the stamp system of dues collection. In his capacity as organizer, he contributed greatly to the cementing of stronger relations between the locals and the national, and was a key figure in negotiations with the secessionist New York plumbers. Finally, as a vigorous author — under the pen name of "Bosco" — of a monthly column in the *UA Journal*, he provided continuous support for reforms that aimed at strengthening the national organization.

The most important reform during John Kelley's presidency was the introduction of the stamp system. This resulted from the recommendations of the nationalization committee presented to the 1898 convention. Under the new plan — actually introduced in January 1899 — the secretaries of the local unions were required to affix dues stamps on membership books upon payment of weekly dues. The dues stamps were, in turn, sold by the national office to the locals at the price of 2 cents a piece. Accordingly, the revenue accruing to the national organization from the sale of weekly stamps would be about 25 cents a quarter.[7]

Since in 1898 the locals contributed 25 cents a quarter for each member, the stamp system did not officially raise the contribution of the local unions to the national organization. But, as Spencer and other adherents of nationalization well realized, the actual effect was that the UA now had much greater control over the locals — control that inevitably resulted in an improvement in the financial position of the national union.[8]

Under the previous system, the local secretaries had considerable leeway in reporting local membership and local dues, and thus in determining the amounts sent to the national as per capita payments. Since the UA had no system of national benefits that called for payments to individual members (sickness or death benefits), the national union had no means of obtaining a completely reliable list or count of membership of the affiliated locals. This situation changed with the introduction of the stamp system. The local members paying their weekly dues naturally insisted on dues stamps. As a result, national revenue from the sale of the stamps revealed more accurately than ever before the actual membership of the local unions. By the same token, the introduction of the stamp system also increased UA revenue derived from the $1.00 national initiation and reinstatement fees — sums that constituted part of the normally larger local fees. This was because the new member booklets had to be obtained from the national headquarters of the UA.

As might be expected, the introduction of the stamp system did not completely eliminate practices of local secretaries or members that deprived the national union of some of its dues.[9] Nevertheless, the degree of control exercised over the accounts of individual local secretaries was considerably increased. Reporting at the 1899 convention, Spencer viewed the introduction of the stamp system as a major factor explaining the "abnormal increase in our membership" that took place that year.[10]

As indicated in the preceding chapter, prior to 1898 the UA was unable to provide any systematic help to its striking locals. With the revival of union activity and increases in membership, the question of strike aid became one of the major problems facing the United Association. But the institution of a workable system turned out to be more difficult than the UA leaders had anticipated.

The moves toward setting up a system of strike aid began with the institution of sinking funds, to be set up by each local union to the credit of the United Association. The nationalization committee of the 1898 convention recommended that each local set aside one sixth of its dues until its fund amounted to $1.00 per member. No specific provision was made for the use of the funds, but the implication was that they would provide a basis for a future system of aid or benefits to be administered by the UA. The recommendation of the committee was accepted by the delegates and became part of the UA constitution.[11]

By the time of the 1899 convention, the problem of aid to striking locals had become sufficiently acute to demand action. The convention's nationalization committee — chaired by Thomas Burke — proposed that the sinking funds of the locals be turned over to the UA for strike aid. The committee also proposed that the locals set up new sinking funds to be maintained through weekly contributions of 5 cents per member. During the debate on the convention floor, some important modifications were suggested, and the delegates finally decided to submit both the committee's proposal and the suggested changes to a referendum vote by the membership at large. The referendum vote approved a plan whereby only 50 per cent of each local's fund would be turned over to the UA for strike help. The members also voted against setting up new sinking funds.[12]

The plan was never carried out. As Spencer explained to the 1900 convention, the funds to which the UA was entitled as a result of the referendum could provide aid to only a small proportion of the striking locals. A selective rendering of strike aid would naturally cause discontent among the affiliated unions. Accordingly, the UA leadership decided not to use the fund until the pending strikes — including a prolonged strike of Chicago plumbers — were settled.[13]

The 1900 convention decided to institute a new program of strike help. The convention's nationalization committee — now under the chairmanship of L. D. Tilden — formulated a program for a national defense fund to be accumulated in the locals to the credit of the UA. Five cents per week per member was to be set aside and added to the existing sinking funds. The UA secretary-treasurer had the power to draw upon these funds to provide strike aid of $1.00 per week per member to the various locals engaged in conflicts with employers. Only strikes that lasted over two weeks and involved more than one third of local members would qualify for aid. The proposal also included a provision calling upon the secretary-treasurer to "equalize" the local funds semi-annually. This meant, in effect, that the funds would be redistributed among the locals in order to provide roughly equal amounts per member in the accounts of the individual unions.

The reception accorded Tilden's proposal reflected the differing attitudes of the delegates toward nationalization. Some argued that the proposal should be submitted to referendum; Tilden, Merrick, and others believed that a referendum meant inevitable postponement of a viable solution; finally, Spencer and a few other delegates argued that, under the plan, the UA would have no means of knowing whether individual locals were actually accumulating their share of the fund, and that, therefore, at least part of the fund should be sent directly to the national treasury to be kept there. In the end, the proponents of the plan won out, and the delegates voted to accept the strike-aid program as formulated by the nationalization committee.

The experience of the following year fully justified Spencer's views. Although the program became part of the UA constitution, only a handful of locals actually set aside their share of the defense fund. As a result, the UA could not help striking locals. Throughout 1901, the executive board approved several strikes but could not provide any guarantee of assistance.

The failure of the defense fund had an important influence on the thinking of UA leaders. By the time of the 1901 convention, president Kelley, L. D. Tilden who in 1900 was elected the UA's secretary-treasurer, and Spencer, now general organizer, became convinced that only an integrated system of benefits — strike, sickness, and funeral — would provide the necessary strength to the national organization. Their reasoning was best stated by Tilden who in explaining the failure of the defense fund to the 1901 delegates indicated that "the U.A. on account of not having any other benefit system is not in a position to dictate or to compel a Local to do any certain act because it cannot deprive a Local of the benefit when it refuses or neglects to comply, except to suspend or expel it and then deprive the member of the benefits of exchanging cards."

The additional benefits — all of them to be provided to individual members — would bring the members closer to the local unions. More important, however, the benefit system would also tie the members of locals directly to the national union and provide the UA with potential sanctions that could be imposed on recalcitrant local unions. From the viewpoint of an individual member, the payment of dues would also mean payment of premium for insurance against sickness or funeral expenses. But these accruing premiums (which theoretically, at least, could be saved for emergencies) would be lost if benefits were withdrawn because the member's local violated some general rules of the UA or seceded from the national union. The benefit system would thus, in effect, increase the interest of each individual member in the continuous good standing of his local in the United Association.

The majority of the delegates to the 1901 convention did not share the views of their leaders, and the recommendations of the UA officers to institute a comprehensive system of benefits were voted down. The convention's nationalization committee under the chairmanship of William Merrick planned to formulate such a system but in view of the delegates' vote found itself without a major assignment. The committee was obligated, however, to present two resolutions to the convention, submitted by a local, proposing sickness and death benefit plans. Somewhat paradoxically the delegates now voted to submit these proposals to a referendum by the locals.

The nationalization committee felt that the official continuation of what was, in fact, a defunct defense fund would only discourage further efforts toward instituting strike aid and other benefit programs. Accordingly, it recommended that the defense fund be abolished, and that such of its funds as were actually set aside be returned to the respective locals. This was accepted by the convention, and the strike-aid program was formally dissolved.

In addition, the only major change during Kelley's presidency was the re-establishment of the office of general organizer. This office — the second fully salaried job in the UA — was instituted in 1899.[14] From 1900 on it was held, as already indicated, by William Spencer.

What then was the progress toward a stronger UA made during

Kelley's presidency? As Spencer, Tilden, and others surveyed the results of the 1901 convention it appeared to them that "all [that] was needed . . . was to abrogate the stamp system and then the organization would be placed in the position it was back in '97 when we were paralyzed both financially and numerically." [15] The 1901 convention — in Spencer's words "a carnival of rebellion against innovations" — seemed to have left the UA further from modernization than it had been at any time during the preceding four years.

In historical perspective, however, it appears obvious that this appraisal was not justified, and that there were at the end of 1901 several portents of the forthcoming period of reforms:

(a) The very same convention that defeated proposals of benefit systems elected officers who were both frmly committed to the program of strengthening the position of the UA, and had considerable experience with such programs. William M. Merrick who succeeded Kelley to the presidency had been a member of the 1900 and chairman of the 1901 nationalization committees. Tilden, re-elected as secretary-treasurer, had been a member of the 1898 and chairman of the 1900 nationalization committees. Spencer, re-elected as general organizer, had been, of course, for years both an advocate of and a participant of nationalization reforms. And finally, Thomas E. Burke, elected now to the relatively minor office of auxiliary secretary-treasurer had also been on the nationalization committees in 1898 and 1901 and, as a business agent of the Chicago local that suffered greatly from a prolonged strike, had a keen appreciation of the importance of aid for the affiliated unions.

(b) In the past, nationalization committees were appointed by the president during the convention. At the end of the 1901 convention, however, as a result of special resolution, Kelley also appointed a nationalization committee whose task was to prepare a plan for the 1902 convention. Both Merrick and Burke were members of that committee, and the three other members were also strong supporters of internal reform.[16] This committee was inevitably in a better position to develop a systematic program of reforms than the temporary committees appointed only for the duration of particular conventions.

(c) As already suggested, the experiences of the strike-aid plans impressed upon the UA leaders the importance of a comprehensive benefit system both as a means of bringing the members closer to the locals, and as a source of potential sanctions against local unions. The prosperous years that lay ahead, accompanied as they were by rising employment and wages, were particularly favorable to the introduction of benefits that could not be gained by workers through the normal process of labor market competition or collective bargaining agreements. In effect then the approach to reforming the UA that the national officers were adopting was particularly well timed in terms of the external economic conditions of the pipe trades.

Major reforms: 1902–1906. As might be expected, the new leadership of the UA took the task of nationalization very seriously, and made systematic preparations before introducing a reform program to the 1902 convention. The proposals of death and sickness benefits that were submitted to a referendum were voted down by the membership, and the nationalization committee proceeded to formulate its own program.[17] A number of articles appeared in the *UA Journal* pointing out advantages of a comprehensive benefit plan, and in June 1902 the *Journal* presented with some accompanying flourishes a tentative proposal formulated by the committee. This proposal was further discussed in highly favorable terms by Spencer in his monthly column and, with some modifications, was eventually presented to the delegates of the 1902 convention in Omaha.[18]

As Thomas Burke, who read and interpreted the benefit program to the delegates indicated, the nationalization committee had studied several systems of other unions, both in the United States and abroad, and had corresponded for weeks with many UA locals concerning the conduct of local union finances. The committee also had met several times with the officials of the Cigarmakers' Union, and it was the benefit program of that organization that most influenced the formulation of the UA plan.[19]

The most striking aspect of the program was the scope of the proposed changes. In line with the thinking of the UA leaders the program proposed the introduction of a comprehensive system of strike aid and other benefits. In addition, the committee tied up the benefit program with a drastic change in the whole system of finances, both at the local and national levels.

The main provisions were: 1) A system of death benefits — amounting to $100 — payable to the heirs of a deceased member; 2) Weekly "sick benefits" of $5.00. Such payments could be received in any one year for a period up to thirteen weeks. A provision was also made that only members, medically qualified as sick, would receive the benefits;

3) Strike payments amounting to $5.00 per member per week for the first sixteen weeks and to $3.00 per week thereafter. All strikes had to be approved by the executive board, and any strike involving more than 25 members had to be approved by a vote of affiliated unions; 4) "Superannuation benefits" to be paid to those who had held UA membership for at least twenty years and were totally incapacitated. These benefits consisted of lump payments varying from $300 to $500 depending on the length of the membership; 5) Financial arrangements to support both the system of benefits and the functioning of the national organization that represented a drastic departure from the per capita system of preceding years. The committee recommended that minimum weekly dues paid to the locals be 30 cents per week, and minimum initiation fees $5.00. The funds accruing from payment were to become, in effect, the property of the United Association. For its running expenses, each local was to be allowed a certain percentage of these funds. This percentage was to vary inversely with the size of the local, with 30 per cent allowed to the smallest unions and 20 per cent to the largest. In addition, the locals were allowed to use for their own expenses whatever local fines or assessments they would impose and presumably (though this was not stated explicitly) any differences between the minimum dues and initiation fees and the actual dues and fees. On the other hand, the locals were not allowed any share of national assessments imposed by the UA. All the funds collected by the locals — whether destined for local or national use — were to be kept locally in banks or securities. But the differences between what was allowed the local unions and what was collected was to be at the exclusive disposal of the UA. These funds could be drawn upon to support the national organization and to pay benefits either to the local where they were actually deposited or to any other local. The program also provided for "equalization of UA funds" (by the end of each fiscal year the secretary-treasurer was to redistribute the funds held locally in such a way that in each local treasury there would be about an equal amount per member); 6) The institution of a sinking fund. Each local was required to set aside a fund that would amount to $2.00 per local member. This fund would have to be replenished through assessments if it fell below the prescribed level. The purpose was to provide a continuous fund at the disposal of the national union.

The program became the subject of prolonged debate on the convention floor. In spite of some opposition by the defenders of "local autonomy," every section of the program was passed. The two major changes introduced during the debate pertained to the minimum initiation fee and to the percentages of UA funds to be allowed the locals for running expenses. The minimum initiation fee was raised to $10.00; and the percentage allowed the locals was made uniform for locals of all sizes, and raised to 50 per cent. This latter change, suggested by former President Kelley, made the nationalization program acceptable to the majority of delegates.

A major debate also developed about the method of introducing the nationalization program. Many of the delegates, and particularly those who defended local autonomy, felt that the entire program — as approved by the convention — should be submitted to referendum by the membership at large. Others, including the strongest proponents of nationalization, argued that a referendum was never really representative of true majority opinion, and that it meant only postponing action on the program. Surprisingly enough, the supporters of the referendum found a strong ally in William Spencer. Spencer argued that the adoption of the program would probably lead to secessions and loss of membership. Accordingly, he advised caution and a trial of the proposed program in a referendum vote. Spencer's views were probably influenced, as he himself claimed, by the introduction of the stamp system when some locals withdrew from the UA. But it is also likely that he was thinking in terms of his future candidacy for presidency and tried to develop a position in which he would not be completely identified with the Merrick administration. Whatever his motivations, Spencer's views played a crucial part in persuading the majority of delegates to change their previous votes, and submit the whole nationalization program to referendum. The convention also decided that, prior to the referendum, special delegates be sent to various locals to explain the basic principles of the nationalization plan.

In addition to the nationalization program, the 1902 convention considered two important matters concerning the government of the national union — the problem of annual conventions and the salary of the UA president.

The conventions have always represented a major expense — the cost of the 1901 convention was estimated at about $17,000 for example. And since the expenses of the delegates were paid by the locals, only a small proportion of the affiliated unions normally sent repre-

sentatives. Thus, in 1902, less than one sixth of the locals were represented at the Omaha convention.

In his report, Merrick proposed that future conventions be held
either on a biannual basis, or, alternatively, only after a referendum
vote decided the need for a meeting. A committee examining the issue
also suggested that at least part of the delegates' expenses be paid by
the UA rather than the locals.

The decision to submit the nationalization plan to a referendum
vote made it difficult for the delegates to take a firm decision on the
arrangements pertaining to future conventions. Accordingly it was left
to the executive board to decide who would pay the expenses of the
next convention, and no change was made in the constitutional provision calling for annual conventions.

More decisive action was taken on the issue of the president's
salary. In spite of its growth, the UA still did not have a fully salaried
president in 1902. This was changed by the Omaha convention. The
delegates voted to provide the president with an annual salary of $1500.
As in the past, he was also entitled to all the expenses involved in the
pursuit of his duties.

The final act of what from an historical point of view was one of
the crucial UA conventions was the re-election of Merrick, Tilden,
Spencer, and Burke. This and the fact that the nationalization committee — never discharged by the 1902 convention — was to continue
its work clearly suggested that the period of major reform was now in
full swing.

The referendum vote on the nationalization plan took place in
November 1902. Slightly less than half the membership officially
claimed by the UA participated in the balloting. However, of those
participating, over 58 per cent voted for the nationalization plan and
it went into effect January 1, 1903.[20]

The introduction of the plan created many difficulties at the local
level. In some locals, there was strong opposition to the new financial
system; in others, the incumbent officers — now faced with new administrative tasks — gave up their offices and were replaced by
relatively inexperienced men; in some the officers, though willing to
cooperate, made many mistakes in the actual administration of the
benefit and financial systems. The UA leaders attempted to cope with
these problems in a variety of ways — through personal visits to the
locals by Merrick and Spencer; through advice by mail and in the

UA Journal; and even by advising the local officers to turn for counsel to the locals of other unions with experience in similar programs, such as ITU or the Iron Molders.[21]

The efforts of Merrick, Spencer, and Tilden undoubtedly contributed to the fact that only a few locals actually defected. Nevertheless, during the first few months, local dissatisfaction was apparently so widespread that the leaders feared that the next convention (planned for August 1903) would either do away with or, at least, considerably weaken the nationalization plan. Under these circumstances, the only remedy appeared to be a postponement of the convention.[22]

The constitution stated that "regular sessions of the United Association shall be held annually." [23] Moreover the constitution had no provisions for any exceptions. Therefore, there was no legal basis for a postponement, but the leaders chose to ignore this. The nationalization committee published a statement with several reasons for a delay. As the committee saw it, the holding of the convention would impose great costs at the time when funds were needed to make the nationalization program work. Moreover, "to make any change in our constitution in August would upset our system" and cause disruption of the progress of nationalization. Accordingly, the committee submitted to referendum questions pertaining to postponement and the keeping on of officers until the next referendum or convention.[24]

As might be expected, the leaders supported the view that the convention be postponed. At the same time, a campaign was conducted, under the leadership of the New York local, which was openly opposed to the nationalization program, for holding the convention.

The outcome of the referendum was a victory for the national officers. By a 2 to 1 majority, the UA membership decided for postponement. A number of locals, including New York, were disqualified from voting because of debts owed to the national union. Still, about 50 per cent of the officially claimed membership participated in the balloting.

The same referendum also decided on two subsidiary issues. The convention was to be postponed for a "definite period" to be decided upon by the national officers, and the incumbent officers were to hold their offices until the next convention or referendum.

The results provided the UA leaders with the time needed for improving and strengthening the actual administration of the nationalization program. By the middle of 1904, however, the feeling apparently was that the danger of revoking the program had passed. The New York local and a majority in the Brooklyn local — unwilling to cooperate in the carrying out of the nationalization plan — actually left the UA, but in other areas, in spite of difficulties and national assessments, the new system was in operation and functioning. Accordingly, in May 1904, the executive board asked the membership to vote on the question of the convention. The majority then voted to hold the convention in August.

The reasons of the UA members who voted for the convention are unclear, but there is no question as to the motives of the national leaders. From the viewpoint of these men, the 1904 convention primarily represented both an opportunity and a vehicle for introducing further reforms that would add to the strength of the national union.

Some of the changes proposed by the leaders — and eventually passed by the 1904 convention meeting in Birmingham — were designed to reduce the expenditures on benefits and to increase the revenue of the national union.[25] Of these, the most controversial was the change pertaining to situations in which a local actually spent less than its allotted share of 50 per cent of revenue from dues and fees. The original financial plan did not specify to whom the unspent funds belonged. But Tilden and Merrick now insisted that the unspent portion of a local's share should belong to the national organization. A special clause — reflecting this view — was then formulated and passed by the convention.

This change was criticized sharply by several delegates and, as later events showed, contributed to the antagonism felt by many locals toward the national administration. For one thing, as some pointed out, the new provision was unwise in that it discouraged economizing in the administration of local affairs. Second, to many the provision appeared as basically "unfair" to the member locals. Any local that spent more than 50 per cent of its revenue was to be penalized, but a local that practiced economy was to be deprived of a reward for its thrift.

The main reforms proposed to the 1904 convention by the national leaders — or actually the nationalization committee — concerned reorganization of the government of the UA. These proposals — passed with only a few amendments by the delegates — introduced the following basic changes in the constitution of the national union: 1) Conventions were to be held only after a referendum. Holding of a convention could be proposed by any local, but before submission to a referendum such a proposal had to be endorsed by at least one fifth of the total number of local unions; 2) Representation at the conventions was to be on a graduated membership basis. The minimum size entitling a local to a delegate was 25 members. The expenses of the delegates were to be borne by the UA rather than the locals; 3) Amendments to the constitution could be introduced through a referendum procedure essentially similar to that pertaining to conventions; 4) The election of national officers was to take place by popular vote of the members. Nominations of candidates were to be made by individual locals, with the candidates receiving the largest number of votes of the locals winning the nominations. The officers were to be elected for a two-year term.

The main reason underlying these drastic reforms appears to have been the desire of the UA officers to minimize expenses in holding national conventions. With the nationalization system in full, and presumably efficient, operation there appeared to be little need for regularly scheduled meetings of local delegates. And providing that the conventions would be held infrequently — perhaps once in ten or more years as Burke apparently preferred it — the United Association would be able to save itself tens of thousands of dollars. The fact that, as the constitution now provided, no convention referendum could be held unless endorsed by one fifth of the locals would have contributed to a relative infrequency of conventions. This meant that it took more than a few large local unions — unions that might have some special interest in a national meeting — to have a convention proposal submitted for referendum.

Popular election of officers to be held biennially was, of course, almost a necessary concomitant of the provisions concerning holding of conventions, and the expectation that the conventions would take place infrequently. Nevertheless, it is interesting to note that the choice of nominees was to be determined by the locals rather than by popular vote. As in the case of convention referendum, this provision in effect reduced the importance of the few large locals in nominating candidates for officers. Moreover, the provision probably increased the chance of re-election of the incumbent officers. The reason was that to the small unions who constituted the majority of the locals and whose vote would be thus decisive in the process of nominations, the best-known leaders were the actual officers of the UA.

The election taking place at the end of the 1904 convention resulted in the victory for the leaders who planned the governmental reforms. President Merrick, running for re-election, defeated William Spencer who apparently did not want to continue in his old position as organizer; Tilden was re-elected secretary-treasurer without opposition; and Thomas Burke, still a key member of the nationalization committee, became organizer. Two men not previously connected with the national administration of the UA were elected to the other main offices: Thomas M. Dooley of Cincinnati became the second organizer, and E. Hobbs of the Chicago Gas Fitters became auxiliary secretary-treasurer.

The 1904 convention was the scene of relatively little controversy. Moreover, the recommendations of the national leadership were adopted with only a few changes and against fairly limited opposition. It appeared that the UA leaders — particularly Merrick and Tilden — were not only in full control of the union but that their conduct met with the general approval of local union leaders and membership. The situation was to change drastically, however. During the two years following the Birmingham convention, dissatisfaction with the UA leadership spread to such an extent that by 1906, as John Alpine later said, "it seemed that nothing but dissolution of this splendid machine [the UA] would be the result." [26]

The dissatisfaction of the locals was caused by a combination of factors.

Many locals — particularly some of the bigger ones — found it difficult to conduct business with the 50 per cent share of revenue allotted them by the constitution. Their financial needs led to the imposition of higher than minimum dues and of local assessments. But such local policies were made more difficult by the fact that the national union itself imposed several additional assessments to cover *its* financial needs.[27]

This happened to some extent, at least, because of the unusual expenditures resulting from the secession of the New York locals, and the attempts of the UA leaders to prevent it. Merrick apparently considered the re-establishment of the UA in New York as a major task of his office. His efforts were only partially successful, and in mid-1906 most of the New York and Brooklyn plumbers were still outside the UA. But in the process of dealing with the New York situation, the leaders spent a great deal of money. These sums — amounting to over $17,000 — were spent not only on the expenses of the national officers (particularly Merrick and Organizer Dooley) but also largely on salaries and expenses of special organizers. Many locals — particularly those with financial difficulties — viewed the expenditures as extravagance or even dishonesty on the part of some UA leaders. This opinion was strengthened by the fact that the results were unimpressive in terms of organization.[28]

Dissatisfaction with the management of UA affairs was increased by some rather arbitrary moves by Merrick and Tilden. Merrick, for example, appointed additional full-time (and fully salaried) organizers for New York and other areas. Such organizers were in the past elected by conventions and under the new rules were to be chosen by popular election.[29] Tilden absented himself from his office for six weeks, as he later explained, to help in an organizing drive in New Orleans. (Originally he went there for short vacations.) But the constitution did not provide that the secretary-treasurer also be organizer.[30] More important, perhaps, Tilden and Merrick eliminated the office of auxiliary secretary-treasurer, although the 1904 convention actually elected Hobbs to that office. While Tilden later attempted to explain this action with flimsy legal reason, no advance explanation was given to Hobbs. And since Hobbs was a member of a Chicago local, and since his office entitled him to a review of financial reports, rightly or wrongly the impression was created among the Chicago journeymen that Tilden and Merrick were trying to avoid a check on their activities.

Several other factors contributed to the spread of dissatisfaction among the UA locals. Some felt that the membership should have been consulted about policies pursued by Merrick toward the International Association of Steam Fitters which at that time was making inroads in the UA ranks; other locals felt that Merrick had no right to appoint delegates to the AFL conventions and to other organizations such as the Structural Building Trades Alliance; among the larger locals — particularly in Chicago — there was dissatisfaction with the new constitutional clauses that, as already indicated, provided that for some purposes each local regardless of its size, would have one vote. In addition, some of the locals became aware that there were some sharp disagreements between Merrick and the other officers — Tilden, Dooley and others — concerning the conduct of policies in New York.[31] This fact undoubtedly contributed further to the view that mismanagement was taking place in the conduct of UA affairs.

The discontent of the locals resulted in mounting agitation for a convention in 1906. The Pittsburgh local — seconded by the union in Milwaukee — sent out a circular to other cities calling for a convention. Over 120 local unions responded favorably. Other UA unions sent out similar letters. The result was that in June 1906 the representatives of several major locals — Chicago, St. Louis, Milwaukee, Pittsburgh, Buffalo and Baltimore — were given a hearing before a meeting of the general officers and of the ten vice-presidents who constituted the executive board. (The membership of the Board was increased to ten in 1900, with two vice-presidents elected from each of five broad regions. By 1906, two of the vice-presidents had to be steam fitters, and one a gas fitter.)

The hearing provided a clear indication of the need to reconsider both the laws introduced in 1904 and the current policies of the UA. All of the representatives of the locals strongly urged the holding of a convention in the immediate future and the delegate of the largest (Chicago) local indicated "that it is the sentiment of Local No. 130 that if they do not have a convention there will be a secession, and that this seems to be the feeling of all members with whom they have had communication."

Prior to the June meeting the national officers strongly opposed holding a convention in 1906. Moreover, a move was also in the making to postpone also holding of elections of officers, the reason being that some constitutional clauses that pertained to such elections contained certain contradictions and had to be amended. But the determined attitude of the major locals and the continuing agitation throughout the UA unions had their effect.

Some members of the executive board — apparently in close touch with local officers — were in favor of a convention from the very beginning. Others, including then Vice-President John Alpine, were clearly swayed by the sentiment expressed among the membership. In the end, faced with a critical situation, the executive board and the officers made a decision that, in essence, ignored the existing constitutional provisions. This was that they themselves submit to the membership a series of propositions concerning the holding of the next convention, the method of financing it and also the method of electing new officers.

The letter which outlined questions submitted to the referendum contained a defense of the past expenses incurred by the UA. It also indicated that if the convention were held at the expense of the UA, as the constitution provided, a special assessment would have to be imposed. But if this text was meant to constitute an implicit argument against a convention, it had little effect. By an unprecedented majority of 6777 to 432, the UA members voted for a convention in September. By an almost 5 to 1 vote they decided that new officers be elected at the convention rather than by popular vote. And finally, by a small majority, the members elected that delegates' expenses be paid by the national union rather than by the locals.

While the results proved the universal dissatisfaction among the locals, they also reflected another factor. The outcome of the referendum was influenced significantly by the relatively heavy participation of the major locals in the voting. For example, Chicago's Local 130 alone provided one seventh of the total vote cast — a much larger proportion than in previous referenda. For reasons indicated before, the large locals opposed the election procedures introduced by the 1904 reforms. Accordingly their members voted almost unanimously to elect the next officers at the forthcoming convention rather than by the methods provided for in the constitution.

Since the delegates' expenses were to be paid by the UA, the 1906 convention meeting in Toronto was attended by a record number of 240 representatives of local unions, and constituted the largest gathering since the founding of the national organization. It is thus of special interest to note the nature of changes in the UA constitution made by the Toronto convention. The convention did away with most of the reforms introduced in 1904. But, while the delegates introduced important modifications in the financial and benefit systems, they left their basic principles unchanged. The fundamentals of the original nationalization plan, introduced in 1902 at Omaha, appeared thus to have gained general acceptance by the UA membership.

The change in system of government instituted in Toronto meant, in effect, a return to a modified pre-1904 system. Under the amended constitution, conventions were to be held biannually, and the officers were to be elected at the conventions. The expenses of the delegates, however, would be paid by the UA, as provided for in the 1904 constitution. The delegates retained also, in a modified form, the clause providing for the possibility of ameding the constitution through referendum. The modification, suggested by the Chicago local, changed the requirement that a proposed amendment should be endorsed by one fifth of all locals to an endorsement by one fifth of all UA members.[32]

The changes made in the benefit and financial system were worked out by the convention's nationalization committee which operated under the chairmanship of John Alpine.

(a) The locals' share of revenue was raised from 50 to 60 per cent, with any unspent portion of that share remaining in the locals. As it had been any difference between actual local dues and fees and the national minima (30 cents for dues, $10.00 for initiation fee and $1.00 for reinstatement) would belong to the locals.

(b) The remaining 40 per cent of local revenue was alloted to the UA. Local secretaries were required to send UA funds to the national office where they would be held. This was a change from the previous arrangement under which these funds, though subject to withdrawals by the UA secretary-treasurer, were kept by the locals. The new system thus meant an elimination of the "equalization" provision.

(c) The benefit payments would normally be forwarded to individual members by the national office rather than paid by the locals from UA funds.

The increase in the locals' share and the elimination of the previous arrangement concerning the unspent portion of that share clearly represented a concession to the demands of the affiliated unions. An additional benefit to the locals was that the UA funds held at the time by the locals would be evenly divided between the locals and the national union. But the locals were not the only beneficiaries. The fact that the UA was now to hold its funds and send out benefit payments to individual members meant that the national union would have a stronger position in administering the benefit and strike-aid systems.

As it was reasonable to expect from the events leading to it, the Toronto convention resulted in personnel changes within the leadership. One could hardly say, however, that a completely new breed of leaders was swept into office. Instead the delegates elected a group of men who had been previously associated with the national administration in what was a second echelon capacity — as members of the executive board (vice-presidents) or organizers. While these men had had actual experience with the conduct of UA affairs, they had managed to avoid identification, in the eyes of the membership, with the policies of Merrick or Tilden and, indeed, were successful, through their contacts with the locals or through activities during the conventions, in building up a considerable following among the officers of the local unions.

Much of the time of the convention was devoted to a critical appraisal of the administration of the UA during the past two years. Criticism voiced during the meetings was given further support by the report of a special committee which had investigated the accounts. No misappropriations were uncovered, but the committee found that "usages and precedents rather than law governed the expenditures of money by our officers." The general conduct of the officers was characterized as "extravagance." From the context of the convention meetings it was obvious that it was Merrick and, to a lesser degree, Tilden who were blamed for the mismanagement. The over-all result was that both men lost their positions. Merrick was not even nominated, and Tilden was defeated, rather narrowly, in two separate elections: first for the office of secretary-treasurer, and then for the office of third organizer — a post newly created by the convention.

The election for the presidency was a contest between the sixth vice-president John R. Alpine and William Spencer who as a delegate from his old local (in Buffalo) became one of the most vigorous critics of the incumbent officers. In spite of his widespread popularity, Spencer was defeated in a close election by Alpine.

The man who defeated Tilden in the election for secretary-treasurer was Thomas Dooley, former second organizer. Dooley was one of the incumbent UA officers who apparently opposed Merrick's tactics in New York. Another former officer, Thomas Burke, was re-elected as organizer. The election for second organizer was won by Edward W. Leonard. Leonard, a member of the Schenectady Fitters' Local, but at that time a delegate of the New England State Association, was previously selected for the job of organizer by the caucus of the steam fitter delegates. His election reflected the fact that, in view of the continuing conflict with the International Association, it was important for the UA to have a fitter on the organizing staff. The post of third organizer was won by John M. Love of Philadelphia, previously the fifth vice-president of the UA. While on the incumbent executive board, Love was essentially a spokesman for the dissatisfied locals, and was a strong advocate for the 1906 convention. To the post of auxiliary secretary-treasurer, the delegates elected E. Hobbs, the man previously kept out of office by Merrick and Tilden.

Consolidation of the UA government: 1907–1914. By the end of 1906, the United Association was in constitutional and organizational structure a very different union from that of pre-Omaha days. In spite of the difficulties and strains during the period of reforms, and in spite of mistakes made by some of the leaders, the locals and the membership accepted, as the 1906 convention showed, a form of organization that made the national union a key element in the administration of the financial and benefit systems. As a result, the national officers were in a dominant position in relation to the officers and members of the local unions. The challenge facing the officers elected in 1906 was that of preventing any retrogression to the previous phase of the UA development and, more importantly, to make the new UA system perform efficiently the tasks it was designed to accomplish.

John Alpine, Merrick's successor to the presidency of the UA, was particularly well suited to undertake the job facing the new leadership. A man of unusual executive ability, Alpine had the gift of differentiating between situations that called for moderation and caution and those that required bold or decisive action.[33] He also had the ability to surround himself with able and devoted coworkers, and to dismiss those who did not measure up to his standards of performance. More wisely, perhaps, than they realized at the time, the delegates at the Toronto convention elected the "right man at the right time." The result was that the election marked the beginning of one of the most successful presidencies in the history of the United Association.

John Alpine was thirty-eight years old at the time of his election. A former president of the Boston Gas Fitters' Union (LU 175) and also of the Boston Building Trades Council, he first attended a UA convention in 1904. At that time he attracted the attention of the delegates by his able discussion of the jurisdictional problems of the gas fitters, and was elected as the sixth vice-president (representing the gas fitters) to the executive board. During the last two years of Merrick's tenure, Alpine also acted as a special organizer, and in this capacity came into contact with many New England locals outside of Boston. By the time of his election to the presidency, Alpine had already had experience in many aspects of management of union affairs.[34]

During the later years of his career, Alpine's abilities were widely recognized outside trade union circles — in the sprinkler fitting industry with which he became eventually associated, and in the federal government for which he fulfilled an important function in 1931. But in the present context, it is important to note the recognition that came to him (and to the UA) in 1908. In that year Alpine was elected as the eighth vice-president to the executive council of the AFL. Re-elected annually, he stayed in that position until 1919 when he joined the Grinnell Company.

Alpine's major achievement in the area of internal union affairs consisted essentially of a vigorous and efficient administration of the existing system of government, finances, and benefits. Taking over the leadership of an organization that had just undergone major transformation, he apparently saw little need for drastic reform in the UA's internal structure. Accordingly, most of the changes that were introduced with the support of the leadership were essentially designed to improve the actual administration of the existing constitutional provisions.[35]

One relatively major constitutional problem that continued to attract the attention of both the leaders and the locals was that of conventions. The reason, as in the past, was the high cost of bringing hundreds of delegates for a week or more of deliberation. From 1908 on, various local unions proposed either that a convention take place only after a referendum decided the need, or that they meet less frequently. The memory of the last two years of Merrick's administration was, however, still vivid, and there was a widespread feeling that holding conventions less often or making them dependent on a referendum vote would unduly strengthen the position of the incumbent officers. Both in 1908 and in 1910, the majority of convention delegates voted down the proposals to modify the constitutional requirements of biennial conventions.[36] In 1912 — at the very end of the successful offensive against the IA — the scheduled convention was postponed for a year through referendum vote. (Officially, the vote was to amend the constitution for that special purpose.) [37] The following year, at the convention in Boston, Alpine recommended that some means of lessening the burden of conventions be devised. Having considered many different proposals, the 1913 convention decided that from that time on conventions would be held on a triennial basis.[38]

During the 1907–1914 period, the United Association also strengthened its organizing staff. The number of organizers was expanded from three to nine, and their salaries were increased from $1500 in 1906 to $2000 in 1913. These changes reflected the continuing growth in the membership of the UA and the satisfactory financial position of the national union.

As Table 2 indicates the membership of the UA continued to increase throughout the entire period of 1907–1913. The increase was relatively large between 1906 and 1908, small between 1908 and 1910, and large again in the years 1910 to 1913. The slowdown in the middle interconvention period reflected a sharp decrease in building construction in 1909; on the other hand, the sizeable increase between 1910 and 1913 is explained in large measure by the affiliation of thousands of former members of the International Association of Steam Fitters.

The 1906–1908 interconvention period was also characterized by a significant improvement in the financial position of the national union. After the first two years of the new administration, Alpine could report that, despite the fact that no national assessments were imposed, the UA had, after all expenditures, a net balance of over $70,000. It was this success, combined with the continuous demand of the locals for more organizing activity, that led to the increase in the salaries of all the officers and a major change in the administration of the organizing staff. The country was divided into six districts, and a full-time organizer was assigned to each of them. This meant doubling the number of permanent organizers.

In spite of this increase in staff, locals in many sections of the country — New England, the south, California — continued to demand more UA Organizers. Since, despite increasing expenses, the UA had managed to accumulate a net surplus after each interconvention period, the number of organizers was increased to eight in 1910 and to nine in 1913.

Some changes were also made in other national offices. The salaries of the president and the secretary-treasurer were increased over the years, and by 1913 they each received $3000. The size of the executive board was expanded to fourteen vice-presidents, and they received a nominal yearly salary of $200. The office of auxiliary secretary-treasurer was abolished when, in 1910, the incumbent, E. Hobbs, decided to enter business and leave the UA.[39]

But perhaps the most important change in the government of the UA was not a result of any specific modifications in the constitution. This was the reduction in turnover among national office-holders, and the accompanying development of a core of men who were, in effect, becoming professional leaders of the national union.

Even prior to 1906, the UA had some officers who could be characterized as professional union leaders. One, of course, was M. J. Counahan, the UA's secretary-treasurer during the 1890's. Spencer, who after leaving office became secretary-treasurer first of the Structural Building Trades Alliance and then of the Building Trades Department of the AFL, would certainly be in this category. But from 1906 on, there developed in the UA a group of officers who normally could and did count on re-election, and whose tenure of office extended for many years. The members of this group — normally exercising considerable authority in dealings with locals — may be described as having collectively represented the management or the administration of the United Association during the 1906–1914 period and the years immediately following.

To be sure, the composition of national leadership underwent changes during 1906–1914. Secretary-Treasurer Dooley died in 1908 during his first tenure; John Love who replaced him resigned after being charged with mismanagement before the executive board by Alpine; a few officers, elected after 1906, left because of illness, entry into business, or for other reasons.[40] And as the number of organizers increased, new men were brought into leadership. But these personnel changes were at no time of a major nature, and several UA officers continued to occupy key positions over a period that eventually stretched into a decade and more.

Alpine was re-elected without opposition in 1908, 1910, and 1913. By 1910, it was apparent that his position was extremely strong, and, for the first time in the history of the union, endorsements of the incumbent president were made prior to the convention in reports and resolutions published in the *UA Journal*.[41] Thomas Burke — closely associated with Alpine — was elected to the office of organizer without opposition both in 1906 and 1908. In 1909, after Love's resignation, Burke was appointed secretary-treasurer by the executive board, and was re-elected without opposition in 1910 and 1913. Another member of the group originally elected in 1906 and closely associated with Alpine, Organizer Leonard, was also re-elected unanimously in 1908, 1910, and 1913.

Some of the organizers added to the staff after 1906 were first appointed to the office by the executive board to fill vacancies due to resignations, and then elected unanimously at the next convention; others who started their work after an election appeared to have had the backing of the UA administration. Except for one man, none of the organizers encountered any difficulties in being re-elected.[42]

The increasing stability in the composition of the UA leadership and the accompanying professionalization of the national officers may be explained in several ways. Some of these factors pertained to the preferences and motivations of the office-holders, and some to the preferences of the locals and the membership at large.

From the viewpoint of the office-holders — or the supply side as economists would say — the national offices of the UA held during the 1906–1914 years were of considerable attraction. For one thing, the remuneration compared favorably with the earnings of a journeyman and probably of many a small employer. In 1910, for example, the salaries of the president and the secretary-treasurer were more than twice as large as the estimated yearly earnings of an average plumber in Chicago, a high-wage city; the salaries of the organizers were more than 80 per cent higher than the plumbers' earnings.[43] Traveling expenses, allowed the UA officers, further increased the relative financial advantage. Secondly, in the post-1906 years, the functions of the officers involved considerable authority in dealing with the locals, in negotiations with employers, and in contacts with the officials of the local, state, and even federal governments. And as the UA grew numerically and financially, its officers were also becoming more important in the trade union movement. This quite apart from financial rewards, the national offices carried with them the kind of prestige and authority that would be attractive to men with a background of journeyman's work and union activity on a local level. All told then, on the supply side, the reduced turnover among the UA office-holders may be explained by the fact that positions in the national union compared favorably — both in financial and nonfinancial terms — with the kind of opportunities that were normally available even to the more active and enterprising members of the UA.[44]

There were several reasons explaining why the UA officers could normally count on re-election.

The problems of administering the affairs of the national union and its relation to the locals and individual members grew in complexity with the financial and benefit reforms introduced during the 1902–1906 years. Similarly, with the growth of unionization and collective bargaining in the pipe trades, the locals began to encounter many complex problems pertaining to matters such as intercraft and geographic jurisdiction, handling of technological changes, contracts with employer associations, and contracts with large employers operating in several cities. All this meant that the national officers — whether chief executives or organizers — needed both experience and competence in a variety of areas in which even a local union leader might not be well versed. The convention delegates naturally felt that, in the absence of special factors militating against the incumbents, the experienced national officers would constitute the best choice for the next tenure of office.[45]

The tendency to re-elect experienced leaders could be expected to operate with special strength in a union like the UA. One reason was that the delegates to the conventions — representing undoubtedly the general attitudes of the members — usually took a very practical and, indeed, businesslike view of the goals and problems of the union.[46] Another related reason was that ideological conflicts pertaining to matters outside of pure trade unionism — conflicts that could lead to factional opposition against otherwise effective union administration — never played a role either in the locals or in the national conventions of the UA.

Incumbent officers facing re-election had other advantages (besides past experience) over potential aspirants who might come from outside the administration group. Because of their duties and travels throughout the country, the incumbents were generally known to the convention delegates and the local union officers; their activities were reported extensively in the *Journal*. In the absence of widespread dissatisfaction, such as that which led to the defeat of Merrick and Tilden, these and other advantages would be hard to overcome. It would be difficult, for example, for a local union officer to become well known and popular in the many small communities that, under the paid system of expenses, sent delegates to the national conventions. The Alpine administration had strong connections with the large locals in Chicago; the New York locals of the UA were divided and had little national influence. Any base for determined opposition to the incumbents would have to be provided by some sort of a coalition of locals in the other large cities. But only in special circumstances would it be possible to create such a coalition against an administration that was both effective and that drew its officers from some of the same cities (Alpine from Boston). Accordingly, the officers in the Alpine administration and the candidates backed by the administration had little reason to expect effective opposition in election.

An additional factor of a more special type probably further strengthened the political position of the incumbent officers. This was the conflict with the International Association of Steam Fitters. As other studies have pointed out, the force of external pressures impinging on a union — that is, opposition of employers — provides one of the reasons for a tendency to avoid internal struggles and to institute a one-party government.[47] During most of the 1906–1914 period, the UA locals were facing, in addition to the normal problems of collective bargaining, external pressures emanating from the dispute with the IA. Moreover, from 1910 on, it was apparent that the UA was gaining the upper hand in this prolonged dispute and moving toward a complete victory over the rival union. These developments could be expected to strengthen the tendency to keep unity within the UA and to re-elect the officers who were actively involved in the fight against the IA.

As already suggested, the developments discussed above — the relative attractiveness of the national offices, the need for experienced leaders, the advantages of the incumbents arising out of their activities in what was now a relatively complex business of administering the national union — have been all connected with, and brought about by, the nationalization of the United Association and its increasing numerical and financial strength. Thus the changes in the internal structure of the UA and the growth of the organization were bringing also a basic and long run change in the actual — as distinguished from formal — position of the national officers, and were creating what in any given period would be essentially a permanent group of professional leaders of the national union.

NATIONALIZATION AND THE LOCALS

During the 1898–1914 period, the UA introduced many provisions that regulated both the relations between the national union and the locals, and the relations among the local unions themselves. While some of these provisions (those concerning strikes) were a concommitant of the over-all nationalization program, others were not related directly to the reforms of 1902–1906. In the final analysis, however, the effectiveness of all the rules of behavior imposed on the locals depended to a large extent on the success of the nationalization program. For these rules would be generally observed only if 1) they were administered by an organization that had, potentially at least, the power to impose sanctions on recalcitrant locals, and 2) if expulsion or suspension from the UA would impose major costs on the particular locals.

As a result of the internal reforms and the accompanying growth in membership and income, these necessary conditions were being, in fact, realized.

(a) As suggested earlier, the existence of the system of benefits — sickness, death, superannuation — provided a source of potential sanctions against suspended locals. The suspension of benefit payments by the national could become a major hardship for many members of the local.

(b) Another sanction was provided by the threat of refusing strike aid. Since under the nationalization system most locals had relatively little opportunity to accumulate defense funds, national strike aid was of crucial importance.

(c) The increase in the number of UA locals and the founding of unions in previously unorganized areas increased the importance of membership as a general passport for traveling journeymen. Accordingly, the loss of clearance and privileges that would follow suspension or expulsion would impose a major penalty on many of the local's members.

(d) Many large construction projects were built by contractors who did business in several different areas. Such multicity contractors — as they may be called — were normally reluctant to antagonize the UA, since this might lead to conflicts with local unions in several areas where the locals were strong. Accordingly, these large contractors could influence local journeymen to come to terms with the national union.

(e) Another potentially effective means of reacting against a local, available to the UA, was the launching of a local union to provide competition to a recalcitrant union. The possibility was facilitated by the existence of full-time national organizers who could be assigned for prolonged periods to an area where the UA was experiencing difficulties. As noted below, this method was, in fact, used in New York.

The powers that the UA could exercise with respect to the locals inevitably increased the personal authority of the full-time executive officers. To be sure, under the constitutional provisions, the decisions of the president and of the secretary-treasurer could be appealed to the executive board. Moreover, further appeals could also be made to the national conventions. But for several reasons the chances of a successful appeal were in most cases small.

Until 1913, the members of the executive board received no salaries, and, after that year, as mentioned, only a nominal pay of $200 per annum. More important, the vice-presidents who constituted the membership of the board lived and worked in towns and cities scattered throughout the country. The result was that the board generally met only once a year, and its members could not participate actively in the actual affairs of the national union. In the early years turnover on the board was very high, and even those members who did not formally resign were at times difficult to reach. In 1896, the president of the UA was given the power to remove any member of the board who neglected his duties.[48] In 1900, a clause was added which provided that in cases in which a precedent was established by a previous decision of the board, the president himself would handle the appeals of locals or individual members.[49]

The rise of a fully paid and relatively permanent executive officers' staff inevitably had its effect on the role of the executive board. The UA constitution provided that, when so assigned, the vice-presidents could act as representatives of the president.[50] This role became more important during and after the nationalization program.[51] What this meant, however, was that assignments connected with UA work given to the vice-presidents depended on the president and his immediate advisers. The executive officers also participated — though without vote — in the meeting of the executive board. Since they represented the actual management of the union, they naturally exerted an important influence on decisions. And since, as a result of their activities, the executive officers had by the time of the post-nationalization period significant political power in the UA, their influence was normally decisive.

In times of dissatisfaction with the national officers (1906, for example), the executive board could undoubtedly become a significant means of checking the actions of the president or the secretary-treasurer. But under more normal circumstances, the board exercised little control over the executive officers, and thus left them in a strong position in their dealings with the locals.

The constitution did not make any provision for an appeal from the decision of the president or of the executive board to the national convention. Such appeals, however, were in fact made from time to time.

Each national convention had a Committee on Appeals and Griev-ances. Individual locals could then submit propositions dealing with the past decisions of the officers and these propositions were con-sidered by the committee. The committee in turn would report on each of the propositions to the convention, recommending either concur-rence or nonconcurrence.[52]

The records of the conventions reveal relatively few cases of success-ful appeals from the decision of the executive board. The UA con-stitution provided that "all committees shall be appointed by the Presi-dent, unless it shall be otherwise directed by the Convention."[53] The convention delegates, however, never exercised their prerogative to change the system of committee appointments. Accordingly, the members of the Committee on Appeals and Grievances, like those of other committees, would be appointed by the president of the UA. The recommendations of the Committee on Appeals were normally followed by the conventions. The reason was that the issues sub-mitted to the committee were generally of such a special character and involved so many details pertaining to only one local or even one mem-ber of a local that the delegates were both unable and unwilling to consider them at length.

The reforms of the nationalization period did not deprive the con-ventions of their crucial role as the courts of last appeal. In fact, in situations where the policies of the UA would be at variance with well-established preferences of the membership, the appeals to the conven-tions — whether submitted to the Committee on Appeals or formu-lated as general propositions — could, and at times did, become a major restraint on the administration of the national union. But under more usual conditions, an effective administration, such as Alpine's, did not have to consider these appeals as a significant check on its routine policies toward particular locals. Thus, it is not surprising to find that Alpine, for instance, felt free to suspend a business agent of a local union even though the suspended officer enjoyed full support of his organization, and, even though, strictly speaking, there was no con-stitutional provision that gave the right of such action to the UA presi-dent.[54]

Traveling members. During the period of nationalization, the UA developed a viable system of arrangements pertaining to its traveling members. However, a number of difficulties had to be overcome. On the one hand, truly effective arrangements meant further restrictions on the autonomy of the locals and the recognition of the supremacy of the national over local membership. But, on the other, a workable system had to take into account that giving UA members an unrestricted right to obtain a travel card or to gain admission to any local could at times cause serious problems.

One of the first issues encountered by the Kelley administration when it took up the problem of traveling members was that of initiation fees. These varied considerably from one local union to another. The locals with high fees insisted that traveling members who carried transfer cards from unions with lower fees pay the difference between the fee of the admitting union and that of the home organization. The argument for such arrangements was well reflected in the statements of R. W. Godfrey, one of the Boston delegates to the 1898 convention:

Take Boston, for instance. We have ten locals in a radius of ten miles, locals in cities from 10,000 to 15,000 inhabitants. One has $2.00 initiation fee. Malden has $5.00, Salem $5.00, Lynn $5.00, Waltham $5.00, Lowell $5.00. Now a man could go to Boston to go on a job, and the first thing we know they tell him to join the union. "What is the initiation fee?" "It will cost you $50.00 to go before the board." He kicks and they say "Well, if you haven't done anything we will let you in for $25.00." What does he do? He jumps to a small town and works in Boston just the same. He works there a short time and gets initiated, jumps back to Boston with a transfer card and we must accept him. . . If you do not do something on this initiation fee matter, you must allow the large locals to charge the difference between the small locals. Why? Because if a man goes to any of the large cities he gets a dollar or a dollar and a half a day more. Our expenses are so that we must keep a business agent; it costs considerable money to keep this work up — to keep the wages up. If we do not have a regular national initiation fee you must allow the large cities to change the difference between the large locals' and the small locals' fee.[55]

As Godfrey's speech implied, a possible alternative to permitting payments of fee differences was a uniform initiation fee. But this was not, in fact, a practical solution. The interlocal differences in initiation fees reflected basic differences among the geographic areas organized by the UA — differences in the demand for and supply of skilled labor, in the local wages, in the strength of the local organization. A fee that would be considered very low in New York or Chicago could cripple local unions in many areas of the country, and make impossible extension of the organization to thousands of nonunion journeymen. Moreover, as also suggested by Godfrey, some locals had in fact not one initiation fee but a range of such fees. Thus in some cities individual applicants for admission were charged different fees, with the amount depending on a number of personal factors. Under a uniform national fee, this discriminatory practice would be abandoned.[56]

The nationalization committee of the 1898 convention followed the arguments of the large locals, and formulated a clause that permitted charging traveling members the differences in initiation fees. This clause was passed by the delegates. At the same time, the clause depriving traveling members of a vote in their new local was dropped from the constitution.

The clause permitting collection of differences in fees stayed in the UA constitution for only one year. It was apparent that with the large interlocal differences in initiation fees and with locals having the right to change these fees at any time, the clause would in effect lead to undermining the privileges of traveling members.[57] Accordingly, the 1899 convention adopted a new solution, and instituted a national minimum initiation fee of $10.00. Local unions had the right to impose initiation fees above the minimum when they admitted new members; but traveling members had to be accepted without paying any differences in fees of the admitting union and the home union.[58]

After this affirmation of the rights of national membership, the UA introduced — as a result of the decision of the 1900 convention — a major administrative reform. This was the inauguration of the clearance card system. Briefly, any member who wished to leave his local was given the right to secure a clearance card. The card could be obtained from the home local union upon the liquidation of any debts (for past dues) that the potential traveler owed to the local. The member had to turn in the clearance card to the local union in the area where he obtained a job. The admitting local would collect any dues for the period that the traveling member was "on the road" — between the day of issuance of the card and reporting to the local. In the case of journeymen who were in the UA less than six months, the admitting local could also collect the difference between its initiation fee and the fee of the home local.[59] This last provision was meant to eliminate purposeful avoidance of paying high fees through temporary joining of locals in small towns.

The clearance card system was a logical development of the principle first introduced in 1896 — namely, that the admitting local should collect any back dues, assessments, or fees owed by the traveling member. But the new system was an important administrative development because it considerably reduced the amount of correspondence between the locals and the secretary-treasurer that was previously required, and because it established simple methods of transferring membership from one local to another.

In the years after 1900, the UA introduced a number of modifications in the clearance card system. The purpose was to make the system more flexible and adjustable to a variety of conditions.

(a) In 1904, locals on strike were given the right to refuse to issue clearance cards. Although members of striking locals could be permitted to seek work elsewhere, they had to send their dues to the home union. The purpose was to limit possible desertions from a local that was in trouble.[60]

(b) In 1908 a "conditional" clearance card was instituted. This card could be issued to a member who had no means to settle his debts with the local but who desired to seek work elsewhere and pay his back dues once he obtained a job. The conditional card was a product of the slowing down of construction activity and, though apparently rarely used, was supposed to help unemployed UA members.[61]

(c) The UA eventually provided for special circumstances under which a local might be justified in rejecting the clearance cards of traveling members. A constitutional clause passed in 1910 gave locals the right to refuse admission of traveling members if such rights were sanctioned by the two nearest local unions, and if the particular local got special dispensation from the executive board.

(d) Another provision pertaining to the right of rejecting clearance cards was passed in 1913. A special clause passed in that year gave the locals engaged in a strike approved by the UA the right to refuse admission to traveling members.

One purpose of the last two clauses was, of course, to provide for conditions under which a local might be unable to absorb new members. But, as the debates of the conventions indicated, there was also another purpose. Since the clauses spelled out the conditions under which locals had the right to reject clearance cards, they also made it explicit that rejection of cards under any other conditions — for instance, during a strike not approved by the UA — would constitute a violation of the constitution.[62]

The development of the clearance card system did not eliminate all the conflicts in the problem of traveling members. Even in 1913 Burke still had to report that "almost every day there is objection or complaint lodged at the general office in relation to the narrow tendencies and feelings of the local unions against traveling members when they enter their jurisdiction seeking work." The instability of employment in construction combined with the desire to limit the local labor supply inevitably led to many attempts to circumvent the obligations imposed on locals by the clearance card system. Moreover, as the large contractors expanded their activities and began to send what was called "fleets" of craftsmen from their home bases to other areas, the issue of traveling members acquired a new significance and raised new problems. Nevertheless, the continuous presence of disputes among the locals should not overshadow the basic fact that the system developed by the UA did work, and did result, by and large, in an orderly transfer of individual members from one local to another. As the lists of names published in the *Journal* indicated, practically every month hundreds of UA journeymen were "admitted by clearance" to the various locals, and hundreds more were being issued clearance cards by their home unions.[63] "There is no craft that travels more than the plumbers and when they come into a town they want to be treated fair," stated one of the delegates debating the issue of travel cards during the 1899 convention.[64] By the end of the 1898–1914 period, the traveling members could expect that, under normal circumstances, they would, in fact, be treated "fair" by the local unions of the towns where they decided to obtain jobs.

Strike control. "It having been clearly demonstrated that strikes are deplorable in their effect, and contrary to the best interests of the United Association and its members, they should be used only as a last resort." [65] This statement — first appearing in the 1891 constitution and then included in each subsequent edition until the time of the 1902 reforms — reflected the concern of the leaders with what Spencer termed as "strikes of hasty and unwarranted nature." [66] As Kelley, Spencer, and other UA leaders of the prenationalization period viewed the strike activities of the locals, they recognized that in many cases the local unions would start or become engaged in strikes that could be avoided. Some of these strikes resulted in the defeat of the union; others, though costly and prolonged, resulted in gains that could have been achieved through peaceful negotiation. Whatever the outcome, many of the local strikes appeared to the UA leaders as unnecessary

◄ CONSTITUTION ►

OF THE

INTERNATIONAL ASSOCIATION, DISTRICT ASSOCIA-

TIONS AND LOCAL ASSOCIATIONS

OF

JOURNEYMEN

Plumbers, Steam Fitters

AND

GAS FITTERS.

———

Adopted at New York City, N. Y., Sept. 25, 26, 27, 1884.

Revised at Cincinnati, Ohio, Sept. 8, 9, 10, 11, 1885.

Also at Chicago, Ill., Sept. 6 to 12, 1886.

Boston Apr. 25th

Richard A. O'Brien Dear Sir and
Brother I take the liberty of
addressing a few lines to you at the
Suggestion of Bro Grace to obtain
your Views as regards the formation
of the United Brotherhood I fully
understand the position you are
placed in and for that reason
anything that passes between us
will be strictly Confidential Here

Both organizations as a Basis to work
on with Such improvements as will
tend to build up a Stronger union
that relying upon your experience
and good judgment I would like
to have your opinion upon what
would be the best methods of uniting
the whole Craft.
Yours Fraternally
P. J. Quinlan

address Vernon Place
Roxbury mass

Letter written April 25, 1889
by Patrick J. Quinlan to Richard O'Brien

CONSTITUTION AND RULES OF ORDER

OF THE

UNITED ASSOCIATION

JOURNEYMEN PLUMBERS, GAS FITTERS,

Steam Fitters and Steam Fitters' Helpers

OF THE

UNITED STATES

AND

CANADA.

———

Organized October 11, 1889.
Adopted Washington, D. C., October 11, 1889.
Amended Pittsburg, Pa , July 28 to August 1, 1890.
Revised Denver, Colo., July 27 to August 2, 1891.

———

DENVER, COLO.
MERCHANTS PUBLISHING CO.
1891.

**P. J.
QUINLAN**
First General
President
United Association

Richard A. O'Brien, First Secretary-Treasurer

WM. J. SPENCER,
Secretary-Treasurer, BUFFALO, N. Y.

John Alpine, General President

Thomas E. Burke, Secretary-Treasurer

John Mangan, General Vice President

John Coefield, President

Power Laboratory in Washburne Training School

and, in effect, detrimental both to the locals and the national union. Accordingly, institution of some sort of control or restraint over initiation and conduct of local strikes was viewed by the national officers as a logical concomitant of a stronger UA.

Any control by the national officers could hardly be developed, however, without a system of strike aid. As related before, under the Kelley administration, the UA was still unable to establish such a system. The result was that, until the nationalization program, the UA could exert very little influence on the strike activities of the local unions.

In the absence of a national aid system, individual locals on strike frequently resorted to appeals for help addressed to other local unions affiliated with the UA. Since the locals that were contacted had no way of checking either the validity of the particular pleas or the amounts that the strikers received from other sources, there were many cases where particular local unions took "advantage of the generosity of sister unions." In 1901, the UA convention passed a constitutional clause which provided that any appeal for strike aid addressed to the locals had to be first approved by the executive board. Potentially, the clause represented a means of extending national control over local strikes; in actuality, it was never enforced. As a result, both unauthorized appeals and donations by various locals continued until the UA instituted national strike aid.

The introduction of the national strike-aid system brought about a drastic change in the relative ability of the UA to exercise control over the strike activities of the locals. By 1913 — after several modifications of the system — the UA had at its disposal effective means by which it could exert influence in local situations where a conflict with employers was either anticipated or actually taking place.[67]

The most widely used means of influence stemmed from the power to approve or disapprove of local strikes. In order to qualify for aid, local unions had to prepare "an application to strike." This application had to be approved by the executive board in conjunction with the general secretary-treasurer. The application had to indicate the wages paid in the local's area, the nature of demands, the number of unemployed members, and so forth. The application was to be considered "with regard to chances of success of the proposed strike or lockout, justice of demands and finances liable to be involved." If the board disapproved an application, the decision could be appealed to a general vote of locals. But to overrule the board, the appealing local had to be upheld by two thirds of the voting locals.

In some situations of anticipated or actual conflict, the UA had a special representative. Any local that contemplated a strike involving more than fifty members had to notify the secretary-treasurer. The secretary had the right, with the agreement of the local, to appoint a special agent who would "represent the interests of the United Association" — investigate the situation, participate in the local meetings, and report his findings to the national office. Since the special representative could through his reports influence the decision pertaining to strike help, he could presumably also exert influence in local deliberations pertaining to the strike.

The executive board of the UA also had the right to appoint a member of the union "with instructions to arbitrate, in conjunction with a committee of local union, any difficulty affecting the members." This meant essentially that the appointed man had the right to change the policy of the particular local. Unless appealed to the vote of all locals, the decision of the arbitrator was to become final. To be sure, in actual practice arbitrators were hardly ever appointed. Nevertheless, the provision did strengthen the position of any UA representative who might be sent to investigate local problems.

The main purpose of these and other provisions was to lessen the cost of the strike-aid system and thus contribute to its financial success. But, by the same token, the provisions gave the national union a considerable measure of control over local strikes. The local union officers had a relatively free hand in ordering limited strikes designed to produce "immediate adjustment of any local trouble." Such strikes — on a particular job site — might be started without any prior notification of the UA, with the possible strike payments from the national office forthcoming after the strike was over. But any major contest required assurance of outside help. The local officers could not count any more on donations from the other locals; moreover, a large part of what in the prenationalization days might become a local strike fund was now paid to the UA. Accordingly, it was essential to any local which contemplated, or became engaged in, a major contest with employers that it have the support of the national union and the cooperation of the national officers. This inevitably meant that the national organization and its officers could exert a great deal of influence on the local decisions pertaining to the undertaking of strikes, the conduct of negotiations with employers, and the terms under which a strike could be terminated.

An additional factor that contributed to the growth of UA influence on local decisions was the increase in the number of organizers and the extension of their activities. UA organizers have always devoted a great deal of their time to negotiations with local employers, the settling of local problems, and intervening in local labor disputes. Indeed, in the view of some UA officers the organizers' main job was not to found new locals but rather to settle strikes and strengthen the existing local unions.[68] Thus the increase in the number of organizers from one to nine inevitably meant that the UA influence on the local approaches to the problem of strikes was becoming more pronounced.

The New York locals. The problems created by the local unions of plumbers in Manhattan and Brooklyn constituted one of the main difficulties encountered by the UA leaders during the years when they were carrying out the programs designed to strengthen the national union. By the same token, the eventual re-establishment of the UA in New York signified the final victory of the nationalization program. During the early 1900's, the New York locals of most construction unions had strong "localistic" tendencies. The control exercised by the national unions over the New York locals was relatively weak, and the locals of such important unions as the carpenters, bricklayers, iron workers, and others were, at one time or another, expelled from their respective national organizations.[69] Accordingly, the fact that the UA — a union that was actually increasing the power of the national body and reducing the autonomy of the locals — was able to re-establish itself largely on its own terms in what one AFL official called the "cradle of rebellion and secession," indicated that in the plumbing trade, at least, the days of loose federations of local unions were over.[70]

During the first presidency of Kelley (1897–1898) the UA had no local union in Manhattan. As already mentioned, former Local 2 left the national organization in 1895 and constituted itself as an independent union — the Amalgamated Society. Early in 1899, a group of members under the leadership of former UA President John Lee seceded from the Amalgamated and established a separate local union in Manhattan — the United Brotherhood of Plumbers and Gas Fitters. The split was the result of purely internal conflict, and neither the secessionists nor the group remaining in control of the Amalgamated had UA sentiments. However, once the United Brotherhood was established — and it was a numerically smaller union than the Amalgamated — it began making overtures to the UA. Kelley and Spencer took advantage of this situation and chartered the Brotherhood as Local 2 of the UA. Thus by March 1899 — after a lapse of almost four years — the UA again had a local union in Manhattan.

During the subsequent three years, New York had two rival unions of plumbers — Local 2 and the Amalgamated. As might be expected under such circumstances, the two unions frequently had jurisdictional conflicts. Moreover, the Amalgamated was also involved in jurisdictional disputes with UA locals in Brooklyn, Long Island, and New Jersey.[71] Local 2 made attempts to use its affiliation with the UA to defeat the rival union, and asked some UA unions in upstate New York to strike the shops of the multicity employers who employed Amalgamated men in New York City. These attempts met with little success. Throughout 1899–1902, the Amalgamated remained as the larger of the two rival organizations in New York.

The conflict between Local 2 and the Amalgamated contributed to a general weakening of the bargaining position of the journeymen plumbers, and, as a result, several attempts were made to establish a unified organization. Since the Amalgamated represented the majority of the organized plumbers, its leaders were particularly interested in a merger of the two organizations rather than in any other arrangements such as "exchange of cards." In 1900 they proposed that Local 2 rejoin the Amalgamated. After this proposal was rejected, the Amalgamated began moves designed to bring about a merger under the auspices of the national leadership of the UA.[72] These moves — made with the support of the New York AFL organization and of Gompers himself — led eventually to the merger of the two New York unions.

A major obstacle to the merger was the difference in conditions under which the two unions were willing to unite. From its very inception, Local 2 was composed of three branches or "councils." Each council held separate meetings in a different part of the city, and each was represented by five delegates on the executive board of the local. The leaders of Local 2 — presumably concerned about the balance of power in the merged organization — wanted the Amalgamated to become a fourth "council" of the local. The Amalgamated, on the other hand, wanted to merge to form a union in which there would be no "councils," and in which the officers would be elected in a popular vote by all members.[73]

The views of Local 2 had little influence on Tilden and Spencer who negotiated with the Amalgamated on behalf of the UA. One reason undoubtedly was that the independent union represented the stronger party among the organized journeymen. But, in addition, Local 2 was also in difficulties with the UA. The local did not introduce the stamp system for dues collection; its financial affairs were in poor shape; and, by 1902, it owed substantial sums to the national organization. Under these conditions, Local 2 had little bargaining power, and the UA officers apparently felt free to negotiate an agreement that, in effect, resulted in a union to be governed according to the system proposed by the Amalgamated.[74]

The merger was accepted by old Local 2, and in March 1902 the united organization was launched as new Local 2 of the UA.[75] The merged union was then represented at the historic convention in 1902 that started the first phase of the nationalization program.

The New York merger was hailed by Spencer as "our greatest achievement." But, as the 1902 convention began to consider the program of nationalization reforms, there were already signs that the UA was to encounter new difficulties in New York. The delegates of Local 2 opposed the introduction of sick and death benefits on the grounds that these were matters of local autonomy. When the majority approved the individual sections of the program, the New York delegates asked that they be permitted to operate under the old system during the following year, and introduce the nationalization system in 1904. The convention, taking into account what was presumably the "special conditions" in New York, agreed to this request.[76]

After the Omaha convention the New York plumbers provided further evidence of their opposition to the reforms that were being introduced in the UA. In the referendum on the nationalization program, Local 2 voted overwhelmingly against the program. And when the UA leaders wanted to postpone the convention until 1904, Local 2 issued a circular — sent to other local unions — which called for immediate holding of the convention, and an election of new national officers.[77]

The final break came early in 1904. Local 2, which was then supposed to come under the nationalization program, refused to conform to the UA system. Moreover, the leaders of the local apparently contributed to the decision of their neighbor Local 1 of Brooklyn. That local, too, decided not to observe the nationalization rules.

Both local unions were willing to stay in the UA and observe the rules of the clearance card system. However, they insisted on specific conditions. One was that they be permitted to exercise complete autonomy in the setting up and administration of their benefit systems. Another was that they pay only a percentage (40 per cent) of what was previously the per capita contribution. These conditions were presented to the executive board and circularized, with additional explanations and arguments, among the other locals.

The leadership of the UA did not accept the conditions. In March 1904, both unions were suspended, and the UA locals throughout the country were notified that the clearance cards from New York and Brooklyn were invalid and were to be rejected.

Viewed against the background of the history of the New York local, the events of the early 1904's appear quite understandable. As already suggested, the original UA affiliation of the secessionists from the independent Amalgamated (in 1899) was a defensive action, motivated by a desire to achieve supremacy in the New York market rather than by a pro-UA sentiment. Analogously, in the 1902 merger the primary motive of the independent union was to achieve unity in New York; affiliation was mainly for that purpose. The characteristics of the New York City labor market — the fact that local unions were both older and stronger than in neighboring towns, the highly developed employer associations, the continuous threat of the influx of both journeymen and contractors from scores of urbanized communities in New Jersey, Connecticut, or upstate New York — fostered a tradition of "localism" in collective bargaining practices and of "local autonomy" in the union movement.[78] The New York plumbers' unions shared in this tradition. But, as a result of a series of developments, they found themselves in 1904 in a national union that was, in fact, significantly curtailing local autonomy. Moreover, the period of transition from virtually complete independence to the point where the national union would strongly influence the conduct of local affairs was very short — less than a year. Accordingly, having once again achieved unity in the local labor market, the New York unions reacted strongly to the program of reforms fostered by the new administration of the UA.

But if the New York leaders thought that the situation in 1904 was similar to that in 1895 when the local could secede and continue as an independent organization without incurring any sanctions from the national union, they were clearly mistaken. For, as events showed, the

UA of 1904 — still undergoing transformation — was able and willing to take decisive steps against a seceding local.

Among the first was the launching of new UA unions in New York. One of them — officially Local 1 — was formed by a local UA leader, George Coddington, in Brooklyn. It laid claim to property, name, and jurisdiction of former Local 1. Another union — Local 379 — was formed by Merrick in the Bronx; it took over some of the territory of former Local 2.[79] By May 1904, the UA thus had two locals in the New York area. While the new unions were weak, they symbolized the determination of the national organization to be represented in the city.

The founding of these locals was followed by the UA's leasing of an office in Manhattan and the organization of a district council of loyal unions in greater New York. The council sent letters to plumbing journeymen and to employers, explaining the position of the UA. More important perhaps, the large plumbing contractors of New York were told by UA representatives that the national union would not tolerate any New York agreement that would exclude UA members from work. If the contractors discriminated against UA men, their work in other cities would be struck. To demonstrate its determination, the UA ordered that projects of New York firms in Hartford, Philadelphia, Pittsburgh, and other cities be struck for a few days by affiliated local unions [80]

As a result of negotiations and strikes outside New York, the UA secured a promise from the association of larger employers that it would sign a contract with a UA local in New York. A few days later, on September 3, 1904, the UA established a new union in Manhattan — Local 480. Most of the members formerly belonged to Local 2.[81]

The large employers tried to arrange a reconciliation between independent Local 2 and the UA. When this failed, they signed an agreement with Local 480 — essentially the same contract they had with the independents.

Although the UA succeeded in founding three additional locals in greater New York, the secessionist leaders were not intimidated. In fact, the leaders of Local 2 were apparently intent on expanding the secession. After some unsuccessful attempts to sway the UA convention in New York state, the leaders of Local 2 founded a new organization — the National League of Plumbers and Gas Fitters. In addition to former Locals 1 and 2, the league also had as an affiliate a former UA union in Staten Island (Local 104) which followed its sister locals in Brooklyn and Manhattan, and a small, newly founded union in Queens.

During 1905, the National League made attempts to establish local unions in the greater New York area, and in Pittsburgh and Cincinnati. While none of these efforts brought a permanent organization into being, each led to jurisdictional conflicts with the established UA locals.

The activities of the independent unions spurred Merrick and the UA administration to stronger measures. Two of the officers of Local 480 and the leader of Local 1 (the loyalist local) were made special agents of the UA, and Merrick and Organizer Dooley personally spent a great deal of time in New York. These efforts had at least limited success. All the loyal unions — each counting several hundred members — appeared to hold their own; and UA members, transferring from outside New York, were able to secure jobs in Brooklyn and Manhattan. But, throughout 1905, the balance of power in the New York market did not change greatly, and the unions of the National League still represented the majority of New York plumbers.

By 1906, as I have pointed out, many UA locals became alarmed at the large expenditures incurred by the national union in New York. Moreover, disagreements developed among the officers over the strategy to be used against the National League locals. In the middle of 1906 — when dissatisfaction within the UA was at its peak — Merrick withdrew from his functions in New York. From that time on, the work was carried by the two organizers — Burke and Dooley.

Burke and Dooley were less involved than Merrick in the personal animosities of the New York conflict and were better suited to carry on organizing. They also benefited from the fact that New York and Brooklyn employers were by this time vitally interested in bringing about unity in the plumbing trade. In July 1906, the National League unions in Brooklyn and Manhattan struck, demanding major wage increases in the next contract. The UA unions took advantage of this situation, and signed an agreement with the employers that called for a somewhat smaller raise than that demanded by the independents. This action — coming after a prolonged period of local conflicts, and after the failures of the National League to expand — demonstrated to the leaders of Locals 1 and 2 the futility of further rivalry. Shortly after the signing of the agreement, Burke and Dooley began negotiations with the officers of the independent unions. The result — in August 1906 — was that the secessionist unions agreed to affiliate with the UA.

Burke and Dooley did not insist that the independent locals merge with corresponding UA unions. Instead, the UA representatives installed former Local 1 as a new UA union, Local 96; and, analogously, installed old Local 2 as a new UA union in Manhattan, Local 498. With the exception of three former leaders of the original secession of Local 2 (who were no longer active in the union movement), all the members of the independent unions were admitted to the new UA locals. While the new unions were granted all the privileges of UA member locals, they also automatically accepted the constitution incorporating the nationalization program.[82]

By the time of the 1906 convention, almost all the organized plumbers of New York City were in locals affiliated with the UA. Shortly after the convention, the independent local in Staten Island merged with a UA union.[83] Thus, just about the time Merrick and Tilden were losing their power in the UA, the New York conflict that significantly contributed to their defeat was drawing to a close.

The affiliation of the New York and Brooklyn locals created a complex union situation among the New York plumbers in construction. By 1907, there were two UA locals in Manhattan, two in Brooklyn, one in the Bronx, and one on Staten Island. In 1907, at Burke's recommendation the UA executive board ordered a merger of the two Brooklyn unions. In spite of strong opposition from old loyalist Local 1, the merger was carried out and the combined unions (Locals 1 and 96) formed a new Local 1.[84] In 1913, the convention ordered a merger of the two Manhattan unions, and this too — though opposed by former loyalist Local 480 — was eventually carried out. Later, the Bronx local was merged with the Manhattan union.[85]

The affiliation of the former National League locals did not put an end to all the problems of the locals in the New York area. Nevertheless, the return of the Manhattan and Brooklyn unions to the UA should be regarded as an important moment in the history of the organization. Quite apart from the fact that the UA was now stronger by about sixteen hundred members, the affiliation marked an end to a conflict which showed that the "nationalized" UA had power that could be used successfully against a recalcitrant or rebellious local union.

Chapter 5

Affiliation of the Steam Fitters

THE FIGHT to eliminate the International Association of Steam and Hot Water Fitters and Helpers as an independent union and to absorb its members constituted one of the major efforts of the UA throughout its entire history. Between the early 1898's, when the UA first proposed amalgamation, and the early 1914's, when the last locals of the fitters joined the national union, UA officers spent a great deal of their time on the problem of the IA; the UA expended thousands of dollars on organizing, legal proceedings, conferences and meetings — all because of the conflict with the IA; at one time some UA officers were indicted in a criminal conspiracy case, and one local officer was found guilty of murder and sent to prison for life; and in the process of the dispute, UA locals either started or indirectly caused strikes affecting hundreds of building projects, involving thousands of workers of all crafts and eventually resulting in months of lost man-days. Moreover, the UA frequently incurred enmity of many local and national organizations of the other building crafts, contractors, employers, and, in some areas, the local press along with public opinion. But, though the costs were heavy, throughout most of the 1897–1914 years the continuation of the fight was viewed by the UA leaders as one of the most important tasks and critical challenges facing the United Association.

The tactics adopted by the UA leadership and its official pronouncements kept changing during the 1898–1914 period depending on circumstances — the internal cohesion of the UA itself, the relative strength of its position within the AFL and in the construction industry, developments at AFL and Building Trades Department conventions, decisions of various special bodies that were supposed to solve the UA–IA issue. There is no question, however, that the basic assumption underlying the long-run policy of the UA was that the IA's very existence was incompatible with the functioning of the United Association as an effective trade union. Accordingly, the goal of the leadership remained the same throughout the period — to bring the organized steam fitters into the UA, and to establish that organization as the union with exclusive jurisdiction over all the pipe trades.[1]

There are several factors that explain this basic policy of the UA.:

From the viewpoint of the UA, the International Association constituted a dual union. The UA from its beginning claimed jurisdiction over all types of pipe fitting and always included among its members steam and hot water fitters as well as plumbers and gas fitters. In the sense that it claimed to cover the pipe trades, the UA could be considered, as one student of unionism termed it, "a limited industrial union." [2] The jurisdictional claims of the IA — covering steam and hot water fitting, sprinkler fitting, and other types of pipe fitting outside plumbing — directly conflicted with UA jurisdiction. More important, the presence of IA local unions always posed the danger of rivalry between the UA and IA steam fitters, a rivalry that could only lead to the undermining of union standards and a weakening of the organization. The actual experience during the 1898–1914 years did, in fact, provide several examples of the effects of interunion competition.[3]

The IA's existence posed a danger not only to the UA fitters but also to the plumbers. As a result of technological changes, much of the pipe fitting performed by the plumbers could also be performed by steam fitters. Large numbers of shops did both plumbing and steam fitting and employed members of both crafts. In spite of attempts to draw strict lines between functions, in many cases plumbers did some steam fitting and fitters, in turn, did pipe fitting in what were considered plumbing installations. To be sure, in many areas the licensing laws and building codes limited the work of fitters to steam and hot water projects or other types of pipe fitting. But in many localities, licensing laws were either nonexistent or not enforced. In such areas, the IA locals of fitters provided a source of labor that could compete with the plumbers organized by the United Association.[4]

The problem was particularly acute outside the major metropolitan areas. In large cities, the large amount of construction work and the specialization of functions permitted the existence of separate locals of plumbers and fitters, locals that could belong to different national unions. In the smaller cities and towns, the total number of pipe-fitting journeymen was small, and the amount of construction was too limited to permit continuous specialization and rigid division between plumbing and other pipe fitting. The UA locals in such areas were usually mixed (plumbers and fitters).[5] IA organizing activities threatened to break up such mixed locals; by the same token, there was the fear that many areas would have two small organizations whose members were ready — in competition with each other — to perform both plumbing and other pipe fitting.[6] Even if the IA had concentrated its organizing primarily in large cities, its very existence would have endangered the viability of the mixed locals in smaller areas. For with steam fitting in the major cities organized by the IA, the UA fitters belonging to the mixed locals would have been largely deprived of the advantages of the clearance cards of their own national union.

In the eyes of the United Association, the threat of the IA was further increased by the appearance of several major jurisdictional conflicts concerning work assignments of plumbers and steam fitters in the construction industry:

As indicated previously, there were some disputes about what constituted the work of the fitter and what of the plumber also in the early period of the UA's existence. But till about 1900 such conflicts were relatively minor. The basic ingredients of the plumbing installations were generally easy to distinguish from the assignments involved in putting in steam or hot water heating.

In the early 1900's the construction of large buildings for commercial and industrial purposes required many piping installations that were, by and large, not obviously identifiable either with plumbing or steam fitting. In commercial buildings, these new installations involved piping for a wide variety of purposes — pneumatic tubing for a carrier system, vacuum cleaning systems (both the so called "dry" and "dual"), fire lines and sprinkler fitting, thermostatic control apparatus, speaking tubes. In the construction of industrial buildings (as well as in some commercial structures) pipe fitting installations also involved piping for humidity maintenance systems; for conveyance of liquid chemicals, syrups, and so forth; for apparatus that supplied lubricating fluid to engines and machinery; for ice making machines; and for many other special purposes.[7]

The reasons why these and other installations resulted in work assignment conflicts are easy to understand.

As a result of pre-1900 technological changes, the plumbers mainly used the kind of pipes — cast iron, wrought and galvanized iron, tinned steel — that were also used in new installations. They also employed methods of connecting and fitting pipes that were applicable to the new materials. Similarly, the steam fitters, normally working with all kinds of iron pipes, were using other methods of pipe fitting besides the more traditional joining of threaded pipes. Both crafts were, in effect, qualified by the nature of required skill, materials, and tools used to handle practically all the newer types of piping installations. As a result, disputes pertaining to craft jurisdiction over particular work assignments became common in many cities.

The work assignments conflicts and disputes took place under a variety of circumstances. In some, the conflict involved a UA plumbers' local and an IA local of fitters; in other cases, both the fitters' local and the plumbers' local might belong to the UA; and in still other situations, the dispute arose among the members of a mixed UA local.[8]

Since the IA represented only the steam fitters, it was always defending and, indeed, fighting aggressively for the jurisdictional claims of that craft. In contrast, the UA could not afford to take either a consistent or decisive stand on the issues. The majority of its members were plumbers; equally important, in several areas — including throughout most of the period cities such as New York or Chicago — all the fitters were in IA locals. Any ruling by the national body of the UA or its officials favoring the fitters would be politically difficult, and would be used by the IA in the local arbitration proceedings where the work assignment conflicts also represented a conflict between the UA and the IA locals. On the other hand, any national decision that favored the plumbers would strengthen the IA in its attempts to organize steam fitters in a separate union and contribute to the secession of fitters from the UA.[9]

In the face of these difficulties, the UA leadership generally avoided formulation of national decisions pertaining to any specific issue of the plumber-fitter trade jurisdiction. Under pressure from the plumbers, the 1906 convention provided that vacuum cleaning piping was within the plumbers' jurisdiction;[10] but, in most other cases, the solution was left to local option and arbitral decisions of local umpires. This general policy — or perhaps lack of policy — could not suffice to counteract IA policies. The appearance of intertrade jurisdictional conflicts played into the hands of the International Association. Since it would consistently uphold any jurisdictional claims of the fitters, it was obvious that as the trade jurisdiction problems continued and multiplied, the IA's appeal to the fitters — whether outside the UA or in it — would grow stronger. Accordingly, any UA policy based on the principle of "coexistence" could be reasonably assumed to lead eventually to the loss of virtually all the steam fitters to the rival union.

The IA also threatened the expansion of the United Association outside the area of construction. In the early 1900's, it was apparent that a union of pipe fitters could also find thousands of potential members in manufacturing establishments, in sprinkler fitting companies, in shipyards, and in railroad shops.[11] Organization of the marine and railroad fitters and of fitters in industrial plants would add to the strength of the United Association. Equally important, the extension of UA organizing into these new fields would prevent potential undermining of union standards in construction through the influx of unorganized pipe fitters into the building firms. The many types of pipe fitters working outside construction were considered by the UA leaders to be covered by the jurisdiction of their union. The same claim was made by the IA. Both organizations had, in fact, local unions that were composed of railroad fitters and of general pipe fitters employed by manufacturing concerns.[12] The presence of the IA created thus, what was from the UA viewpoint, dual unionism in all the branches of pipe fitting except for plumbing proper and for the rapidly declining craft of gas fitting.

While it thus seems obvious that the elimination of the IA was of paramount importance to the UA, there is still the question of the reasons underlying the stubborn and prolonged resistance of the International Association. In spite of its organizational progress, the IA remained throughout 1898–1914 a relatively small union, probably never exceeding 7000 members.[13] The power and prestige of such IA leaders as John Mangan came primarily from their positions in strong local organizations rather than in the national union. At the same time, the UA continued to make amalgamation proposals providing for considerable autonomy of the fitters' organization within the larger and consolidated union. Why then had the IA leadership resisted to the very end — and at very considerable cost — the attempts of amalgamation?

As the IA leadership — and probably most of its members — felt, the UA's fight for amalgamation essentially represented an attempt on the part of the plumbers to acquire control over all pipe fitting for the benefit of their own craft. In their speeches, publications, and testimonies IA leaders continuously emphasized that the technological changes in plumbing had revolutionized the craft and reduced demand for skilled journeymen. As a result, the plumbers began to look for job opportunities in steam fitting. In order to expand these opportunities — the IA leaders argued — it was necessary for the plumbers to control the steam fitters.[14] In an amalgamated union the plumbers would constitute a large majority; moreover, their jurisdiction was being protected by licensing laws that barred steam fitters from performing any work even remotely connected with plumbing.[15] Accordingly, amalgamation could only lead to a continuous invasion and erosion of the jurisdictional rights of the steam fitters. As one of the local IA leaders put it during the bitter conflict with the Cincinnati UA union: "The steam fitters are well aware that it is not their organization that the plumbers want, but their work."

The IA leaders also believed that their organization had a strong "constitutional" basis derived from the principle of trade autonomy, presumably promulgated by the AFL and organized labor in general. In this view, the steam fitters represented a distinct craft entitled to a separate national organization. Their relation to the plumbers was not closer than that of the printing pressmen to the printers or of the core makers to the moulders — all of them crafts with their own unions. The amalgamation moves were thus considered by the IA leaders as a step back to the early experiences of the Knights of Labor.

These factors do not of course, provide a complete explanation of the attitudes and behavior of IA leaders or, for that matter, of many of the members. Such men as John Mangan, William Onstott, or Thomas Kinsella — all veterans of many years of unionism — had strong attachments to their organization and were proud of the unions they helped to build. Inevitably they felt that they were fighting for a "right cause" against organizations that compromised the principles of trade unionism.[16]

The course of the struggle between the UA and the IA constitutes a complicated story of many moves and countermoves, of joint conferences and meetings of the two unions, of decisions of the AFL and the Building Trades Department, and of local strikes and legal proceedings. In recording the main aspects, it will be useful to divide, in a somewhat arbitrary fashion, the 1898–1914 struggle into three phases — the first one covering 1898–1903, the second 1904–1910, and the third 1911–1914 period.

THE FIRST PHASE OF COEXISTENCE: 1898–1904

The story begins appropriately with the UA's offer of amalgamation. Following the instructions of the UA's 1897 convention, W. J. Spencer contacted the leaders of the IA and proposed that it affiliate as a unit with the United Association.[17] No immediate answer was given, but the next convention of the IA meeting in Toledo, in November 1898, "decided, after a careful consideration, not to affiliate itself with the United Association, but to remain in an organization of its own." [18] The same convention also decided that the IA make an application for membership in the AFL, and empowered John Mangan — leader of the Chicago Steam Fitters' local — to represent the IA at the forthcoming AFL meeting in Kansas City.

The IA application led to the first confrontation of the conflicting claims of the two unions before a leading body of organized labor. Because of the dispute over the jurisdiction of the UA — already a member of the AFL for a year — the executive council of the AFL refused to issue a charter to the IA. The Kansas (1898) convention of the federation took a more friendly position. The delegates voted that Mangan be heard on the floor, and he delivered a spirited defense of his national union as a distinct trade. The UA's reply — delivered by William J. Spencer — emphasized the close relation of the two trades and the frequent interchangeability of work and common employers. Spencer repeated the offer of amalgamation, with equal representation of the fitters on the UA's executive board and autonomy in decisions pertaining to steam fitters. He also urged that the executive council of the federation draft a proposal for amalgamation.[19] The majority of the delegates were unconvinced by Spencer's arguments. By a vote of 27 to 20, the convention passed a motion that a special committee be formed to investigate the question of amalgamation and of separate charter to the IA. The recommendations of the committee were to be reported to the president of the AFL and then to be taken up by the federation's executive council. The convention appointed George W. Perkins of the cigar makers, T. J. Elderkin of the coast seaman, and O. E. Woodbury of the carpenters to the committee.[20] Perkins later resigned, and his place was taken by Daniel J. Keefe of the longshoremen.

The committee — after several sessions in April and May of 1899 — recommended that "the Steam Fitters be granted a national charter." [21] The recommendation included however what turned out to be important conditions: 1) the UA had the right to retain all its steam fitters without any interference on the part of the IA, but the fitters could withdraw voluntarily from the UA to join the other union; 2) in areas where there were not enough fitters to form an IA local, the journeymen were allowed to join the UA.

This provided the basis for the admission of the IA to the federation. After some hesitation and an unsuccessful effort to find another solution, the executive council of the AFL granted the IA a "conditional charter." [22] The conditions were actually undefined, but the presumption was that they were those spelled out by the Keefe committee. Thus "paradoxically," as one student termed it, the AFL recognized two organizations whose jurisdictional claims overlapped to a significant extent.[23]

The decision of the AFL represented, of course, a victory for the IA. Nevertheless, the steam fitters felt restricted, since, under the conditions of the charter, they were presumably barred from exercising organizing initiative in many areas where the UA had either mixed locals or separate locals of fitters. Accordingly, in 1900 the IA asked for a "constitutional" (regular) charter from the federation.

The 1900 convention of the AFL refused, but called for a meeting of the IA and UA representatives with a committee of the executive council of the federation to reconcile the "existing differences." [24] The committee, composed of Samuel Gompers, Thomas Kidd and John Lennon (the president, the vice-president, and the treasurer of the federation), met in May 1901 in Chicago with the leaders of the two unions and found that no mutual agreement could be reached. The committee reaffirmed, therefore, in a rather strong tone what it conceived to be the original restrictions imposed by the charter issued to the IA, and emphasized that "these conditions already indicate that the International Association of Steam and Hot Water Fitters and Helpers under no circumstances (other than the voluntary act of the United Association of Plumbers, Gas Fitters, Steam Fitters' Helpers, as such) has the right to interfere with the membership of the United Association . . . or to persuade them from their allegiance to the said United Association." [25] Significantly, the Gompers group did not mention that, according to the original recommendations of the Keefe committee, individual UA fitters were permitted to leave the UA voluntarily and form an IA local. Instead, the committee concluded that the IA's right to form locals "cannot be construed to permit the organization of locals of steam fitters of those who are already members of the United Association."

Although something of a setback for the IA, the decision of the Gompers committee had no immediate influence on the fortunes of that organization. In 1900–1901, the IA established several new unions in areas where the steam fitters previously belonged either to a mixed or a separate local of the UA. This activity continued after the statement of the Gompers committee.[26]

To some extent, the fitters' secessions from the UA were an immediate result of IA organizational activities which ignored the geographic restrictions on territory. But there were also other reasons. As the new pipe fitting installations became more frequent, jurisdictional conflicts pertaining to work assignments provided the fitters with a strong stimulus to form separate locals under the aegis of the IA; many fitters long felt that the UA was dominated by the plumbers and acted exclusively on behalf of that craft; the fact that the IA was recognized by the AFL as a legitimate union of the distinct craft of steam fitting increased its prestige and attractiveness in the eyes of the minority craft of the UA. Because of these factors, in many areas there was no need for the IA organizers to instigate a secession. The very existence of the IA on the national scene was sufficient in many cases to cause the fitters to leave the United Association.

As indicated previously, the UA was unable to develop a policy on the work assignment issues that would provide an effective defense against the IA. But at the urging of John Kelley, the UA began moves to make the organization more attractive to the steam fitters. In 1899, two steam fitters were elected for the first time to the executive board of the UA, and in 1900 the constitution was amended so that at least two members of the executive board *had* to be steam fitters.[27]

In December 1901, during the Scranton convention of the AFL, the UA requested that the IA charter be revoked. The main reason was that the IA had violated its charter by establishing a local composed of men who scabbed on UA work; another was that the IA had added to its title the term "General Pipe Fitters." The Executive Council denied the request but ordered that the IA release all members admitted in violation of the conditions of the charter, and drop the new term from its title. The council also ordered that the two organizations meet in conference and arrange for exchange of cards "and such further agreement as may restore peace and harmony between the two unions, or bring about an amalgamation." [28]

The decision of the executive council was upheld by the AFL convention. However, the delegates added a clause providing that, in case of failure of an agreement, the matter be taken up by a three-man committee of the executive council to act as umpire.

The result was another meeting between UA and IA representatives. The IA delegates agreed to relinquish one of the new locals (the one composed of "scabs"), and to abandon the new title. But they refused to surrender the charters of other new locals — including those in Indianapolis, Kansas City, Oklahoma City, and Denver. The IA also rejected the proposal of an interchange of cards. Instead, the representatives proposed that the UA have complete jurisdiction over plumbers and gas fitters and the IA over steam fitters. The conference ended in complete disagreement.[29]

In accordance with the decision of the Scranton convention of the AFL, the issue was turned over to the committee of the executive council. This committee — meeting in Chicago in March 1902 — was again composed of Gompers, Kidd and Lennon. It met with the representatives of both unions and, acting as arbitrator, issued a decision to settle the matter.

The statement issued by the committee was sharply critical of the IA. But the decision was not very different from that made by the executive council of the AFL. All steam fitters, now members of the IA, who were admitted contrary to the conditions of the IA charter were to be released and restored to UA membership within sixty days after such request was made by the president of AFL. The UA was asked to specify each case in which the IA violated the charter, and the validity of such claims was to be determined by the committee. Finally, the committee decided that in case of noncompliance on the part of the IA, the IA charter would be revoked.[30]

As in the case of the previous decision by Gompers and his colleagues, this decision had little immediate effect on the actual course of events in the pipe trades. The IA held on to the previously organized locals and, in fact, formed new ones. However, the two national unions made another attempt at reconciliation. As a result of a suggestion made by the IA, the 1902 convention of the United Association decided that a special committee meet with IA representatives.[31] Another fruitless conference took place in September 1902. Th UA representatives essentially wanted the affiliation of the IA as an autonomous subdivision of the United Association; the IA proposed a loose alliance of the two unions for the purposes of cooperation and definition of jurisdiction of the two crafts. After a two days' discussion the conference adjourned without agreement.[32]

The conflict was taken up again at the 1902 convention of the AFL in New Orleans. The executive council reported that, since the UA had not yet provided information on areas where the IA violated its conditional charter, the question of revoking that charter had to be postponed. The IA in turn, offered several resolutions reflecting its own position in the dispute. During the ensuing debate, Thomas Dooley, one of the UA delegates, made a motion that another meeting — consisting of two delegates from each of the unions and a referee appointed by the president of the AFL — meet within sixty days and settle the matter. This was passed by the convention.[33]

The outcome of the AFL convention was to the UA just another instance of the failure of the federation to come to grips with the issues and to adopt a decisive policy.[34] As it turned out, however, the decision of the 1902 convention led to important developments.

President Gompers appointed as referee Frank A. Rist (from the ITU local in Cincinnati). Rist met with representatives of the two unions in January 1903, and held sessions for over four days. As he later reported to Gompers: "From the start it was noticeable that no mutual agreement could be reached." He also became convinced that "both organizations treated each other's members as outlaws, and to continue in this industry without change of conditions would prove disastrous not only to the trade interested, but to the general labor movement as well." Rist thus concluded that the only remedy was the affiliation with the United Association on terms previously specified by the UA (with considerable autonomy), and issued a decision "in favor of merging both organizations into one body and jurisdiction." [35]

The International Association protested vigorously. As Onstott, Mangan, and other IA leaders saw it, the question of merging was not discussed at the 1902 convention of the federation and was not submitted either to the committee or to the referee. Accordingly, in making the decision for amalgamation, Rist exceeded his authority.[36] The executive council of the AFL took a different position. In April 1903, the council decided to sustain the Rist decision, and called for a meeting of the two unions. The council also decided that in the event of the IA's failing to comply with the decision, "the conditional charter now held by the International Association be revoked." [37]

As might be expected, the IA refused to comply, and its charter was revoked. The matter then came up for final consideration before the 1903 convention of the federation. The IA itself had no accredited representation, but it had many supporters among the delegates. In fact, the convention's committee on the executive council's report recommended that the case be reopened and that a charter be granted to the IA. This was decisively defeated by the convention, and the delegates then went on to sustain the decision of the executive council of the federation.[38]

By the end of 1903, it appeared that the major phase of the UA–IA conflict was over. The UA — with a much larger membership than its rival — was now the only union in the pipe trades recognized by the AFL. As the leaders of the UA began moves to have the IA locals unseated in city central unions, Spencer could say, not without some justification, that, though the IA was dying hard, "they are dying just the same." [39]

THE SECOND PHASE OF COEXISTENCE: 1904–1910

The revocation of the IA charter initially appeared to constitute an important factor strengthening the position of the United Association. In several areas, the local bodies of the federation unseated the IA, and, partly as a result of these moves, the UA organized some new locals of steam fitters.[40] But even as the IA charter was being revoked and during the immediate period after that event, the IA organized locals, composed of former UA men, in such important areas as Pittsburgh and Baltimore.[41] IA organizing continued, of course, after its charter was reissued. Indeed, despite its nominally strong position at the beginning of the period, the UA was, through most of the 1904–1910 years, essentially on the defensive in the area of steam fitters' organizations. The relative weakness of its position in steam fitting and its inability to take full advantage of the AFL decision was a result of several factors.

Perhaps the first and most important reason was the internal situation within the United Association. As described previously, during the early years of the 1900's and particularly in 1904–1906 the U.A. was undergoing a transformation that produced major internal strains.

The attention of its officers was largely absorbed by the problems raised by the "nationalization" program and by the secession of New York. And even in 1906 when John Alpine took over the presidency, the internal problems of the United Association constituted the dominant issue facing him. As a result, the leaders of the UA could not devote their main efforts to the fight against the "dual" union.

A second reason was that the IA had many supporters among the building trades and other unions affiliated with the AFL.[42] Some of the federation's leaders — like James Duncan of the granite cutters — were strongly in favor of amalgamation; and Gompers himself appeared, at least at times, to lean in that direction.[43] But the IA organizations were firmly established and had a long tradition in such important cities as New York, Chicago, and Boston, and the union inevitably had many friends among local union officials and national representations at the AFL convention. Thus the UA could not count on overwhelming support of organized labor.

A third reason was that in the early 1900's the federation frequently had little actual control over the action of its local bodies. In spite of the revocation of the IA's charter, several local bodies did not comply with the official requests for unseating of the Steam Fitters; in other areas the unseating procedures took a long time. And even where the IA was eventually compelled to leave a local body, this did not mean that the locals of the Federation-affiliated unions would refuse to have its members working alongside the I.A. men.

The position of the United Association was further weakened by disputes pertaining to trade jurisdiction over various types of piping. Indeed the 1904–1910 years witnessed some major conflicts. In Chicago, the disputes about work on vacuum cleaning systems and pneumatic tubes led to arbitration decisions that generally favored the IA, and increased its prestige among the steam fitters; in other cities, such as Pittsburgh, the conflicts contributed to the secession of the fitters from the UA.[44]

As a result of the Rist decision, the IA was kept out of the AFL for two and a half years. In 1905, the fitters applied for another charter but were refused one by the executive council. During the 1905 convention of the federation, however, the St. Louis Central Trades Union — which previously refused to unseat the fitters — introduced a resolution calling for issuance of a charter to the IA.[45]

AFL Vice President John Mitchell pointed out that this resolution raised some important constitutional problems. For one thing, the Louisville convention of the AFL adopted a resolution that once a dispute was decided upon by the convention, it should not be taken up again within a period of three years. Secondly, a charter that might be issued to the IA would presumably trespass on the jurisdiction of an affiliated union (United Association). In spite of these objections, the 1905 convention passed a resolution recommending to the executive council that it "grant a charter to the Steam Fitters' organization." [46]

The council did not immediately follow this recommendation. Faced with the vote of the convention on the one hand, and a potential constitutional problem on the other, it decided to call another conference with UA and IA representatives, hoping that some agreement could be reached. The meeting with the two unions — in May 1906 — produced no positive results.[47] Thereupon, after considerable debate, the executive council decided by a 4 to 3 vote to restore to the IA the conditional charter which the fitters previously held.[48] The action of the council was in effect upheld by the 1906 convention of the federation which rejected the resolution of the UA calling for revocation of the IA's charter.[49]

The AFL decision constituted a victory for the IA. Nevertheless, since the conditions of the original charter also applied to the new charter, the IA felt restricted in its organizing activity. Accordingly, at the 1907 convention of the AFL, the IA representatives submitted a resolution calling for a removal of the conditions attached to its charter "thereby granting the IA full jurisdiction and absolute control of their trade." The resolution also called upon the UA to remove the words steam fitter from its charter.

The IA resolution was never submitted to the vote of the delegates. Instead, the convention approved a report of the Adjustment Committee which called for a meeting of the representatives with Gompers "for the purpose of arranging an agreement defining the jurisdiction of the two organizations." In case of a failure to agree, the executive council was empowered to define the jurisdictional lines.

This meeting like the previous meetings ended without agreement.[50] Accordingly, following the decision of the 1907 convention, Gompers referred the matter to the executive council of the AFL. In June 1908, the council decided that the whole matter be referred to the next convention of the federation, with the recommendation that it be further referred to the next convention of the Building Trades Department.[51]

The Denver (1908) convention of the AFL upheld the decision of its council, and the whole matter went to the convention of the Building Trades Department. The convention — meeting immediately after that of the AFL — ordered that the two organizations meet in January 1909 to work out a mutually acceptable solution. The official decision of the Building Department's convention did not spell out what would happen if no agreement were reached. But, as the discussion on the floor suggested, the presumption was that, if this were the case, the executive council would draw up a solution to the jurisdictional conflict of the two unions, and then enforce it through the action of its local bodies.[52]

Following the decision of the Building Trades Department, the UA and the IA representatives met again — this time in Washington. Both organizations came with essentially the same proposals that they had offered at previous meetings. The International Association wanted complete jurisdiction over fitters in all areas where the number was sufficient for a separate local; cessation of organizing fitters by the UA; right of the UA fitters to join the IA. The United Association brought its old proposal of amalgamation which granted autonomy to the fitters within the combined organization. The meeting — under the chairmanship of President James Kirby of the Building Trades Department — lasted three days and, as was already becoming customary, produced no agreement.[53]

Since the meeting of the two unions failed to produce a solution, the executive council of the Building Trades Department, meeting in Pittsburgh in February 1909, made its own decision. This so-called "Pittsburgh agreement" was in the form of a mandatory decision. The main points were 1) each of the organizations was barred from organizing fitters "where the other organizations have already covered the territory in accordance with its own laws"; 2) in areas where both unions controlled work the organizations were required to establish common standards of wages and hours as well as initiation fees; 3) unorganized localities were to be "a legitimate field for organizing work of the organization whose representatives shall first commence the work of organizing"; 4) a permanent joint committee of the two unions was to be established, with an impartial umpire, to adjust any grievances; 5) if either party failed to participate in joint conference the subject matter was to be referred for final decision to the executive council of the Building Trades Department.

The "Pittsburgh agreement" constituted a decision highly favorable to the United Association. For one thing, the "agreement" disposed decisively of the IA's claim of complete jurisdiction over the steam fitters. More important, the agreement imposed conditions on the IA that were much more restrictive than those of the AFL charter. In 1909 the IA claimed to have about 100 local organizations. The UA had close to 500. The plumbers naturally constituted a majority of the UA members. But most of the UA locals — about 400 — were "mixed" in the sense that they either had, in addition to plumbers, representatives of the other crafts among the members, or that their charters provided for membership for all the pipe fitting journeymen. Thus in areas where such locals existed, the territory was presumably covered by the UA "in accordance with its own laws," and the IA was barred from conducting organizing activity.[54]

The implications of the "Pittsburgh agreement" were immediately perceived by both unions. The UA accepted the agreement at once; the IA, on the other hand, appealed on the grounds that the agreement was not in accordance with the mandate of the department's convention.[55]

The International Association also continued its organizing activity in areas which, according to the Pittsburgh agreement, constituted territory covered by the UA. New IA locals were organized in Syracuse, Salt Lake City, and Spokane, and attempts to establish locals — sometimes through direct contact with fitters belonging to the UA — were made elsewhere. The UA complained to the executive council of the Building Trades Department and, as a result, the IA was ordered to annul the charters of the new locals. The IA was also requested by the council to meet with President Kirby and "show cause why it should not be suspended from membership in the Department." [56]

Any suspension procedures that the council had in mind were postponed by the action of the Building Trades Department's 1909 convention in Tampa. The report of the convention committee supporting the actions of the executive council was upheld by only half the delegates. Following this, the delegates passed a substitute motion referring to the UA–IA conflict. According to this, the two unions were required to meet once again with the executive council of the department to work out an agreement. However if that meeting failed, the "Pittsburgh agreement" would be recognized as the legal and final solution.[57]

The meeting of the two unions took place in December 1909. The

IA delegates — for obvious reasons, in a much more conciliatory mood — did not press for complete jurisdiction, and merely offered a proposal of mutual cooperation, with full freedom of organizing on the part of both unions. But the UA delegates refused to agree to anything more favorable to the IA than the conditions of the Pittsburgh agreement.[58] The meeting ended in failure — an outcome both expected by and welcomed by the UA.[59]

After this, the executive council of the department officially announced that the "Pittsburgh agreement" was now in force. The International Association refused, however, to recognize it as valid. In June 1910, the council met in Atlantic City and, after taking testimony from the representatives of both UA and IA, decided to refer the "grievance" against the IA to the next convention of the department with the recommendation that if the IA still refused to comply, it should be suspended from the Building Trades Department. As a result of this decision, the 1910 convention — meeting in St. Louis — again took up the matter of the UA–IA conflict. This time, however, it acted in a decisive manner. After a brief debate, the majority of delegates followed the recommendation of the executive council, and voted to suspend the IA from membership in the department.[60]

As already indicated, during most of the 1904–1910 years, the UA was essentially on the defensive in its conflict with the IA. Indeed, it should be recalled that the developments eventually leading to the suspension of the IA from the Building Trades Department started with the IA's demand for complete jurisdiction over the steam fitters. What is, then, the explanation of the change in the relative position of the two unions — a change that was explicitly revealed in the "Pittsburgh agreement" of 1909?

The answer appears to be the growing strength of the United Association and the desire of the building trades unions to limit jurisdictional warfare.

By the 1909–1910 period, the United Association emerged successfully from the experience of internal reforms and nationalization. In terms of membership and financial position, it was stronger than ever. Moreover, it was gaining influence in the councils of organized labor: John Alpine was a vice-president of the AFL, and William Spencer was secretary-treasurer of the Building Trades Department. Thus, it was probably apparent to many union leaders that a proposal totally unacceptable to the UA could not provide a viable solution to the conflict in the pipe trades.

The prolonged dispute between the UA and the IA involved both the problem of jurisdiction over a craft (steam fitters) and jurisdictional disputes over work assignments (plumbers versus steam fitters). The numerous local conflicts resulting from this naturally affected the other building trades. For one thing, the walkouts of either plumbers or fitters — walkouts resulting from the dispute between the two unions — involved stoppage of work by other crafts. In some cases (for instance, in the construction of a new Marshall Field building in Chicago), the resulting stoppages were very costly.[61] The contests between the UA and the IA actually weakened the local building trades councils.[62] The fight between the UA and the IA said AFL Vice President Duncan, "has caused some of the worst contentions in the building industry." [63] By the end of the 1904–1910 period many of the building trades' leaders were thus determined to take decisive steps to solve the UA–IA problem.[64] But as, already suggested, a pragmatic solution had to be acceptable to the stronger and more influential of the two unions — i.e. the United Association.

THE UA OFFENSIVE AND VICTORY: 1911–1914

The suspension of the IA from the Building Trades Department marks an end to the previous policies of the United Association. After that decision — beginning in early 1911 — the United Association mounted an organizing offensive that, combined with more decisive actions on the part of the federation, led to complete defeat of the IA. By the end of 1910, the International Association was still at its peak of membership; three and a half years later — in the middle of 1914 — virtually all the IA locals were either affiliated with the UA or merged with UA locals. In view of the prolonged history of the struggle between the two unions, the UA's victory was thus achieved in a remarkably short time.

One of the major factors that contributed to this success has already been suggested — the condition and the leadership of the United Association. In 1910, the UA was a strong union, with a membership of 25,000 and average annual income of over $200,000.[65] It was led by skilled men firmly in control of the national organization, and it had available funds for special organizing activities and for financing legal procedures. With a staff of eight full-time organizers, in addition to the services of Alpine and Burke, the UA also had the manpower resources for negotiations with and the organizing of IA locals.

As a result of its strength and widely scattered membership, the UA was also able to exert pressure on some IA locals analogous to the pressure used in dealing with the New York union. In several cities — Boston, Providence, Richmond, Cincinnati and others — large projects were being constructed by firms that normally did business in many other areas. These firms were sensitive to the threats of boycotts and strikes that could be initiated by plumbers in the many areas where the UA had strong locals. As a result, the large contractors frequently yielded to Alpine's pressures to dismiss IA men and employ UA steam fitters.[66] This, in turn, put additional pressure on the local fitters to affiliate with the United Association.

Another factor that helped the UA to some extent was the aid of the Building Trades Department. The suspension of the IA meant that the local Building Trades Councils were required to expel the IA unions and to provide support to the UA. In some areas — Kansas City, Cincinnati, Worcester and others — the actions of the local bodies proved to be of importance either in inducing the IA locals to affiliate or in persuading employers to employ UA fitters.[67] There were, however, cities like Boston where the local building trades bodies were badly split, and where the UA could count on the help of only a limited number of other construction unions.

Much greater help than that of the Building Trades Department was given to the UA by the AFL. The policy of the federation became a particularly important factor inducing local affiliation of steam fitters with the UA in the period after the 1912 AFL convention. During that convention, the federation revoked the charter of the International Association, and announced its full support of the UA as the only legitimate union in the pipe trade.

The revocation of the IA charter by the AFL constituted a final development in a chain of actions following the suspension of the steam fitters from the Building Trades Department. The 1910 convention of the department recommended that the IA also be suspended by the federation. Accordingly, Spencer acting as a secretary of the department transmitted this recommendation to Gompers. After some delays — and one more meeting of Gompers with UA and IA representatives — the executive council of the AFL replied that a charter could be revoked only by two thirds of the federation's convention. But at the same time it made public its view "that the best results to the workers of the industry would be best conserved by all being united in the one general organization of these [pipe] trades, namely, the United Association." [68] The very same pronouncement was submitted by the executive council to the 1911 convention of the AFL, with the further request that the council "be instructed to carry this [amalgamation] . . . into effect." [69] A committee of the convention (building trades committee) decided to concur both in the policy pronouncement and in the request of the executive council. Its report was, in turn, upheld by a majority of the convention delegates. In effect then by the end of 1911, the AFL officially supported the UA as the legitimate union in the pipe trades.

Following the 1911 convention, Gompers called a meeting of UA and IA representatives to work out a plan of amalgamation. The IA representatives refused to confer with the UA men, and asked the executive council to formulate a plan.[70] The plan — essentially calling for affiliation of locals and individuals with full rights of membership — was then submitted to both organizations with a terminal date for acceptance. Since the IA failed to accept it, the executive council decided that, as of May 1912, the AFL would accept per capita tax from only one organization in the pipe trades — the UA. This decision was then publicized in a circular sent to affiliated unions.[71]

The final action took place, as indicated above, at the Rochester convention of the AFL in 1912. Following a prolonged debate, the convention voted to refuse seating of IA delegates and to approve the previous action of the executive council. The convention then voted by an overwhelming majority to revoke the charter of the IA and to recommend the amalgamation plan previously formulated by the executive council.[72]

As the IA's experience in 1903 showed, even a small union could at times survive expulsion from the federation. But in the conditions of 1912 — with the IA locals encountering strong organizing by the UA and with the growing reluctance of employers to antagonize the plumbers and the other building trades — the final decision of the federation proved to be a crucial factor in persuading fitters' locals both in smaller and larger areas to affiliate with the bigger union. The revocation of the IA charter, said John Mangan, dealt "to our local a blow that was difficult to overcome, and we were forced by circumstances and not by our free will to join the United Association." [73] Many IA officers and members throughout the country undoubtedly felt the same way.

An overwhelming majority of IA locals affiliated with the UA — or merged with the UA fitters' locals — without any major show of strength such as strikes or boycotts. Thus throughout 1911–1913, IA locals were being brought into the UA through negotiations and agreements in a wide variety of areas — from Waterbury, Connecticut to San Francisco. In some areas (Nashville, for example) the IA local would take in the fitters from the mixed UA local and affiliate with the United Association; in other areas (like Indianapolis) the IA fitters would join the already existing UA local of steam fitters or (as in Waterbury) the local union of plumbers; in still other places, such as San Francisco, the fitters' local would simply leave the IA and affiliate with the UA. [74]

But peaceful affiliation of IA locals was not universal. In a few major cities, IA locals affiliated with the United Association only after a period of bitter conflict — conflict reflected in strikes and boycotts that involved, in addition to plumbers and fitters, most of the other building trades.

Of these conflicts, by far the most important took place in Chicago. The Chicago interunion fight was important not only because of its duration and scope — it lasted over seven months, and at one time it caused unemployment for several thousand workers — but also because of its timing. [75] Since the battle was started, essentially through UA action, in February 1911 — shortly after the IA's suspension from the Building Trades Department and before any IA locals changed their affiliation — it demonstrated to the organized building trades and to the federation the determination of the UA leaders to carry on a vigorous and costly offensive.

Chicago's steam fitters and helpers were organized in 1911 by two IA locals: Local 2, the union of journeymen, and Local 4, the union of helpers. Local 2, founded in 1885, was the second oldest and the second largest fitters' union in the country. The home local of the outstanding IA leader John Mangan, Local 2, had, in 1911, 600 to 700 members and was under the leadership of Charles M. Rau. IA Local 4, with a membership of about 400, was in 1911 still led by

Martin "Skinny" Madden, prior to 1900 a powerful figure in the Chicago building trades.[76] The United Association was represented in Chicago by a local of plumbers (Local 130) with a membership of about 1500, and by two smaller locals of about 200 members each — the gas fitters (Local 250) and the sprinkler fitters (Local 281).[77]

Until 1911, the UA had no organization of steam fitters in Chicago. In February of that year, however, Alpine and Organizer Leonard instituted a local union of fitters, composed of men who previously worked on the so-called "permit system" of the IA Local 2, of some fitters brought by the UA to Chicago from outside locations, and of a few former members of the IA in Chicago.[78] In view of the long history and firm position of the IA in Chicago, the formation of this union — Local 520 as it was officially called — represented a sign that the UA was intending to take over the initiative in the conflict with its rival.

Virtually all the unionized steam fitting contractors employed IA fitters. In order to compel the contractors to employ the members of Local 520, the UA barred its plumbers, gas fitters, and sprinkler fitters from working on projects where steam fitting was done by IA fitters. The strikes of plumbers and other UA men were successful in several cases in securing jobs for Local 520 men. Moreover, the UA action had the official support of the Chicago Building Trades Council. But some unions like the carpenters did not belong to the council and were sympathetic to the IA; also, certain unions affiliated with the council, the brick layers, for instance, decided to support the IA fitters. The result was that the hiring of UA fitters caused walkouts by the building crafts supporting Locals 2 and 4 of the IA. To make matters more complex, the UA was, in turn, supported by other Chicago unions — among them the iron workers, sheet metal workers, and electricians — who refused to work alongside the IA men.[79]

At the request of the IA the local court issued a general injunction restraining the UA in its activity against the steam fitters. Because of the number of unions involved and the number of projects affected, the injunction appeared, however, to be ineffective in stopping strikes.

In March 1911, a new element was added to the Chicago conflict — the use of physical force. The professional "sluggers" who took part in several fights were considered both by the Chicago newspapers and by the police as connected with some of the leaders of UA Local 520, and with "Skinny" Madden's local of the steam fitters' helpers. However no evidence was ever produced that either the national leaders of the UA or, for that matter, of the IA were directly involved in hiring the "sluggers." [80]

The conflicts existing in the building trades were also reflected in barroom fights. In one, a "slugger" connected with "Skinny" Madden was mortally wounded. A few months later, in connection with another shooting, the police arrested and charged Maurice Enright, the business agent of UA Local 520, with the crime. In addition, three officers of the UA's plumbers' local were arrested on charges of conspiracy to kill. The charges were soon dismissed because of lack of evidence. Enright, however, was later found guilty and sentenced to life imprisonment.[81]

The strikes and work stoppages caused by the conflict continued during the summer of 1911. Contractors employing IA fitters were struck by unions loyal to the AFL Building Trades Department; contractors using Local 520 men were, in turn, struck by the unions helping the IA. After several unsuccessful efforts to settle the matter, a truce, negotiated with the help of the executive council of the Building Trades Department, was finally established in September.[82]

The agreement on which it was based was essentially the principle of toleration. Local 520 men — numbering according to the UA about 500 — were permitted to work wherever they had contracts.[83] But the IA fitters — and they still represented an overwhelming majority of the craft in Chicago — were also permitted to work without interference on the part of the UA or other unions wherever the IA had the contracts. Thus, though the UA succeeded for the first time in establishing a fitters' local in Chicago, it still failed in dislodging the IA from its dominant position in steam fitting.

Although the agreement was signed on the IA side only by Madden, it was observed by both the UA and the IA, and by the other crafts. Shortly after the revocation of the IA charter by the AFL, local UA officers and leaders of the two steam fitters locals began negotiations concerning affiliation with the UA. The result of the negotiations, later joined by President Alpine and Organizer Leonard, was an agreement specifying work jurisdictions of plumbers and fitters. This paved the way for affiliation of the two unions. On February 5, 1913, IA Local 4 — by then under new leadership, since Madden died in 1912 — was formally installed as Local 598 of the UA. A day later, Local 2 — Mangan's and Rau's union — became Local 597 of the UA.[84]

After the affiliation, the Chicago locals organized a Pipe Trades

Council consisting of all the UA unions. Local 520 — originally instituted as a weapon against the IA — was ordered to disband, with its journeymen members joining Local 597 and its helper members joining Local 598. In spite of the protests of leaders of Local 520 this merger took place shortly after the 1913 convention of the United Association.[85]

The Chicago experience was repeated on a much smaller scale in St. Louis and Boston. In both cities, UA members struck projects on which IA men were employed, and these strikes in turn led to walkouts by the other construction unions divided in their sympathies. The Boston conflict also involved an injunction against the UA and the direct intervention of Gompers. The disputes ended in a truce and the eventual affiliation of the steam fitters with the UA (in January 1913 in St. Louis, and in June of that year in Boston).[86]

By the time of the 1913 convention of the United Association, meeting in Boston in August, John Alpine was able to claim that the battle "has been practically disposed of." [87] Some steam fitters were still outside UA locals in Toronto and in Newark; and in Detroit the old IA local was still negotiating about the condition of affiliation. However, the problems in these areas were being resolved. The only city where the old IA organizations were still in full control of the fitters was New York. But, as Alpine correctly foresaw, these fitters were to affiliate with the UA in a short time.

The New York steam fitters and helpers were organized into two unions affiliated with the IA. One — the Enterprise Association or Local 1 — was the oldest and largest of the former IA locals. Its membership consisted entirely of journeymen. The second — the Progress Association or Local 80 of the IA — was a helpers' local. The two organizations — believed to have included over 2000 members — were firmly entrenched in steam fitting and had for years negotiated agreements with the New York employers. The fitters' locals had also had several jurisdictional disputes over work assignments with the New York plumbers, with some of the major ones resolved through arbitration awards.[88]

As Alpine realized, the Enterprise and Progress Associations were in such a strong position that an outright confrontation resulting from the launching of a competing UA local would have been very costly.[89] Accordingly, until 1913 the UA took no action against the New York steam fitters.

In May 1913, Alpine began exploratory talks with the leaders of IA locals. As these talks continued, he was joined by leaders of the New York plumbers' unions. About the same time, the UA established a branch office in Manhattan, and began to issue circulars presenting its position to the New York fitters.[90]

The main subject of the negotiations with the steam fitters — negotiations that lasted for seven months — was the subject of jurisdiction over various types of piping. In January 1914 the talks broke off. The reason was a disagreement about jurisdiction over pneumatic tubing, air piping, piping for syrups and other liquids, and fire lines.

Alpine and Leonard took the position that, as a result of precedents or previous arbitration decisions, the disputed items belonged to the steam fitters. Accordingly, as representatives of the UA, they signed an agreement in March 1914 that defined the jurisdiction lines in a way acceptable to the fitters, and provided a plan for affiliation of the Enterprise and Progress Associations with the UA.

One of the UA unions — Local 1 of Brooklyn — joined Alpine and Leonard in signing the agreement. However the two UA unions in Manhattan — Locals 480 and 498 — vigorously protested Alpine's action, and refused to become party to the agreement.

The Manhattan locals were also joined by the employers. Some of the large firms in New York, knowing the strength of the UA outside the city, were sympathetic to the affiliation. But the master plumbers — most of them presumably doing work only in New York — felt that the jurisdictional agreement negotiated with the fitters was detrimental to their business. Thus, apparently at the instigation of the officers of Local 498, the New York Master Plumbers' Association applied for an injunction that would restrain Alpine and the Manhattan locals from carrying out the agreement with the fitters.

In spite of these difficulties, Alpine and Leonard proceeded with the affiliation of the fitters' unions. As a result, in April 1914, the two former IA locals officially joined the UA — the Enterprise Association becoming Local 638 and the Progress Association becoming Local 639.

Since the efforts of the New York plumbers and their employers failed, the April 1914 affiliation marked the end of the UA conflict with the International Association. From then on, the United Association was to be in a real sense the national union of virtually all the pipe trades.[91]

In view of the preceding narrative, it is not necessary to emphasize the heavy costs borne by the UA — both financial and in terms of effort — that led to final victory. It is appropriate, however, to indicate some of the major organizational and legal changes introduced by the UA and several of its major locals — changes introduced as a direct result of extending UA organization in the field of pipe fitting.

(a) The drive to win the allegiance of the steam fitters was reflected in further modifications in the composition of the UA's executive board. In 1902, the UA constitution provided that only 2 of the 10 board members be steam fitters. By 1913, as a result of these changes, 5 of the 14 members — over one third — had to be steam fitters. As in previous years, each of the minor crafts — the gas fitters and the sprinkler fitters — was entitled to one member of the Board.[92]

(b) To assure the steam fitters of greater autonomy rights, the constitution was amended to facilitate formation of separate fitters' locals. Specifically, if two thirds of a craft organized in a mixed union wanted a separate local, the UA was obligated to issue a charter.[93]

(c) The IA conflict brought new awareness of the complex issue of intercraft disputes over work assignments. In 1908, the UA convention added a special constitutional clause dealing with this issue. The clause provided that in case of a local dispute between UA members a final decision would be made by an umpire appointed by the president of the UA. In view of the touchiness of the subject during the struggle with the IA, this arbitration procedure was not extensively used. In 1913, however, the clause was strengthened by a provision giving the president the right to issue a final decision in cases of local jurisdictional disputes among UA members.[94]

(d) As already indicated, the affiliation of steam fitters' locals in Chicago and New York was preceded by agreements that specified in some detail the respective jurisdictions of the plumbers and the steam fitters. Analogous agreements preceded affiliation of former IA locals in several other cities — Milwaukee, Cincinnati, St. Louis, Washington, Baltimore, and others.[95] These agreements differed somewhat, depending on local conditions and previous arbitral decisions. But they were normally signed not only by the local unions but also by the national officers of the UA. Accordingly, the local agreements were frequently viewed as part of the general legal framework of the national organization.

Chapter 6

Some Important Issues
In the Period of Nationalization

THE PROBLEMS of nationalization and of the conflict with the International Association clearly dominated the 1898–1914 period of UA history. But at the same time the organization had also to face a host of other problems. From the viewpoint of the development and future policies of the national union, the most outstanding among these problems were: the matter of the regulation of extending jurisdiction over the sprinkler fitters; apprenticeship; and the policy toward the so-called "exclusive agreements" between local unions and local employer associations.

AFFILIATION OF THE SPRINKLER FITTERS

During the last two years of John Kelley's presidency (1899–1901), the United Association extended its jurisdiction to cover the youngest and the least numerous of the pipe trades — the sprinkler fitters. This move represented an important step in the UA's development as a national union of all the pipe crafts.

Sprinkler fitting became a distinct occupation in the 1880–1890 decade. Beginning then, installations of automatic sprinkler systems were spreading to industrial plants, warehouses, theaters, hotels, and other commercial establishments. Quite apart from the obvious benefits, these installations were also encouraged by insurance companies which began charging reduced rates in places equipped with the systems.[1]

Recorded attempts of using sprinkler apparatus to fight fires date to early decades of the eighteenth century. But the modern automatic sprinkler systems trace their origin to a series of developments by American inventors and manufacturers during the 1870's and 1880's, and particularly to the work of Henry S. Parmelee and Frederick Grinnell.[2] As it does today, the automatic sprinkler apparatus of the 1890–1914 period consisted essentially of a system of pipes connected

with an outside water supply — fire pumps with city water connections, steel tanks, wooden tanks placed on the roofs of the buildings;
of valves whose purpose was to activate electric or other fire alarm
gongs; and of sprinkler "heads" (devices that automatically released
streams of water in case of fire). The various improvements in the
sprinkler systems from 1870 to 1914 pertained primarily to the development of sprinkler heads that would be more reliable in their automatic response to conflagrations, and more effective in scattering full
streams of water. These and other technological changes had only a
limited impact on the basic functions of the sprinkler fitters — the
men who were employed in installation of the sprinkler apparatus.

Their work — installation of piping, placing of tanks and pumps,
and attaching of valves and sprinkler heads — involved the kind of
skill and experience that were an integral part of the training and work
of plumbers and of steam and gas fitters. In fact in the early 1900's
large numbers of sprinkler fitters were recruited from those who gained
their first experience in pipe work in the older trades. But in some
important aspects, work conditions of the sprinkler fitters differed considerably from those of the other pipe trades.

The manufacturing of automatic sprinkler apparatus was concentrated in a few firms, firms that had, through developmental work and
patented devices, brought about the major improvements in the fire
fighting systems. These firms not only manufactured the apparatus but
also installed it. Hence, one difference between sprinkler fitters and the
other pipe trades was that most of the sprinkler fitters were employed
by a few large manufacturing firms.[3]

Another difference was that sprinkler apparatus was normally installed only in industrial and commercial structures. This meant that
only in a few large cities was there a permanent need for a pool of
fitters specializing in installing fire protection apparatus. Elsewhere,
installations of sprinkler apparatus were carried out by special crews
recruited and sent out by the sprinkler manufacturing companies. The
result was that most of the sprinkler fitters were, in effect, "road men"
who moved from one area to another following the jobs offered by
the manufacturers.[4]

Compared with the other pipe trades, sprinkler fitting was difficult
to unionize. The few large firms which did business over a wide area
were less sensitive to local union pressure than the small local employers of the other trades. Moreover, the fact that the bulk of sprin-

kler fitters was continuously on the move made it difficult for any local union to control them. As a result, sprinkler fitters could be organized at first only in a few large cities. In the early 1890's, independent locals were established in New York, Chicago, and St. Louis. By the time the UA joined the AFL, all three unions — with a total membership of about 250 — were directly affiliated with the AFL as federal locals.[5]

Until 1899, the UA showed no interest in extending its organization to sprinkler fitting. In contrast, the International Association — or at least some of its local unions — claimed the work as part of the jurisdiction of steam fitting. The IA Chicago local became involved in a bitter conflict with the Federal Union of Sprinkler Fitters. This conflict provided the reason for the affiliation of two sprinkler fitting locals with the UA.

At the 1989 convention of the AFL — the same convention that first considered the admission of the IA — the sprinkler fitters' locals asked the AFL to condemn the Chicago steam fitters as strike breakers. This happened in time, but, in the process of the floor debate and of some parliamentary maneuvers, it became apparent that many delegates believed that, assuming that the IA would join the federation, the three federal locals should be absorbed by the steam fitters.[6]

Leaders of the sprinkler fitters' locals thought that they could retain greater autonomy in the UA than in the IA. Accordingly, after a special AFL committee recommended that the steam fitters be issued a conditional charter, the sprinkler fitters asked the UA for a conference to arrange affiliation. The Peoria convention of the UA (1899) decided to refer the matter to the incoming executive board.[7]

After the IA had been admitted to the AFL, the federation's convention (1899) ordered that the sprinkler fitters' locals and the IA hold a conference "to devise ways and means by which the Sprinkler Fitters may come under the jurisdiction of the International Association." [8] This order eventually resulted in the affiliation of the New York sprinkler fitters with the IA. But leaders of the Chicago and St. Louis locals disregarded it, and continued their negotiations with the United Association.[9]

With the sharpening of the conflict between the UA and the IA, UA leaders became convinced that it was essential to "take in" the sprinkler fitters. As Kelley, Tilden, and Spencer saw it, sprinkler fitting represented one of the several branches of pipe fitting that evolved from the original lead work of the plumber; accordingly, it was essential for the UA to control it in order to preserve the jurisdictional lines among the pipe trades. Moreover, it appeared that if the sprinkler fitters were not admitted, they would either join the IA, or form another national union.[10]

Some UA members opposed the admission of sprinkler fitters because they considered the occupation as one of little skill, and one that had little in common with plumbing; others feared that, once admitted to the UA, the fitters would encroach upon the plumbers' jurisdiction. But the UA leadership was able to overcome these objections. The St. Louis local affiliated in mid-1901 as a result of direct negotiations; the Chicago sprinklers were admitted in August of that year after the UA's Buffalo (1901) convention voted to issue them a charter.[11]

Once the sprinkler fitters were admitted the AFL took the view that the problem of their affiliation was just another aspect of the UA–IA dispute, and that its solution depended on the resolution of the basic conflict. To be sure, in the 1902 settlement proposal of the AFL executive council's committee, the UA, was to turn over the sprinkler fitters to the IA. But since, as we have mentioned, the IA did not accept the major points of that settlement, the recommendations pertaining to the sprinkler fitters were not considered seriously either by the two national unions or by the sprinkler fitters' locals themselves. The UA changed its constitution to recognize its jurisdiction over sprinkler fitting in 1904 — at the time when the International Association was out of the AFL.[12] And in the following years — when the IA had been granted a second AFL charter — the issue of jurisdiction over sprinkler fitting was overshadowed by the larger aspects of the UA–IA battle.

The affiliation of the sprinkler fitters' locals had little immediate effect on the extent of unionization in the craft. Throughout the 1899–1914 period, in most areas, sprinkler fitting continued to be poorly organized Unions were well established in Chicago and St. Louis; in a few other major cities the sprinkler fitters were organized in "mixed" locals (together with steam fitters and plumbers); and new unions of sprinkler fitters were eventually organized in Kansas City, Milwaukee, and Minneapolis. But in most localities the work was done by traveling crews of non-union men, recruited and employed by the few large manufacturing concerns.

Strong demands were usually made at the UA conventions that UA plumbers and steam fitters not work alongside nonunion sprinkler fitters. But these had hardly any effect. The UA locals felt that they could not insist that employers use union sprinkler fitters if there were no sprinkler fitters' organizations in the area. And the sprinkler fitters normally stayed too short a time in a locality to make it feasible for the UA locals to organize them.[13]

The UA leader always recognized the special difficulties of organizing sprinkler fitters. But it remained for John Alpine to initiate a policy that eventually established the UA as a full-fledged organization of the craft. This policy was essentially based on two principles: 1) given the conditions of the sprinkler fitting industry, the most effective way to unionize it was not by locals in numerous areas but through direct negotiations between the national officers of the UA and the management of the few dominant firms; and 2) the UA's strength in these negotiations stemmed from its position in the relatively few major industrial areas where local workers were unionized (and could thus strike the relevant firms), and where the principal employers were doing a great deal of installation of sprinkler apparatus.[14]

Alpine's approach proved successful. In 1915, after many conferences, the UA and five dominant firms signed a national agreement under whose terms practically all the fitters employed by the firms — both those in major areas and those "on the road" — were to be organized by the United Association. (The agreement excluded the cities where the UA already had sprinkler fitters' locals — for example, Chicago. The locals in these cities had their own contracts with the companies.) The 1915 agreement represented, of course, a major development in the sprinkler fitting trade; but, equally important, it also reflected a new role played in collective bargaining by the national union and its officers.

APPRENTICES AND HELPERS

Regulation of apprentices — an issue so crucial in the earlier years of the UA — continued to be one of the national problems for the union also in 1898–1914. By the end of that period, most of the agreements negotiated in the plumbing trade had at least some provisions that regulated the institution of apprenticeship. But these provisions, essentially the result of local initiative and reflecting the relative strength of the local unions, varied widely from area to area. In spite of several attempts, the UA leadership was unable to institute a national system of apprenticeship regulation.

Like their predecessors, the UA leaders of the 1898–1914 period realized that national control of apprenticeship required cooperation of the employers' association. But they were also unable to enlist such cooperation. Many employers were keenly aware that unlimited entry into the plumbing craft would also lead to increased numbers of shops, particularly "one-man" shops.[15] But since training apprentices conferred certain advantages, other employers were reluctant to observe the kind of regulations that would be acceptable to the UA.[16] The result was that the National Master Plumbers' Association was unwilling to commit itself to any firm program of national control of apprenticeship. During each of the three administrations of the period — Kelley's, Merrick's, Alpine's — there were conferences with the NMPA concerning the issue of apprenticeship. None of these, however, produced any viable results.[17]

The UA leaders also realized that the locals could not possibly enforce the highly restrictive apprenticeship rules that, since the Milwaukee (1896) convention, had been incorporated into the constitution. In 1899 the old provisions were repealed, and from then on the executive board of the UA was supposed to select the areas where it would be feasible to eliminate all apprentices.[18] Actually, however, the executive board left the matter entirely up to the local unions. This change of emphasis was specifically recognized in 1904 when a completely new constitutional provision was written. It simply stated that "it is the opinion of the United Association that local unions throughout our jurisdiction should use their best efforts and endeavor to abolish Plumbers Helpers and Apprentices, so far as possible." In 1910, the term "to regulate" was substituted for "to abolish," and a clause was added which, in effect, permitted up to four apprentices per shop.[19] However, no attempt was made to enforce even this very general provision.

As the above suggests, such progress as the UA made toward the regulation of entry into plumbing was primarily the result of a general strengthening of local organizations and their increased ability to negotiate with the local employers rather than of new policies evolved by the national union.

Until the time of the Alpine administration, the UA leadership had shown little interest in formulating national policies concerning the helpers in steam fitting. To some extent, this neglect reflected the predominant position of plumbers in the union. But there was also another reason. Since the steam fitters normally handled very heavy pipes, they had continuous need for and, in fact, demanded, the assistance of helpers.[20] Under these circumstances, the UA policy which aimed at abolishing, or at least severely restricting, the number of plumbing apprentices did not appear applicable to fitters' helpers.

By the time of the Alpine administration, however, technological changes in heating apparatus resulted in a much wider use of smaller diameter pipe, and reduced the need for assistance to the journeymen installing steam and hot water heating. This contributed to the change in the attitude of the UA leadership toward the problem of helpers. As Alpine, Burke, and Leonard saw it, the helpers represented a potential increase in the number of journeymen steam fitters; their position was quite analogous to that of the plumbing apprentices, and called for similar policies. Accordingly, by 1913, the UA leaders were urging locals to adopt policies that would drastically reduce the number of steam fitters' helpers.[21]

The view that the helpers were essentially the equivalent of plumbers' apprentices was also reflected in a constitutional provision passed by the Boston (1913) convention. An old clause in the constitution provided that, in order to be classified as a journeyman, a steam fitter's helper had to pass an examination. This was amended to the effect that, in addition, the helper had to serve five years in the trade before qualifying as a journeyman.[22]

"EXCLUSIVE AGREEMENTS" AND "MATERIALS CLAUSES"

In the late 1890's and early 1900's, many local unions — both in major cities and smaller areas — signed the so-called "exclusive agreements" with local employers' associations. These were contracts with a clause providing that members of the employers' association would use only the members of the particular local, and that the local members, in turn, would work only for the shops that retained good standing in the association. Many of these agreements also contained a clause specifying that UA members would not install or handle any material or fixtures not purchased by their immediate employers (master plumbers or master steam fitters). These "materials clauses" — as they may be called — were also incorporated in a few agreements that did not have the more common "exclusive" clause.[23] As indicated previously, both clauses constituted key features of what the UA leaders publicized in 1891 as a "model agreement." But after only a few years' experience with these "model" provisions, it became obvious that, while highly beneficial at times, they could also raise difficult problems both for the locals and for the national organization.

From the viewpoint of the locals, the exclusive agreements could, under certain conditions, provide important benefits. The most crucial was, of course, the provision instituting closed shop among the members of the employers' association. In areas where the employers' association provided all the major sources of employment, institution of closed shop through an exclusive clause was likely to be an important factor strengthening the union. This was particularly true of areas where union organization was weak. In such places, a closed shop might well have been, as a Providence UA leader put it, "the only thing that holds them" in the union.[24] Both the provisions limiting union employment to members of the association and the materials clauses were, primarily, a *quid pro quo* for concessions granted by the employers. But as pointed out below, given appropriate circumstances they could also benefit the unions.

The exclusive agreements and the material clauses benefited the members of the local employers' associations for several reasons:

(a) By signing the agreements, the associations secured for their members the exclusive right to employ what in many areas was the bulk of the available supply of skilled plumbers or steam fitters and, frequently, the bulk of the only craftsmen who could be put to work on a construction project where the other crafts were unionized. In situations where the employer associations also limited their membership — through high initiation fees or in other ways — this exclusive right provided means of limiting the number of local competitors.[25]

(b) The exclusive right to employ local union members also provided means of strengthening the discipline among the individual members of the local employer associations. As might be expected, local associations would normally attempt to establish standards of behavior that would regulate or control competitive pressure among their members. The exclusive right to employ union members provided a means of enforcing these standard, since, under the provisions of the union contract, an employer who lost his standing in the association would automatically face a strike.[26]

(c) The "materials clauses" were an important means of retaining for the plumbing and steam heating contractors the function of retailing equipment and supplies. Where the employers also had an exclusive agreement, the clauses provided additional instruments for enforcing association codes of behavior on members. For instance, a master plumber subcontracting for a building owner who himself purchased sinks, bathtubs, and so forth, would expose himself to the danger of a walkout even if his own association took no specific action against him. And the materials clauses were even more important where there was no exclusive agreement. In such areas there were normally many employers who, for one reason or another, did not belong to the association. But the materials clause made the union a crucial means of extending one of the association codes to these unaffiliated master plumbers. In either case, if the materials clauses were observed, they would clearly contribute to a stronger financial position of the members of the association that signed the contract with the UA local.

Lessening of competitive pressures among employers would normally result in less downward pressure on wages, and would thus put the union in a stronger position to maintain standard rates and conditions in the local shops and to negotiate further wage gains. And there would be the same result if, by expanding their retailer functions, employers derived satisfactory profits from the sales of plumbing and steam fitting supplies. Accordingly, the benefits accruing to the employers also provided important advantages to the unions. But the exclusive and materials clauses also posed special problems for the locals. The reason was that observance of the clauses was frequently inconsistent not only with maintaining job opportunities for all of the local UA members but also even those jobs that were already held by union craftsmen.

The problems arose in a variety of circumstances. In some areas, certain employers were expelled from their association because of internal conflicts or unwillingness to abide by its codes of behavior; in other areas, employers who were paying union rates were barred from joining the association; and in still others certain employers — both inside and outside the association — violated the local version of the materials clause. In all these cases the local union was obligated under the contract to order some of its members to leave what were frequently considered steady, well-paying jobs. In view of the personal hardship to the workers, these orders were frequently disregarded. Recalcitrant workers were then fined and, if the fines were not paid, suspended by the local. In this sense then, as one UA leader put it, these contract clauses had the effect of forcing "good union men to become scabs." [27]

The difficulties posed by the clauses were forcibly brought to the attention of the national union in 1899. This happened as a result of developments in Omaha and Denver. In both cities, plumbing shops were opened which apparently had direct financial connections with N. O. Nelson, a large wholesale supply firm operating from St. Louis. The local employers viewed this entry of a wholesaler into their industry as a violation of the "regular channels of trade." The Denver local had, in effect, an exclusive agreement with the employer association from which the Nelson-sponsored firm was excluded. And after the founding of the new firm, the Omaha local signed an agreement containing a very broad materials clause. In addition to the usual provision about ownership of materials, this clause also stated that the union members would not work for "any concern owned, operated or controlled in whole or in part by anyone engaged in manufacturing, wholesaling or jobbing business." Although the Nelson-sponsored firms paid union rates and were willing to observe all the union rules, the Denver and Omaha locals ordered their members to stop working for them. When the men refused, the locals imposed high fines.[28]

Both cases came before the Peoria (1899) convention because the UA executive board rescinded the fines, and the locals, in turn, appealed the decision to the convention delegates. The Omaha case was further complicated by the fact that the strike against the Nelson-connected firm was ordered before the actual agreement with the employers was signed, and that the original fines were followed by a series of further fines, and a major internal fight in the local UA organization.

As reflected in the decisions to rescind the locally imposed fines, the UA leadership was becoming aware that the exclusive and materials clauses could pose serious difficulties for the union. In his presidential report, Kelley explicitly opposed both clauses as unduly strengthening the employer organizations. He also argued that the agreements were "practically assisting trusts and combinations to compel the general public to pay an exorbitant price for the construction of our work . . . which will inevitably lead to curtailment of such work in the future." [29]

The Peoria (1899) convention disagreed sharply with the leaders. The Omaha and Denver locals were upheld primarily on the principle of local autonomy. But the convention also passed a constitutional provision that represented a rather extreme form of the materials clauses incorporated in local agreements. This provision stated:

No member of this Association shall be allowed to work on any job where the material has been furnished directly to the owner or general contractor, except on work for the Federal, state, county or municipal governments.[30]

This provision thus made the observance of what the employers termed as "the regular channels of trade" part of the constitution of the national union.

The materials clause remained in the UA constitution only for one year. In 1900, several factors helped the UA leaders to persuade the Newark convention that, as Kelley put it, the clause was "a positive menace" and that it should be eliminated. The Chicago plumbers, then engaged in a bitter conflict with the local employers, attributed some of their difficulties to the fact that, through materials clauses and exclusion of supplier-connected shops, the union helped to build a strong employer association with a tight hold on the local jobbers. (During the 1900 lockout the jobbers refused to sell supplies to any shop that might employ union men.) In other cities, UA locals found that the materials clause barred their members from obtaining jobs in breweries and other manufacturing plants that normally bought their own supplies, or from working directly for large general contractors. And last, the UA leaders were also supported by Gompers who in his convention address argued strongly that materials clauses and boycotts of supplier-connected shops paying union rates ultimately aided the enemies of organized labor. Responding to these arguments, the majority of the delegates decided, after a lengthy debate, to strike out the materials clause.[31]

President Kelley was not successful, however, in his attempt to introduce some national restrictions on the way locals administered their exclusive agreements with employer associations. In 1900, Kelley argued that, while local unions should be permitted to make such agreements, they should not be permitted "to promiscuously expel our members who may chance to be working in a shop whose proprietor declines to join the Master Plumbers' Association." But the Newark (1900) convention refused to impose any restrictions on the locals.[32]

The matter of exclusive agreements came up again a year later, during the Buffalo (1901) convention. As the debate revealed, there was a sharp division of views on the issue. Some delegates opposed the agreements on the grounds that they deprived union men of job opportunities and strengthened the employers; but others found them essential to the maintenance of strong union organization. The result was sort of a compromise. The delegates tabled a proposal that would prohibit locals from signing exclusive agreements, but the convention did pass a resolution that put it on record as "not being in favor of such agreements."

Without a specific mandate to combat the exclusive agreements signed by the locals, the Kelley administration could do little more than publicize the unfavorable effects of such agreements. The executive board which had to consider the appeals of the UA members who were fined by their locals for working for shops that did not belong to (or were expelled from) the employer associations normally upheld the locals. But in its decisions it also expressed its disapproval of the basic nature of the exclusive agreements.[33] And the *Journal* carried editorials opposing the agreements and publicized the previously mentioned resolution of the Buffalo convention. These efforts, however, could exert little effect on the actual results of local bargaining.

During the Merrick administration and under much of the Alpine presidency, the UA leadership was too concerned with other matters to attempt to work out a consistent policy on materials clauses or exclusive agreements. But in 1913, UA attention was attracted to an issue closely related to the basic problem. This was the question of UA policy toward those of its members who worked directly for general contractors rather than for master plumbers or steam fitters.

In most cases, general contractors subcontracted pipe fitting work to plumbing or steam fitting shops. But in some situations they found it more economical to employ journeymen directly, under the supervision of foremen permanently attached to the firms. The mere possibility of such practice increased pressures on the price bids of plumbing or steam heating contractors, and, when the practice was actually carried out, it deprived the shops of business both as employers of journeymen and as retailers of supplies and equipment.[34]

Some UA members considered working for general contractors consistent with the interests of the union. But others argued that it undermined the position of the local shop and harmed the unions that signed contracts with master plumbers and fitters. In the latter view, the UA firms had a vital interest in protecting "the men who stand by us — that is, the master fitters and the master plumbers who run the legitimate shops."

Officially, at least, the Alpine administration did not take a strong stand on the issue. But Edward Leonard, a close associate of the UA president, urged that the Boston (1913) convention give the problem serious consideration. The Alpine-appointed Committee on the Officers' Report recommended "that we should do all in our power to discourage our members from working directly for general contractors." The recommendation was then adopted by the vote of the delegates.[35]

This passing of what was essentially a very diluted and limited form of a restrictive clause underscores the fact that, during the 1898–1914 period the UA was unable to develop a decisive and consistent policy on the question of whether it should support local measures, of the type here discussed, that were designed to reduce competitive pressures among the employers. This is not surprising since the problem was complex and difficult. The local unions and the UA itself could clearly benefit if the various restrictive measures — exclusive agreements, materials clauses, refusals to work directly for general contractors — would, in fact, result in lesser price competition in the plumbing and steam fitting industry. But, as experience showed, benefits could be offset by other results of the restrictive measures — reduced employment opportunities for some UA members and strengthening of the bargaining power of the local employer associations. Under these circumstances it was difficult to evolve a policy that was equally suitable to all areas and all periods of time, and that could be readily accepted by all the locals.

Chapter 7

Beyond Nationalization:
The Government of the UA, 1914-1924

THE DECADE 1914–1924 showed decisively that the UA, as it emerged from the period of nationalization reforms and the resolved conflict with the fitters, was a viable national union, an organization fully capable of dealing with difficult issues — internal and external. Of course, not all of the problems confronting the UA in its post-nationalization decade were completely eliminated by 1924, or, for that matter, in later years. But at the same time, none of them — no matter how difficult or intractable — seriously threatened to undermine the UA position as the recognized organization in the pipe trades, and one of the truly strong unions of the period.

The course of UA history in this decade was heavily influenced by the sharp economic fluctuations of the period.[1] The American economy, depressed in 1914, revived rapidly in 1915 as a result of a growing demand for U.S. exports and then, further stimulated by the war-generated expenditures, continued on an upswing until late 1918. Construction activity also revived but declined again in 1916, as the resources of the country were mobilized for war production. However, the impact on construction workers was offset by employment opportunities in war plants and shipyards. The signing of the armistice was followed first by a mild slowdown, and then by an inflationary boom that lasted until early 1920. By that time, the country experienced the first signs of severe deflation and recession. The construction industry, which expanded rapidly in 1919, began to decline earlier than other industries, and in 1920 its level of activity was lower than in any previous year since the depression of 1914. It revived in the spring of 1921, and this marked the beginning of a general recovery. The continuously rising level of building activity became, indeed, one of the key factors in the ensuing prosperity that, except for relatively minor interruptions, lasted through the 1920's.[2]

The influence of economic fluctuations can be seen in the changes in

UA membership. The official UA records provide membership figures for only a few of the years of the period 1914–1924. But with information gained from studies of union growth and statements of UA officers, it is possible to obtain a fairly clear picture of the changes in the membership of the UA during its post-nationalization decade.

Membership in 1913 was 35,768; in 1917, 41,239; 1919, 58,322; 1921, 51,016; 1924, 52,268.

As these figures indicate, the years 1914 through 1919 were a period of rapid growth in membership. Other sources strongly suggest that the union also increased its membership in 1920, with the total figure probably around 60,000.[3] This paralleled the enormous gains made by all the American unions during the 1915–1918 prosperity and the postarmistice boom. Strong competition for labor, friendly policies of wartime government agencies, and the relatively tolerant policies of employers were the major factors that contributed to a doubling of total union membership between 1915 and 1920.[4]

While the 1921 membership figure indicates a reduction from the peak of 1919–1920, it does not show the full decline that took place after 1920. Since expulsions, suspensions, and withdrawals were reported with a lag, the full impact of the 1920–1921 depression was recorded in the early 1922's rather than in mid-1921. And according to UA statements some years later, in early 1922 official membership (in good standing) amounted to only about 42,000.[5]

The sharp drop during 1921 was not, of course, unique to the UA. Virtually all the unions suffered major losses, and between 1920 and 1922 total union membership declined by over a million, or about 20 per cent.[6] The reasons were the sharp depression, and the reduction in employment in war manufacturing and shipyards where the unions previously made important gains. And there were also other explanations — the change in the policies of the government, and the many "open shop" and anti-union drives by employers.[7]

By the fall of 1924, UA membership counted over 52,000 — about 10,000 more than its low point, in early 1922. This large gain reflected primarily the continuous prosperity in the construction industry.

UA membership gains made in 1922–1924 were in sharp contrast to the over-all record of American unions. In spite of prosperity, the decline in total union membership, beginning in 1921, continued throughout the 1920's. Faced with a generally unfavorable socio-political environment, American unionism was losing most of the gains made during 1915–1920. The UA was also exposed to developments that tended to weaken its position — a rapid and lasting lack of employment in shipbuilding where it had many members, a series of wage reductions in 1921, a record number of strikes, and employer drives for open shop. But the UA was so firmly established in the important trades over which it exercised jurisdiction that it was able to derive a major advantage from the continuing prosperity and expansion of the construction industry.

The end of the UA's post-nationalization decade also marked the fortieth anniversary of national unionism in the pipe trades. As it happened, the United Association could celebrate this event at a time when its membership was both prosperous and growing, and its position as a national organization of the pipe crafts more secure than ever before.

The leaders and their constituents. The problems that confronted the Alpine administration from 1914 on were certainly less critical and challenging than the issues during the period of nationalization. Nevertheless, Alpine continued to guide the national government of the UA with the energy and decisiveness that characterized his previous years in office. One of his most successful moves was the negotiation of agreements with companies manufacturing and installing automatic sprinklers. As indicated in the preceding chapter, this agreement eventually resulted in the unionization of the sprinkler fitters. Another decisive move was the suspension and then reconstitution (under new leadership) of Local 1 in Brooklyn. The reason was that the former business agent of the local attempted to break the agreement negotiated by Alpine and Leonard with the steam fitters. Still another achievement was the merger of the two UA locals in Manhattan. In the fall of 1916 — three years after the original order of the Boston (1913) convention — Local 480, the old loyalist union, finally yielded to UA pressure and merged with Local 498 to form a new New York organization — Local 463.[8]

As the resources of the country were being mobilized for defense and war, the federal government began to enlist the active cooperation of both business and organized labor. John Alpine was highly thought of in the AFL, particularly by Gompers. As a result, he was called upon to serve as labor representative or adviser on several bodies concerned with the war effort.

Alpine's first appointment to a public body — to two subcommittees of the Labor Committee of the Council of National Defense — was perhaps not of unusual importance.[9] But his second assignment, as labor representative to the Cantonment Adjustment Commission (later renamed Emergency Construction Commission), was significant. The task of this board was to set wages and conditions, and adjust disputes on construction work on military facilities; moreover, its creation was an important precedent since it was formed as a result of a specific agreement between labor unions and the U.S. government — the first such agreement in the history of the country — and since it was a forerunner of other tripartite bodies based on similar principles.[10] Finally, Alpine was also appointed (in May 1918) as labor adviser to the War Labor Policies Board — a committee whose purpose was to evolve and coordinate broad labor policies of various federal agencies, and whose membership included among others Felix Frankfurter and Franklin D. Roosevelt.[11] This last post clearly reflected the prestige that the UA president had gained in the course of his work.

While some of Alpine's renown undoubtedly rubbed off on the UA, the union probably also benefited in a more direct way. In 1917–1918, much of the attention of the UA officers was centered on problems relating to the conditions and the wages of UA members in shipyards, war plants, and other defense facilities. Alpine's new position and his government connections were undoubtedly helpful in the many conferences with federal officials and others in charge of defense projects.[12]

In many ways the years between the Boston (1913) and the Toledo (1917) conventions should be viewed as a highly successful period in the development of the UA. By the time of the Toledo meeting, the Alpine administration was able to report a significant increase in membership and, despite large payments of strike, sick, and death benefits, a sizable balance in the union treasury; the UA members were fully employed under a variety of union contracts and were receiving the highest wages in the history of the trade; and, finally, the affiliation of the fitters was turning out to be a success, with the former IA members fully integrated into the organizational structure of the union. Yet, despite this record, the Toledo convention confronted Alpine with what was, in effect, the first significant opposition to his administration.

Judging from the speeches and remarks of the delegates, the opposition was motivated by several factors — a conviction that the UA should not be run by a "political machine"; by resentment of the high costs of union administration, and particularly of the special assessments; by concern about the influence presumably exercised by the large locals; by dissatisfaction with the activities of some of the organizers; and to some extent, at least, by a reformist zeal that characterized segments of the union movement during World War I (some of the most vocal opposition came from delegates from the northwest). These and other factors also provided a basis for criticism in previous conventions. But the difference was that in 1917 the delegates who wanted to introduce major changes were more numerous than in any of the previous three conventions of his administration; that some of them corresponded with each other prior to the Toledo meeting; and that, while in Toledo, they held caucuses to work out programs and strategy.[13]

The "progressives" — as the opposition referred to themselves — presented several proposals for reform. Their main effort was concentrated, however, on an attempt to make the system of referendum and initiative the basis of the UA government. Under the opposition proposal most, if not all, conventions would be abolished; officers would be elected by popular ballot; and major governmental changes would be made through the process of initiative and referendum. As the "progressives" argued, this system would produce true democracy and reduce administrative expenses. None of the speakers made a specific attack on the officers of the national union. Nevertheless, the various references to "political machine" and "slate making" clearly suggested that the attempt to introduce major reforms was directly related to the experiences with the administration in office.

In spite of their preparation — and many eloquent speeches — the "progressives" were unable to win over the majority of delegates. The Alpine administration mustered all its forces and influence, and, as a result, the referendum proposal was defeated by a vote of 296 to 172.[14] The administration forces also defeated the other proposals of the "progressives," and won a complete victory in the election of national officers. The "progressive" candidate for the presidency — nominated, as his own supporter publicly announced, "really as a protest to the present administration of this association" — was decisively defeated (by a vote of 360 to 100); Burke, Leonard, and a few other officers were re-elected unanimously; and the other candidates of the administration slate also secured the offices for which they were nominated.[15]

Early in 1919 — only a year and a half after the defeat of the "progressives" — Alpine and his fellow officers were faced with another attack. This was initiated and directed by Local 110 of Norfolk, Virginia. The local's action proceeded along two lines: First, it sent out to other locals a circular, which, among other things, asked for contributions to help fight the administration. Second, it submitted, under existing UA laws, several propositions for membership referendum. There are no available copies of the circular, but from indirect evidence it appears that it cited specific instances of alleged misconduct of UA officers, and that it called for support of referendum propositions. The propositions, in turn, if passed were to accomplish three purposes: increase the power of small locals at the convention (a ten-man union would send one delegate, and no union could send more than two); call a special convention in November 1919; and make possible a suspension of national officers charged with violation of the UA constitution by at least twenty locals, and then a recall of the accused officers through popular ballot. The leaders of Local 110 evidently felt that, if the propositions were passed, the special convention would be under the domination of the small locals and that the Alpine administration could be ousted; and that the recall provision would provide another means of removing the officers.

Local 110's campaign elicited favorable response from many other local unions. One hundred and thirteen of them — mostly small locals — made donations, and these made possible not only further circulation of anti-administration literature but also speaking tours by William Morlock, the leader of the Norfolk union. Indeed, Morlock later claimed that as many as 241 locals assured him that they would vote for the referendum propositions.

In spite of this apparent support, the campaign turned out to be a failure. Only 30 locals actually participated in the referendum, and the total vote for even the most popular of the propositions fell far short of the 20 per cent required to put the Norfolk proposals on a final ballot. Very few of the large city locals bothered to vote; and the administration was also apparently able to persuade most of the unions that originally supported the Norfolk program to change their minds.

The publication of the results of the referendum — in October 1919 — put an end to the Norfolk campaign. A few months later, the anti-administration leaders of Local 110 resigned from the union, and the local was taken over by officers loyal to the national leadership.

Just about the time the results of the referendum were published, Alpine resigned from the UA presidency. It seems likely that the Norfolk campaign influenced the timing of this move (Alpine resigned as a vice-president of the AFL the previous July); but the decision itself appears to have been unrelated to any of the anti-administration efforts. For several years, Alpine had negotiated with the major sprinkler companies on behalf of UA sprinkler fitters. He then joined one of these firms — the Grinnell Co. — to become an assistant to its president, and to work in the area of labor relations.[15]

Following his formal resignation, the UA executive board elected John Coefield, the first vice-president of the union, to fill Alpine's unexpired term of office. The UA constitution did not specify how to deal with a presidential vacancy occurring during an interconvention period. But there was an historic precedent going back to the tenure of the first president. In 1891, John Lee, first vice-president, filled the unexpired term left by the ailing President Patrick Quinlan. Thomas Burke was thus justified to state in his official announcement that the Coefield election was made "in accordance with the laws, usages and precedents that have been established by the United Association." [16]

At the time of his election, John Coefield was fifty years old, with many years of experience in the union movement. A plumber by trade, he left his native Pennsylvania early in life and after several years "on the road" settled in San Francisco. There he became one of the leaders of an independent union of plumbers which became, after 1903, Local 442 of the United Association. Active also in the union movement outside his own local, he became in later years a business agent of the San Francisco Building Trades Council. In December 1911, Coefield was elected by the UA executive board to fill the vacancy left by the death of First Vice-President O'Connell (O'Connell was also a member of Local 442). In 1913 Coefield was unanimously re-elected to the first vice-presidency by the delegates to the Boston convention.[17]

During the 1917 convention in Toledo, Coefield was the chairman of the Committee on Law which examined the program of the "progressives" and then recommended its rejection. Nevertheless, Coefield's handling of the issues apparently left a highly favorable impression even on the anti-administration forces. His nomination for the first vice-presidency was strongly seconded by one of the "progressive" speakers, and he was re-elected without opposition.[18] At the time of his elevation to the presidency, Coefield was thus well known and respected not only among the UA leaders but also among the many local officers who attended the Toledo convention.

Coefield's experience as president and his high standing among the UA leaders led to his running for re-election at the next (1921) convention. His opponent was Edward W. Leonard, Alpine's close associate, and one of the best-known UA organizers. Although Leonard had a considerable following — particularly in the east and among the steam fitters' locals — Coefield defeated him decisively by a vote of 381 to 209. The election was thus a vindication of the original choice made by the UA executive board in 1919.

The elections that concluded the 1921 convention also resulted in a complete victory for the incumbent officers. Almost all were re-elected, many without opposition. Among the latter were Thomas Burke (secretary-treasurer), and the defeated presidential candidate Edward Leonard who was re-elected, with Coefield's support, as a national organizer.

For Coefield himself, the 1921 election constituted the only election for a national UA office in which he had an opponent. As noted before, his re-elections to the vice-presidency — in 1913 and 1917 — were unanimous. He was also re-elected without opposition to the presidency at the three consecutive conventions after 1921 (1924, 1928, and 1938). At the time of his death, in February 1940, he had held the office for nearly 21 years.

Financial problems. One of the major problems encountered by the UA in its post-nationalization decade was that of maintaining financial solvency. The basic reason lay in factors that reflected the rapidly changing economic environment — fluctuations in size of membership, sharp rise in the cost of running the union, and, perhaps most important, the waves of strikes in 1920 and 1921. By late 1921 these difficulties put the UA in a critical financial situation. The construction boom which reached full scale in late 1922 provided a favorable environment for a financial recovery. Equally important however, were the remedial actions taken by the UA — introduction of fiscal reforms, and a special assessment of the membership. The result was that at the time of the 1924 convention in Atlantic City the UA was in the strongest financial position since its founding.

The Alpine administration first encountered some financial difficulties during the depression of 1914. As unemployment spread, the receipts of the UA fell sharply, and the national union had to suspend strike and sick benefit payments to the locals. The problem disappeared, however, with the beginning of the economic expansion in 1915. High employment and rising membership brought about increases in receipts; the cost of strike benefits stayed at a relatively low level (See Table 3); and further financial support was provided by a special $3.00 assessment of the membership. In August 1917, Secretary Burke could report to the Toledo convention that, after fulfilling all its obligations (including the repayment of the debt to the locals) and meeting all its expenses, the UA had $95,000 in its treasury.[19]

TABLE 3. UA Receipts and Expenditures on Benefits Paid to the Locals, 1913–1924.

Period [a]	UA receipts	Death benefits	Strike benefits	Sickness benefits
1913–1917	$1,162,905	$ 87,800	$121,094	$275,392
1917–1921	2,118,810	164,700	561,061	375,366
1921–1924	2,525,955	182,347	441,228 [b]	315,477 [c]

[a] From July 1 of the earlier year to June 30 of the later year.
[b] Includes $214,247 owed to the locals, most of which was for strikes in 1921.
[c] Includes $69,480 owed to the locals, most of which was due in 1921.

Sources: Journal, August 1917, pp. 10–11; Proceedings, UA (1921), pp. 68–69; (1924), pp. 67–68.

The difficulties which culminated in the next suspension of benefit payments — in 1921 — had their origin in several developments. To some extent, the UA financial position was impaired by the sharp rise — indeed a doubling — of prices between 1915 and 1920. The inflation was reflected in higher costs of union administration — publishing the *Journal*, travel expenses, AFL dues, supplies and other items (including the costs of new UA headquarters). Moreover, in 1920, there were increases in some death benefits (as a result of a decision of the 1917 convention), and in officer salaries (as a result of a special referendum vote). Yet, throughout the inflationary period, membership dues and other local contributions to the national union remained at the level fixed in 1906. The lag in fiscal arrangements thus reduced the advantages derived by the UA from its 1915–1920 rise in membership.[20]

More important was the effect of the two waves of local strikes — in

1919–1920 and in 1921. The strikes of 1919–1920 reflected essentially union efforts to catch up with the sharp rises in the cost of living. From 1915 on, wage increases for plumbers and steam fitters and of the other building trades lagged way behind the rises in prices.[21] The 1919–1920 revival in construction provided an opportunity for recouping some of the losses. The strikes were almost universally successful, and between 1919 and 1920 wages rose to a greater extent than prices.[22] But the cost to the United Association was very heavy. In 1920 alone, there were 261 UA-approved strikes, and the strike benefit payments amounted to $246,000, more than twice the payments made during the entire 1913–1917 period.[23]

In contrast to the previous conflicts the 1921 wave of strikes represented a defensive effort against wage reductions. The postwar (1920–1921) slump was accompanied by an enormous drop in prices, and this, in turn, impelled the employers to lower wages. The employers were supported in many areas by a general campaign against "union power" and for "open shop." But it was virtually inevitable that these moves would encounter strong resistance from the unions which only recently (i.e. during the post-armistice boom) experienced high demand for the work of their members.

Even during the slump, building employers were optimistic about the future recovery; moreover, many strikes were taking place during the industry's early stages of revival. These factors undoubtedly contributed to the relative success of the strikes. The negotiated wage reductions (on the average about 10 per cent) were much smaller than the drop in cost-of-living; in many areas there were no reductions at all; and almost everywhere UA locals retained a union shop. But again the cost to the national union was very high. In the first seven months of 1921 the UA paid $212,000 in strike benefits and, as indicated later, this was only part of the bill. In addition, the UA was being deprived temporarily of dues normally paid by the striking members.[24]

Another factor that aggravated the financial position was unemployment during the 1920–1921 period. As noted previously, the unemployment resulted in a significant drop in the number of members in good standing (i.e. those who paid dues). And, as in previous recessions, it led to an increase in sick benefit payments, since some locals sick benefit payments from national headquarters were used as initial aid to unemployed members.[25]

Deteriorating finances compelled the UA to call for special assessments. Two $2.00 assessments were levied on the members in 1920, and one $3.00 assessment in 1921. In addition, a $5.00 assessment was also imposed in 1921 (as a result of a referendum vote) to pay for the forthcoming convention. These measures were not sufficient, however, to bring about solvency. When the delegates to the Providence convention met in September 1921, the UA had only $163,000, of which almost all ($154,000 — as it turned out) would have to be spent to pay for the convention itself. At the same time, the UA's indebtedness to the locals amounted to $221,000 ($181,000 for strike benefits and $40,000 for sick benefits).

This convention, it will be recalled, was the scene of the contest between Coefield and Leonard. But, remarkably enough, the political contest did not affect the convention's decisions about measures necessary to bring about financial recovery of the UA. J. A. Sullivan, the chairman of the committee to examine the programs of fiscal reforms, was a strong Leonard supporter (Sullivan was a former leader of the International Association). On the issue of fiscal reform, however, he was in complete agreement witch Coefield, Burke, and the other members of the UA administration. The proposals of the UA leadership naturally did run into some opposition. But the majority of the delegates — including those from the large locals in Chicago and New York — were willing to support most of the fiscal changes proposed by the officers. As a result, the convention made a series of constitutional changes that finally led to a significant increase in the revenue of the national union.

The major points of the fiscal program passed by the Providence convention were:

Minimum local dues were raised from $1.30 to $2.00 a month, and minimum initiation fees from $10.00 to $20.00.

The national union's share of the minimum of monthly dues, initiation fees, and other fees was raised from 40 to 50 per cent.

The strike benefit payments for the first sixteen weeks were raised from $5.00 per week to $6.00. But the new law eliminated national strike benefits after the first sixteen weeks of a strike. (Previously, they amounted to $3.00 per week, without any limit on duration.)

Two new funds were created, each to consist of 10 per cent of total receipts of the UA. One of these — the Convention Fund — was to provide for expenses of both conventions and meetings of the executive board; the second — the Reserve Fund — was to remain intact, unless the executive board decided otherwise.

These reforms were introduced at a highly appropriate time. By September 1921 the economy was in the early stages of recovery, and thus, in a relatively short period after the Providence convention, the UA could count on significantly larger receipts from its locals. And as the economic situation continued to improve, the union took further action to strengthen its financial position. In August 1922 it levied a $9.00 assessment to be paid in three installments. The purpose was to provide funds for eliminating UA indebtedness to local unions. As it turned out, however, the receipts — $392,000 — were over a hundred thousand dollars larger than the $284,000 owed to the locals.[26]

Between 1921 and 1924 employment in construction grew by 50 per cent; and, while the cost of living actually declined (by about 6 per cent), union rates of the pipe trades rose by 12 to 17 per cent. In these circumstances the UA was able to reap full benefits from the fiscal reforms introduced in Providence. In the three-year period between the Providence and the Atlantic City (1924) conventions the national union not only repaid its debts and met current obligations but also accumulated a cash balance (inclusive of the special funds) that amounted to $748,000 — about 40 per cent of its total disbursement during the entire interconvention period.[27]

National conventions. One of the characteristics of the developing UA was a tendency toward longer periods between conventions. Originally, it will be recalled, conventions met annually; after 1913, the constitution required only triennial meetings. In 1914–1924 the trend to reduce the frequency of national conventions continued.

The major reason was expense. The Boston (1913) convention cost the UA over $72,000, the Toledo convention (1917) over $96,000 and the Providence (1921) convention a record $154,000. As a result, there were continuous pressures from the locals to make the national meetings less frequent.

Moves to reduce the frequency of conventions were supported by UA leaders. Quite apart from the heavy financial burden, the stronger and more settled position of the national union itself justified making the conventions less frequent. In earlier days, the conventions — a combination of constitutional assembly, parliament, and high tribunal — were a key instrument in strengthening ties between locals and the national organization. The convention played this role also in 1914–24. But, with a well-organized internal system that bound the locals and the UA, there was no need to hold them as often as in the past.

According to the constitution, a convention was supposed to take place in 1916 — three years after the Boston meeting. But in January 1916, the executive board decided that the question be decided by referendum vote; the board also indicated that, should the membership vote for a convention, a special assessment would be necessary. The membership voted overwhelmingly against the convention, and the meeting was postponed by a year.[28]

At the 1917 convention in Toledo, the UA leaders recommended that the constitutional provision regarding conventions be made more flexible. Under the proposal, a referendum could be held two years after the preceding convention to determine whether a convention should take place during the coming year (three years after the previous meeting). If the membership voted against the convention, the procedure was to be repeated each year until an affirmative vote (a majority of at least 55 per cent of total membership) were obtained. This was accepted by the Toledo (1917) convention and became part of the UA constitution.[29]

Two more changes pertaining to conventions were made after 1917. In 1921, the UA added a constitutional clause making it possible for a local union to submit to national referendum a call for a special convention.[30] And in 1924 — at the Atlantic City meeting — the delegates voted to extend the minimum period between regular conventions to four years. The basic principle of the 1917 clause was retained; but the question of holding a convention during the coming year was now to be submitted to the membership at the end of the third rather than second year after the previous national meeting.[31]

Other changes made after 1917 resulted in an increase in delegates to the conventions. In 1921, as a consequence of an organized effort of smaller locals, the minimum size entitling a local union to representation was reduced from 25 to 20 members. At the same time the convention also voted to give locals one additional delegate for each 100 members in excess of twenty. (Previously, in order to qualify for two delegates, a local had to have at least 200 members.) And, in 1924, small locals which together might have counted twenty members were permitted to combine their membership for the purpose of sending a joint delegate. The changes in the basis of representation for conventions did not have a major effect on the UA government. But they did make the national conventions somewhat more representative of individual local unions.

Suspensions, expulsions and consolidations. During the post-nationalization decade the UA also made a number of constitutional changes concerning the power which the national officers could exercise with respect to locals and individual members. Some of these put in legal form the existing practices of the union; others specifically extended the area of UA jurisdiction.

Since 1902, the UA constitutions provided that local unions would be suspended for violating the national constitution. This provision was, however, very general, and none of the procedures relevant to the suspension, its revocation, or any other aspect — such as appeals — were specified. In actual practice, the original decisions on suspension were made by the president or one of the organizers, with an implicit right of appeal to the executive board. And presumably, as in any other major case, the local could make a final appeal to the national convention. (It will be recalled, however, that though the convention provided, in fact, the opportunity for last appeal, this was a result of custom rather than of any specific constitutional provision.) [32]

A series of changes made in 1921 and 1924 clarified the legal status of these procedures. The president and the organizers were given the right to suspend locals that violated the constitution and the UA law; the executive board was to determine when suspension would be revoked; and if the local persisted in its presumably unconstitutional behavior, the president had the right to revoke its charter. The president's decision, in turn, could be appealed to the executive board.[33]

In 1921 the UA also passed a provision that any decision made by the executive board could be appealed to the next national convention. (This was later amended to specify that, until the convention decided on the appeal, the original decision of the board would stand.) The convention thus became formally — as it had been in practice — the court of last appeal.[34]

The formalization of the procedures concerning suspensions and expulsions strengthened to some extent the position of the national leaders. Their position was also strengthened by two other constitutional changes made under the Coefield administration.

In 1921 the Providence convention added a clause dealing with what was officially termed as "Falsifying Circular Letters." It stated:

Any member of the United Association found guilty of sending out circular letters of falsehood and misrepresentation shall be expelled, and the local union that permits such action shall also be expelled.[35]

The passing of this clause was a direct result of the 1919 campaign of the Norfolk local. The fact that the campaign — carried out largely by mail — enlisted the support of many local unions apparently made a deep impression on the UA officers. After the defeat of the Norfolk proposals, the executive board decided to make "secession" and soliciting funds for this purpose a subject for expulsion. And in its report to the 1921 convention, the board condemned the activity of the Norfolk opposition and recommended that the delegates "take the strongest and most drastic action . . . to curb this damnable evil of allowing such conspirators to send out broadcast, as the spirit moves them, to our local unions, circular letters of falsehood and misrepresentation." [36]

Some of the Providence delegates objected to the wording of the "falsifying letters" clause and argued that, once in the constitution, it could be used to suppress proposals for reform. But the UA leaders defended it strongly, and it was passed without major opposition.

As it happened, Coefield's strong and successful administration did not need the protection (from opposition) offered by the new constitutional clause. Nevertheless, its existence did, at least strengthen potentially, the position of the UA leaders.

The Providence (1921) convention also added a clause giving the UA President the power to order two or more locals to consolidate, and to take measures to enforce such consolidation. The president could call for a merger whenever he believed that such action would be "for the best interests of the organization locally or at large." However, any consolidation of locals also had to be approved by the executive board.[37]

In the past, the UA often took an active part in inducing or even enforcing mergers of local unions. But these were special situations — resulting either from an aftermath of secessions (in New York), or from the conflict with the International Association (in Chicago). In more normal circumstances, consolidations were the result of decisions made by the local unions. The consolidation clause thus gave the national union a new prerogative.

As the post-1921 history of the UA showed, the consolidation clause enabled the UA President to intervene in many situations where interlocal competition and conflicts weakened the position of the union, or where economic changes in the area required a consolidation of bargaining in one organization. From the viewpoint of the local unions, however, the clause constituted another step in the direction of reducing their autonomy, and increasing the power of the national leadership.[38]

Chapter 8

Beyond Nationalization:
Challenges and Solutions, 1914-1924

JURISDICTIONAL PROBLEMS AMONG THE PIPE TRADES

IN 1924 the UA officers for the first time devoted one of the major sections of their convention report to the problem of "Jurisdictional Affairs in Our Own Association" — that is, essentially the problem of conflict over work assignments between UA plumbers and fitters. The particular section of the report, a sober discussion of the ways in which the UA had attempted to deal with the issue, indicated clearly what had been apparent for some years to both leaders and members of the union — namely, that jurisdictional conflicts in the pipe crafts presented one of the really stubborn and difficult problems confronting the United Association. In three consecutive conventions, between 1913 and 1924, the UA had been setting up procedures designed to provide methods of settling the issue; none of them was very successful. By 1920 — several years after the bitter struggles preceding the IA affiliation — jurisdictional conflicts between plumbers and fitters were actually increasing in frequency. And, by the mid-twenties, some of the unresolved disputes — grown over time in both complexity and scope — were creating a potential danger to the maintenance of satisfactory work and union relations among the crafts not only in particular areas but, indeed, throughout the entire jurisdiction of the United Association.

As in the past, the conflicts arose in situations where the pipe work was not readily identifiable with the traditional installations of either plumbing or steam fitting. Indeed, several of the jurisdictional disputes and conflicting claims pertained to the same type of work — vacuum cleaning pipes, pneumatic tubes, fire stand pipes — that were contested by the crafts prior to the affiliation of the steam fitters.[1] New disputes arose, however, during the construction of chemical plants and other manufacturing and service establishments requiring extensive piping systems.[2] Here, too, there was no obvious answer to the question of jurisdiction over work. In the view of the plumbers, the new installations essentially involved the same materials and tools and called for the same skills as plumbing; accordingly, the plumbers were entitled to claim the new installations as falling within their jurisdiction. From the standpoint of the steam fitters however, what counted was not the materials or the tools used in the installations but the nature of the piping systems. As John Mangan and others argued, the new work — whether piping for vacuum cleaning or for gas by-product plant — was not covered by the plumbing laws, and was not subject to examination by the plumbing inspectors; accordingly, it belonged to the craft which for years claimed jurisdiction over all kinds of piping *other* than plumbing — the steam fitters.[3]

It is apparent that these conflicting claims could not be resolved in a simple manner. What underlay the rise of the jurisdictional disputes was essentially a complex of technological changes. As indicated previously, some of the earlier changes significantly reduced the differences in the materials, tools, and work techniques used by the plumbers and the fitters. The more recent technological changes were creating new processes and products that, in turn, required the kind of installations which could not be classified easily along the established jurisdictional categories of plumbing and steam fitting.

The jurisdictional conflicts of the post-nationalization years were inextricably connected with the issue of the agreements on demarcation of work. These were the agreements that were signed in several cities by the representatives of the UA and the local unions at the time of the affiliation of the IA fitters.

As mentioned earlier, the demarcation agreements spelled out in some detail the jurisdictional boundaries of steam fitting and plumbing. Inevitably, in view of the complexity of the issue, some of the sections were too general or too vague to provide the kind of answers that were necessary to settle specific disputes.[4] And, since the agreements were signed in 1913–1914, they could be of little help in settling many conflicts pertaining to the jurisdiction over newer types of installations. Yet, in many other respects the agreements were so specific on the demarcation of the craft jurisdictions that, if generally accepted as valid, they could, indeed, provide a basis for both avoiding and settling many disputes. As it turned out, however, the very validity of the agreements became itself a major issue in the jurisdictional conflict between the two crafts.

During the first few years after the IA affiliation, the intercraft conflicts did not appear to pose a particularly grave issue for the UA. Some difficulties arose, in 1915–1918, in a few areas where, under a new constitutional provision, the steam fitters decided to leave a mixed local and form their own UA union. In the same period there were also a few plumber-fitter disputes over work assignments — both in commercial and in industrial construction.[5] But in the context of the past experience of the crafts these disputes were not considered unusually serious. Indeed, what was more noteworthy perhaps was the relative harmony in relations between the various plumber and fitter locals.[6]

Yet, even during this period, the UA leaders became aware that local conflicts over work assignments could have serious ramifications. As we have pointed out, the 1913 convention made the president of the UA the final arbitrator of jurisdictional disputes. By 1917, however, the administration concluded that this was a mistake, and recommended to the Toledo delegates that the UA go back to its pre-1913 procedures. Under these procedures, a dispute was first considered by a local committee composed of representatives of the affected crafts. If the committee could not settle the issue, the president was to appoint an umpire who would then make a final decision.[7] The UA officers did not spell out the reasons for their dissatisfaction with the 1913 system, but the implication was that it created "doubt and misunderstanding" — presumably because presidential decisions in certain local cases might be interpreted as having relevance to jurisdictional demarcation in other areas.

The matter of craft jurisdiction normally aroused convention delegates to lengthy arguments and debates. It was perhaps characteristic of the relatively harmonious intercraft relations of the 1914–1917 years that the officers' recommendation elicited no discussion, and was passed by the Toledo (1917) convention without opposition.

By the time of the postarmistice boom, the problem of jurisdictional conflicts became more acute, and it grew in seriousness during the 1920's. The main reason was the shift from wartime industries to peacetime construction, and particularly to the expanding industrial and commercial sectors with large amounts of the newer types of pipe fitting installations. From the viewpoint of the UA, however, the overall issue was also aggravated by the developments concerning the Chicago agreement on demarcation of work.

The Chicago agreement was signed in 1913 by the UA locals of plumbers and gas fitters, by the two former IA locals (which merged in 1915), and by Alpine, Burke, and Leonard on behalf of the UA. For several years no question was raised officially by any of the parties concerning the adherence to the agreed upon jurisdictional lines. But among many members of Local 130 (the plumbers' union) there was apparently a feeling that the agreement gave away some of their work to the steam fitters. Specifically, certain installations over which the plumbers claimed jurisdiction — vacuum cleaning systems, gasoline piping, iron pipe railings, fire standpipes, and others were made optional by the agreement — that is, could be performed by either craft. And some of the clauses of the Chicago agreement appeared to the plumbers as giving the fitters jurisdiction over most, if not all, piping in industrial and power plants not subject to the plumbing laws of Illinois.

In 1919 the elections in Local 130 were won by officers who were committed to the view that the Chicago plumbers should not observe the agreement as it was originally written. The new officers proceeded then to publicize their stand among the members of Local 130 and among the interested parties in the Chicago construction industry — contractors, architects, and building owners.[8]

The postarmistice expansion in Chicago construction led to several jurisdictional disputes between plumbers and fitters. Some of these could not have been resolved by reference to the 1913 agreement in any case.[9] But, in view of the new policy of Local 130 toward the originally accepted demarcation lines, settling of jurisdictional conflicts became more difficult than at any other time since the IA affiliations. In some cases, in fact, disputes between the UA plumbers and fitters gave rise to work stoppages and strikes.[10]

Before long the developments in Chicago created repercussions in other areas. The leaders of Local 597, the Chicago steam fitters' union, saw the action of the plumbers not only as a violation of a local agreement but also as a potential first move in a general campaign to abrogate all the existing agreements on demarcation of work. Accordingly, several communications were sent to the steam fitter locals throughout the UA jurisdiction, acquainting them with the events in Chicago (as Local 597 viewed them), and alerting them to the possibility of further moves on the part of the plumbers.[11]

The Chicago communications aroused major concern among the

steam fitters. The demarcation agreements were formulated, with the help of Alpine and Leonard, at a time when the UA was trying to induce the former IA unions to affiliate. As in the case of Chicago, the agreements conceded mort to the fitters' jurisdiction than the local plumbers' union would be willing to grant under more normal circumstances. In New York, in fact, the two unions that eventually merged to form Local 463, refused to sign the demarcation agreement as it had been formulated by the UA officers and the fitters' locals. (Brooklyn Local 1, signed it, however.) The demarcation agreements also listed as steam fitters' duties several kinds of industrial installations — and this could be interpreted as providing a basis for jurisdictional claims over the newer types of piping in chemical, power, and other plants. In the context of the jurisdictional conflicts arising in many areas, the Chicago move thus offered evidence that the UA plumbers would not be satisfied with jurisdiction over the traditional types of plumbing, and that they were determined to claim at least some of the installations on industrial and other projects not subject to the state plumbing laws. Accordingly, the issue of the agreements became of vital concern not only to the steam fitters' locals which had actually signed them, but to all UA steam fitters.

The result of the communications from Chicago and of ensuing letters was a meeting of several steam fitters' unions in New York to consider the problem and to map out joint strategy. The decision of the meeting was that the issue be submitted to the forthcoming convention. Specifically, the fitters' locals were going to ask the UA, as one af the signatories, to enforce all the demarcation agreements.

The intercraft disputes and the issue of the demarcation agreements placed the UA officers in a difficult position. The plumber-fitter conflicts were harming the union in many ways — by weakening its cohesion at a time when it was facing many serious issues, by imparing relations with employers whose projects gave rise to the disputes, and by damaging UA standing in the labor movement — particularly among the other building trades.[12] Yet, for a variety of reasons, the UA could do little at the time to settle or even alleviate the internal strife.

For one thing, direct intervention by UA officers could easily enlarge the scope of the disputes and sharpen individual conflicts. The locals directly involved were among the largest and most influential in the organization. Any move on the part of the national officers that would decisively support a particular local (whether one of the plumbers or of the steam fitters) would thus not only alienate another major UA union but also upset the delicate balance of intercraft relations throughout the UA jurisdiction. Second, under the constitution, the national officers had limited power to interfer in jurisdictional disputes. While the president was supposed to appoint an umpire, he had no power to enforce the umpire's decision. And the constitution was, of course, silent on the problem of enforcing the demarcation agreements. Moreover, there was also another factor. Since, in 1920–1921, Coefield had held his office as a result of an appointment by the executive board, and since he still had to face the test of a convention election, he was not in a very strong position to take decisive steps in the sensitive matter of jurisdictional conflicts.

The UA leaders did make several attempts to bring about a settlement of the Chicago dispute.[13] These attempts were fruitless, however, and by 1921 it was apparent that, quite apart from any other considerations that made the problem so complex, the UA actually lacked adequate means to deal decisively with particular disputes. Accordingly, the national officers recommended that the Providence (1921) convention strengthen the constitutional provision dealing with the issue of jurisdiction.

The gist of the officers' proposal was that the decision of the umpire in a jurisdictional case would be binding, and would remain in "full force" at least until the time of a possible appeal to the next national convention. Any local that refused to abide by the decision would be automatically suspended; and if it persisted in the refusal, the national officers had the power to take away its territorial jurisdiction and establish another union in the area.[14]

The recommendation of the officers was only one of several subjects pertaining to craft jurisdiction to be considered by the Providence convention. In accordance with the decision of their meeting, the New York fitters submitted a resolution calling for UA enforcement of demarcation agreements; the Kansas City and New York plumbers asked, in turn, that the agreements be annulled; and Local 597 (the steam fitters) brought up the matter of the Chicago dispute.

It was this last move that produced a rather surprising development. While at the convention, the leaders of Local 597 and Local 130 agreed, apparently with assistance from various UA officers, on a program to settle the Chicago dispute. Under this program, the dispute would be first considered by a joint committee of the two unions; if the committee could not settle the dispute, it would then select an umpire to make the decision. His decision would, in turn, be enforced essentially in the same manner as recommended by the UA officers.

In a move that was hailed by Coefield as settling "the most acute jurisdictional dispute ever occurring in this or any other organization," the convention unanimously approved the program of the Chicago unions. However, the other resolutions concerning jurisdictional issues and demarcation agreements resulted in a lengthy and frequently bitter debate. The representatives of the plumbers' locals argued that the agreements were made obsolete by technological changes; that, as interpreted by the steam fitters, they deprived the plumbers of work that was theirs; and that, in any case, they were not valid because they had no expiration dates. Accordingly, the plumbers' view was that each case of a jurisdictional issue should be decided on its own merits, regardless of past agreements. To the steam fitters, on the other hand, the agreements represented a fundamental condition under which they agreed to affiliate with the UA and an instrument in the effort to claim their craft identity. In this view, the UA had a moral obligation to uphold and enforce what was essentially a contract between the crafts and the national union.

In spite of a basic difference in views, the UA leaders managed to bring the debates to what seemed a harmonious conclusion. At the recommendation of the UA leaders, the delegates decided that the steam fitters and plumbers in New York and other cities resolve their differences by resorting to "the mode of procedure" adopted in Chicago; the resolutions calling for enforcement of demarcation agreements were eventually withdrawn; and the convention adopted a new provision to deal with jurisdictional problems. This incorporated the procedures of the Chicago program. The choice of the umpire in a jurisdictional case was thus left to the locals, and the role of the UA was to be limited to enforcing his decision.[15]

The Chicago "mode of procedures" and the new constitutional provision were apparently observed in a number of areas, and facilitated the settlement of some disputes. But in other cases, where the relations between the locals were particularly strained, or where the issues were especially acute, the parties would not agree, either on the principle of arbitration or the choice of the arbitrator or would, at times, even ignore the umpire's decision. As a result, some of the jurisdictional problems grew into major conflicts. In New York, for example, a plumber–fitter dispute about the installation of a cast iron pipe in the Hell Gate Power House led to a plumbers' strike that cost thousands of dollars and attracted wide attention. In spite of the intervention of Coefield and the New York Building Trades Council, the strike lasted for several months, and was eventually brought to an end with the assistance of public officials.[16]

The most conspicuous failure of the new procedures was in Chicago. As one of the leaders of Local 130 later said, "When the boys got back to Chicago, they did not even get to the first base." [17] No umpire was selected, the problem of the agreement remained unsettled, and conflicts about work assignment kept arising. Indeed, what was already the most serious dispute within the UA grew further in complexity as a result of a new issue — the question of the status of Local 250, the union of the Chicago gas fitters.

Local 250, one of the two UA unions composed exclusively of gas fitters, merged with Local 597 (the steam fitters) in November 1920, during the postwar depression. Under the conditions of the merger, the gas fitters were granted full rights to work at steam fitting; in return the steam fitters took over the jurisdiction of work and territory of Local 250, with gas fitting being added to the "Duties of a Steam Fitter." At the time, at least, the merger was highly advantageous to the gas fitters who, over the years, were losing work as a result of the expansion of electric lighting. A special aspect of the merger was that it was kept secret. As later explained, the reason was that, as two separate unions, the fitters would have more votes at the Providence convention where Local 597 intended to support Organizer Leonard for the presidency. It seems likely, however, that another reason was the concern that the transfer of jurisdiction over gas fitting to Local 597 would complicate the dispute over the demarcation agreement.

Sometime in 1922 William Guenther, the business agent of the gas fitters, and his fellow members decided to return to their previous status as a separate local. This was strongly opposed by Local 597. But, as the facts of the merger became known, the gas fitters gained support both from Local 130 and from the plumbing contractors.

One reason for the decision of the gas fitters was that Local 597 accepted the arbitration award of Judge Landis. The award, originally expected to deal only with the issue of wage reduction, abolished and modified many of the prevailing union work rules. Most of the

Chicago construction unions reluctantly accepted it to retain closed shop. But fifteen other unions — including the plumbers — repudiated it on the grounds that the arbitrator exceeded his authority. Because of the high demand for construction labor, the members of these fifteen "outlaws," as they were called, had little difficulty in finding jobs with employers willing to ignore the conditions of the award. The gas fitters claimed that they could not tolerate the changes in the work rules made by the Landis award, and that, once separated from Local 597, they would continue working under their old rules.[18]

A second — and probably more important — reason for the gas fitters' decision was that, once the news of the merger was out, they had difficulties in securing jobs with employers who normally did the bulk of gas fitting — the master plumbers. The master plumbers were refusing to employ members of the steam fitters' local, and were assigning gas fitting work to the plumbers.[19]

To some extent, the policies of the plumbing contractors reflected the pressures emanating from Local 130 (the plumbers). The plumbers claimed that, once Local 250 merged with Local 597, it was they and not the steam fitters who were heirs to jurisdiction over gas fitting. But, in addition, the master plumbers had their own interests at stake. For if, as a result of the merger, gas fitting was to be recognized as one of the duties of a steam fitter, the installations of gas fitting would be eventually taken over by the main employers of the membership of Local 597 — the steam fitting contractors.

The issue of the merger was eventually taken up by the UA executive board, first in May and then in August of 1923. In spite of the support given to the gas fitters by Local 130 and by the representatives of the master plumbers, the board decided to uphold Local 597 and formally approve the merger.[20]

The decision of the board hardly contributed to an improvement in relations between Locals 597 and 130. The steam fitters welcomed it. But, in the view of the plumbers, the transfer of jurisdiction over gas fitting to Local 597 meant that the board took away "the inalienable rights of the plumbing trade." [21]

At its August 1923 meeting, the executive board also took up the issue of basic disputes between the Chicago crafts, and ordered Locals 597 and 130 to carry out their Providence agreement.[22] However, in the context of the Chicago situation — aggravated now by the gas fitters' issue and the split over the Landis award — the board's order could hardly lead to positive results. The dispute remained unsettled, and by the time of the 1924 convention relations between the Chicago plumbers and steam fitters were probably at the lowest point in a decade.

The experience of New York, Chicago, and other cities convinced the UA officers that the national union had to take a larger role in the settlement of jurisdictional disputes. The issue was, however, so sensitive that the officers were not willing to commit themselves to any particular method of dealing with the disputes. Instead, the previously mentioned report to the Alantic City (1924) convention presented four alternative proposals for changes in the constitutional procedures. While differing in some respects, each of the proposals would give the national officers considerably greater power to intervene in jurisdictional disputes than provided by the clauses passed in 1921.[23]

The issue of changing the provisions attracted major attention at the Atlantic City convention. From among several suggestions, the Committee on Laws eventually recommended a modified version of one of the proposals made by UA officers. According to this proposal the locals engaged in a dispute were given forty-eight hours to appoint a joint referee committee; if the committee could not agree, it was to choose an umpire within another forty-eight hours. If no umpire was chosen within the assigned time the president would appoint one. The umpire was to make a decision within seven days and, as in the previous provisions, the UA President was given the power to enforce the decision by disciplining any of the recalcitrant parties. In essence, then, the recommended clause was meant to put strong pressure on the locals to reach a quick solution; and, in case of failure to agree, to give the UA power to prevent the disputes from developing into lengthy conflicts and work stoppages.

The main issue concerning the recommended provision was whether arbitration would also apply to interpretations of the existing agreements. The question was vital to the plumbers, and a delegate from Local 463 named George Meany offered an amendment stating that the section "applies to all classes of work in which dispute arises, whether covered by agreement or not." Amended in this way, the proposal of the Committee on Laws was passed by the delegates and became part of the constitution.[24]

Most of the discussions pertaining to this change took place in committee meetings, and the UA officers managed to avoid an open, and potentially bitter, debate over jurisdictional issues. They could not avoid it, however, when, as a result of an appeal by Local 250, the convention had to take up the problem of the Chicago gas fitters. The convention's Committee on Appeals recommended sustaining the decision of the executive board on the grounds that the merger agreement was made in good faith and should be honored. But the decisive factor turned out to be the jurisdictional implication of the case. The delegates of the plumbers were influenced by the fact that, as a result of the merger, the Chicago jurisdiction over gas fitting would be transferred to the steam fitters. And they apparently agreed with a Local 130 delegate who argued that the Chicago case would set a precedent for the rest of the country. The result was that after a four-hour debate, the majority of the delegates voted to reverse the decision of the executive board, and to reestablish Local 250 as a separate union.

As a result of constitutional provisions passed in 1924 the UA had more effective means to cope with the problem of jurisdictional disputes than at any previous time. The procedures established by these provisions turned out to be in fact, highly useful in settling most of the plumber-steam fitter conflicts occurring in the years immediately following the Atlantic City (1924) convention. Indeed, the only major conflict of the period where the newly established procedures failed to produce a settlement was between the two unions in Chicago — Locals 130 and 597.

The Chicago dispute was finally settled in 1929, that is, in a period of UA history not covered by the present study. But since this dispute was so important during the early 1920's, and since it raised important issues pertaining to the status of the demarcation agreements, it is appropriate to recount the story of its settlement briefly.

The settlement was a direct result of measures taken by the 1928 convention.[25] The delegates who met in Atlantic City in 1928 found that, although in most localities the conflicts that had plagued the UA unions for years were resolved, the Chicago business was no closer to settlement than it had been in 1924. In these circumstances, the 1928 convention decided to resort to a direct way of dealing with the drawn-out and, by that time, bitter conflict. Following the suggestion of the UA officers, the convention's Committee on State of Association recommended that all disagreements and disputes over jurisdiction be settled in an irrevocable manner by a National Jurisdiction Committee. The Committee was to be composed of three plumbers and three steam fitters to be appointed by the president of the UA; the president was also to act as chairman of the Committee, and was to be vested with the power to cast the deciding vote in case of a tie. As originally recommended, the National Jurisdiction Committee would have had the power to consider any jurisdictional conflict in the pipe trades — whether in Chicago or elsewhere. Many delegates feared, however, that a creation of a body with such comprehensive authority would lead to new claims and new conflicts in areas where plumbers and fitters had been able to work out satisfactory solutions to the problems of intercraft jurisdiction. Accordingly, a delegate from the local of the New York plumbers (LU 463) proposed that the authority of the committee be limited to the Chicago dispute. The convention accepted this amendment and then voted unanimously to create a National Jurisdiction Committee.

Following the convention President Coefield appointed six UA members (three plumbers and three steam fitters) to the National Jurisdiction Committee. In April 1929, the committee, under the chairmanship of Coefield, met with representatives of Locals 130 and 597, and began to hold hearings pertaining to the dispute between the two unions. After more than two weeks of hearings — and an examination of extensive briefs and documents — the committee rendered a decision (on May 21, 1929) acceptable to both plumbers and steam fitters — thus providing a settlement of what had been for years the most serious jurisdictional dispute between UA locals.

The decision of the National Jurisdiction Committee consisted essentially of two parts. First, the committee found that the agreement on demarcation of work, originally drawn up in 1913 when the steam fitters joined the UA, was to be considered as a valid agreement among all its signatories (all the UA locals in Chicago). Second, the committee decided that some sections of the original agreement required special interpretation. Accordingly, it provided the two locals with interpretations pertaining to 11 of the 34 articles of the 1913 agreement. These 11 articles covered a wide range of work — power piping, air piping, piping in gasoline stations, and many other pipe installations.

The decision of the National Jurisdiction Committee was important not only because it settled a drawn-out dispute between two major locals but also because it clarified — by implication — the status of the demarcation agreements. Although the decision pertained only to the Chicago dispute, it clearly implied that demarcation agreements signed during the affiliation of the IA locals had to be considered by UA unions as valid documents, and should provide a continuous basis for the settlement of intercraft disputes over work assignments.

The UA experience with jurisdictional conflicts between the plumbers and the steam fitters should be viewed in proper perspective. As the preceding discussion indicates, during the post-nationalization decade the UA was only moderately successful in its efforts to institute quick settlements of jurisdictional disputes between the pipe trades. Yet, given the structure of its membership and the inevitable changes in technology, it is difficult to see how the union could have achieved greater success in dealing with the complex and difficult issue.

The UA, as it emerged from its formative period, was essentially a multicraft organization. Its members were not only conscious of the economic significance of craft jurisdiction but were also strongly attached to the traditions and customs of their own crafts. The national union itself was deeply committed to the position, as stated by the UA officers, that "each trade, as it were, has a property right in its jurisdiction of work." For reasons indicated previously, the members of the UA were continuously encountering issues pertaining to the demarcation of work along jurisdictional lines. Under such conditions — and with only limited experience in dealing with conflicts among its own locals — the union could hardly be expected to devise an easy solution to a problem that has plagued the labor movement for years, and that has been justifiably termed "a pervasive feature of our highly organized society." Indeed it is noteworthy that even the most serious of the jurisdictional conflicts did not lead to any serious movement toward secession or for a breakup of the organization, and that they did not prevent the UA from introducing reforms that resulted in an over-all strengthening of the national union.[26]

THE UNIONS OF THE SPRINKLER FITTERS

As indicated in Chapter 6, the efforts of Alpine and his colleagues resulted, in 1915, in a collective bargaining agreement with the six major firms that manufactured and installed automatic sprinklers. The agreement, signed for four years (July 1915–July 1919), covered all journeymen fitters employed by the firms except for workers in cities where there already were UA locals consisting exclusively of sprinkler fitters. The agreement set the wage rate at $4.00 a day but retained the higher rates that were being paid in several cities (See Table 4). It also provided for wage re-openings, with a scheduled wage increase in 1918, and for an eight-hour day, overtime, and the right to engage in a sympathetic strike.[27]

A unique feature of the agreement was its provision concerning the unionization of the workers. All the journeymen covered by the agreement were to join the United Association. However, instead of joining one of the regular locals, they were to become members of what was described by the UA officers as "a general union with control from the headquarters of the United Association, and under the direct supervision of [the] general officers." In effect this provision made the UA officers the representatives of the covered workers in any negotiations with the sprinkler firms.

In accordance with the terms of the agreement, the UA, in June 1915, established Local 669 — the "general union" to which the newly unionized sprinkler fitters were to belong. The office of the union was in Chicago, in the headquarters of the United Association.

In the following months, it became apparent that the contract provisions pertaining to Local 669 had to be modified. As originally instituted, Local 669 was in many respects an appropriate organization to represent the "road men" — fitters who had no permanent work attachment to one locality, and who were members of the traveling crews installing automatic sprinklers over a wide area of the country. However, the agreement with the sprinkler companies also covered a few hundred fitters who "did not go on the road," and who worked only in the cities where they resided. In several of the places covered by the agreement, many of the resident fitters were members of mixed UA locals (usually predominantly steam fitting locals); other fitters, though nonunion, were undoubtedly familiar with the usual form of local union organizations. The UA leaders apparently realized that it would be difficult to keep the fitters of the industrial areas in an organization that had presumably an office in Chicago but no such institution as local officers, meeting halls, scheduled meetings, and so forth. Accordingly, with the consent of the sprinkler firms, it was decided that Local 669 would have its own local branches in selected cities — to be called Auxiliary Locals 669 (the Boston branch, for instance, would be called Boston Auxiliary Local 669). These auxiliaries were to serve as local unions of the sprinkler fitters residing in the larger industrial centers.[28]

TABLE 4. *Daily wage rates negotiated in the sprinkler industry by Local 669 (Road Fitters and selected cities with auxiliaries),* [a] *1915–1924.*

Location	July 1915	July 1916	July 1917	July 1919	January 1920	July 1922	July 1923	July 1924
(Road fitters)	$4.00	$4.00	$4.50	$6.40	$7.00	$7.20	$8.00	$9.00
Baltimore	4.00	4.50	5.50	6.40	7.00	7.20	8.00	9.00
Boston	4.50	5.00	5.50	6.40	7.20 [b]	7.20	8.00	9.00
Cleveland	5.00	5.50	5.50	6.40	8.00	7.20	8.00	9.00
Newark	5.50	5.50	5.50	6.40	8.00	7.20	8.00	9.00
Philadelphia	4.00	4.50	5.50	6.40	7.00	7.20	8.00	9.00
Pittsburgh	5.00	5.50	5.50	6.40	8.00	7.20	8.00	9.00

[a] By 1924 there were also Local 669 auxiliaries in Buffalo, Detroit, Los Angeles and Providence. The rates in these cities were the same as in the other locations of auxiliaries.
[b] The $7.20 rate was only till April 1922. After that date it went up to $8.00.
Sources: *Journal*, July 1917, pp. 9–10; August 1917, p. 9; *Proceedings, UA* (1917), p. 142; *Journal*, August 1919, p. 8; February 1920, p. 4; *Proceedings, UA* (1924), p. 79.

The first auxiliaries were established in mid-1916, in Baltimore, Boston, and Cleveland. At about the same time, the UA announced that it had secured special wage increases from the companies for Local 669 fitters in these and other cities where auxiliaries were being instituted. This move undoubtedly persuaded many sprinkler fitters to join the new organization. Indeed, in at least one case the wage increase was specifically conditioned upon the sprinkler fitters' transfer from a mixed local to Local 669.

The founding of the auxiliaries completed the structure of sprinkler fitters' unionism that was to continue for years. These were its basic features:

(a) In six cities — Chicago, Kansas City, St. Louis, Milwaukee, Minneapolis, and San Francisco — there were regular UA unions composed exclusively of sprinkler fitters. These locals had their own officers and business agents and signed their own contracts. However, as time went on, the national officers who in the meantime became familiar with the industry began to take an active role in resolving conflicts and facilitating agreements between the six unions and the sprinkler firms.[29]

(b) In several other cities (ten, by the end of 1924) the sprinkler fitters belonged to the auxiliaries of Local 669. The auxiliaries did not bargain directly with employers, and were obligated, in fact, to accept contracts negotiated on behalf of Local 669 by the UA officers. As it turned out, however, the representatives of the auxiliaries were normally consulted prior to the signing of the 669 agreement. In all other respects, the auxiliaries had the rights of regular UA locals. They retained a percentage of the initiation fees and dues; held regular meetings in union halls; and (after 1921) sent delegates to the national conventions.[30]

(3) The road men constituted the third and numerically largest group of UA sprinkler fitters.[31] Completely unorganized prior to 1915, they became members of Local 669 as a result of the agreement signed by the national officers and the companies. It was originally intended that the road men would be initiated into Local 669 by organizers who were to acquaint the journeymen with the institution and principles of unionism. In practice, however, arrangements on joining Local 669, and on initiation fees and dues were normally made by the officials of the sprinkler companies. The result was that the road fitters, although unionized, knew very little about the nature and purposes of

their organizations. In 1921 Vice-President Joseph Vallila, himself a sprinkler fitter and one of the signers of the 1915 agreement, described the position of the road men in the following way:

They have never seen an officer of the United Association since they joined. They have paid their dues 100 per cent to the United Association and they pay all the strike assessments and convention assessments and they never get any representation; they don't hold any meetings and they don't know anything about the union or what rules are. Your general officers make the working rules for them and the working rules are then given to the companies to present them, and they are transmitted to the men on the job that way. They get their orders from the company instead of from the union officials.[32]

Vallila's description also applied to the position of the road men after 1921. Throughout the post-nationalization decade and, indeed, into the 1930's, the road fitters continued to be essentially passive recipients of whatever was negotiated on their behalf by the UA officers.

Within a short time, the agreement came under sharp criticism from a variety of sources. By 1917, several UA locals complained that the road fitters sent to their areas by the companies were working on nonunion projects, and that the locals had no jurisdiction over them; Local 669 auxiliaries in several cities felt that they could accomplish more for their members if they became regular UA locals; and some of the sprinkler fitters organized in regular UA locals claimed that the relatively low-paid road men were being sent by the firms into their geographic jurisdiction. The UA officers acknowledged that the agreement was short of ideal. But at the 1917 convention Alpine and his supporters were in a strong position to defend it. Shortly before the convention the companies granted a wage increase — a year ahead of the agreed-upon schedule — to both road fitters and the auxiliaries. (See Table 4.) And, as Alpine claimed, despite the flaws in the agreement, the situation would have been worse had the road men remained unorganized. The result was that the Toledo (1917) convention approved the sprinkler contract.[33]

In 1919 the basic principle of the sprinkler agreement was extended to Canada, and the UA established in its Chicago headquarters a general union for the Canadian road men — Local 379. However, difficulties soon developed over the new terms of the Local 669 contract.[34]

The original contract with the sprinklers expired in June 1919. The UA officers called in the representatives of the auxiliaries and,

after a joint session, signed a new three-year contract (July 1919–
July 1921). Under its terms wages of all auxiliaries and road men
were raised to a uniform rate of $6.40 a day. In addition, for the first
time, the contract set a rate — $4.00 a day — for sprinkler fitters'
helpers who worked with the members of the auxiliaries. (The helpers
of the road men were not covered by the contract.)

During the months following the signing of the contract the postwar boom got underway. The regular sprinkler fitter locals won — in
some cases after a strike — significant wage increases from the companies. Although the auxiliaries were presumably working under a new
Local 669 contract, in December 1919, they now demanded additional
increases. In spite of the admonition of the UA they also struck thus
violating the agreement with the companies. Threat of suspension
from the UA brought the auxiliaries back to work. However, within a
few days after the end of the strikes, Coefield and Leonard negotiated
new wage changes that resulted in significant pay increases for both
auxiliaries and road fitters. (See Table 4.)

In spite of this success the auxiliaries continued to be deeply dissatisfied with their status in Local 669 and, indeed, with the nature of
the sprinkler fitter agreement. Accordingly, they submitted to the
1921 (Providence) convention resolutions requesting that (1) the
agreement not be renewed; and (2) that the auxiliaries be granted
separate charters as regular UA locals, with jurisdiction over sprinkler
fitting in their respective areas.[35]

The resolutions won a sympathetic audience at the convention.
The reason was not only the special complaints of the auxiliaries but
also the fact that the delegates had been subjected to some very sharp
criticism of the agreement by many plumber and steam fitter locals.
As at the preceding convention, the attacks were essentially aimed at
the special position of the road men. As permanent members of Local
669, the road men were free from the obligation to report to, and deposit their cards at, the local UA unions in areas where they were sent
by the employers. Moreover, since they were generally ignorant of UA
rules and customs, the road fitters were usually willing to work on nonunion and "unfair" projects, and to use several helpers per journeyman.
Accordingly, the UA locals felt that they had no control over these
supposedly UA members; and that frequently, when sent on their
projects, the road sprinkler fitters were, in fact, undermining the
conditions established by the local organizations.

Coefield defended the agreement, and implied that the problem of road men could be handled more effectively in future contracts with the sprinkler companies. However, he offered no defense of the institution of the auxiliaries, and the convention thus voted that, after the expiration of the current contract (on June 30, 1922), the existing auxiliaries be granted regular UA charters, and that new regular sprinkler fitter locals should be set up wherever there were "not less than twenty five bona fide sprinkler fitters and they request a separate Local Union."

As it turned out, however, the decision of the convention was never carried out. In May 1922, after some preliminary conferences with the employers, Coefield, Burke, and Leonard met in Washington with representatives of the auxiliaries. Although economic improvement was under way, unemployment in construction was still high and, because of over-all deflation, wages were being reduced throughout the country. Under these conditions the representatives of the auxiliaries were persuaded to empower the UA officers to renew the current agreement for one year "with the understanding that the present wage is to be maintained." The representatives also recommended that, in view of the depressed conditions in the industry, "the resolutions adopted by the Providence Convention (1921) . . . regarding the issuance of separate charters be held in abeyance for the one year period." In the following days the UA officers met with the companies, and negotiated an agreement that called for a uniform daily wage of $7.20 for all Local 669 fitters, and for a $4.50 daily wage for the auxiliary helpers. For some of the auxiliaries — and for the road fitters — the new rate actually represented a slight increase; for other auxiliaries it meant only a 10 per cent reduction (the helpers' rate in most cities was unchanged). In the circumstances, the results of the negotiations were thus very favorable, and the new contract was readily approved by the auxiliaries.[36]

During the early months of 1923, the UA officers again held conferences, first with the companies and then with the representatives of the auxiliaries. The result was that, in April, the parties agreed to renew the Local 669 agreement for three years. As shown in Table 4, both the initial wage increase (in July 1923) and the subsequent raise, negotiated in 1924 under the annual wage reopening clause, were very substantial.[37]

The record of the successful negotiations assured that both the sprinkler agreement and Local 669, as originally set up, were to be continued in the future.

At the 1924 convention there were still a few resolutions concerning the employment of helpers by the road fitters, and one of the auxiliaries asked for a separate charter. But, in contrast to the preceding convention, these matters evoked no debate or criticism of the sprinkler agreement. Instead, the delegates passed a resolution which instructed the incoming officers to consult with the representatives of the road fitters and the auxiliaries, and to take into account the results of these consultations when a renewal of the sprinkler agreement was negotiated. The officers were also urged "to install some educational plans for road man that will create a desire to further his knowledge in unionism." [38]   The resolution thus recognized that the UA would retain the basic form of the Local 669 contract.

The sprinkler agreement and the institution of Local 669 represented a pragmatic solution to a rather special situation. As a result of its basic features, the agreement benefited both the employers and the union.

(a) From the viewpoint of the companies, it was advantageous to have a national contract that applied uniformly to each of them. The sprinkler industry was dominated by a few firms that competed over wide geographical areas. The union contract thus introduced an element of stability (in wage costs) in a situation where competitive bidding by rival firms could easily undermine the price structure of the industry. Another advantage was that the contract was negotiated and administered by the UA officers. These were in the best position to bring about effective uniformity of union rules throughout the jurisdiction of the agreement, and to discipline any group of workers that might refuse to observe the contract. Finally, the companies also gained from the fact that, after the first unsuccessful attempt (in 1919), the UA officers and the firms were eventually able (in 1922) to institute uniform wage rates for all journeymen covered by the agreement. As a result, the firms were given flexibility in moving workers from one installation to another — within broader regions, between cities, and within large metropolitan areas.[39]

(b) The major benefit to the UA was the unionization of the road men. In many areas the road men posed a potential — and at times actual — danger of competition with the UA sprinkler fitters, and it was important to have them working under union conditions. It is unlikely, however, that they could have been unionized without the consent and direct assistance of the employers.

The road fitters were, in effect, migratory workers, and the structure of the UA — based as it was on local unions and on a transfer of members from one local to another — was not suitable for their organization. Moreover, the road men had no experience with, and no interest in, union organization. Under these circumstances the institution of Local 669 — a union that under the direction of the national officers negotiated on behalf of these traveling journeymen — represented the most practical way of establishing union conditions in the particular sector of the industry.

Most of the sprinkler fitters in major industrial areas could be organized along the conventional lines of the UA locals. But the existence of many locals with separate charters and autonomous rights of collective bargaining could undermine the viability of the national agreement as it was instituted by the companies and the UA officers. The auxiliaries of Local 669 thus represented a compromise between the needs of resident fitters to have local organizations and the needs of the firms and the UA to have a national and uniformly administered contract.

It should be apparent, however, that the institution of Local 669 did have certain aspects that could create problems for the national union.

(a) Local 669 and its auxiliaries represented an institutional invention that essentially existed outside the UA constitution. To be sure, there was no clause that prohibited the setting up of a local to be run permanently by the national officers. But, on the other hand, there was also no clause that provided for the institution of such a union.

(b) The structure of Local 669 did not provide any specific means whereby the workers could voice their preferences as to the terms of the contract. In the 1920's the UA leaders would normally consult with the auxiliaries prior to the negotiations with the companies. But the road men had no effective means to indicate their demands or grievances.

(c) The structure of Local 669 made it very difficult to educate the road men in the principles of unionism. Yet, apart from any other considerations, the UA members had an economic interest in making the road fitters good "union men." In the course of their work the road men would be sent to many areas where there were UA locals. Accordingly, depending on their behavior with respect to such issues as employing helpers or working alongside nonunion men, the road men could either harm or help many local organizations.

As the resolution passed by the 1924 convention indicated, the UA was well aware that the institution of Local 669 presented certain problems of its own. Yet, given the rather special characteristics of the sprinkler industry and its workers, these issues could not be resolved easily, and it took many years of experience before the union was able to deal with them in an effective manner.

REGULATION AND TRAINING OF APPRENTICES

The years 1914–1924 constitute an important period in the history of apprenticeship in the pipe trades. No moves were made at that time to establish a nationwide system of apprenticeship regulation. But in a number of cities, the UA locals of plumbers and employer organizations developed highly effective and systematized programs of apprentice training. Equally important, the largest UA local of steam fitters abolished the institution of "helper" and established, in cooperation with the employers, a system of apprentice education that, as the employers themselves acknowledged, "has raised the standards of workmanship and at the same time has provided an ample number of new workmen to meet new demands." [40]

The record of these programs indicated that the UA unions and employers could cooperatively establish a system of training that would be acceptable to and welcomed by both parties. Accordingly, the programs developed in 1914–1924 may be properly viewed as having prepared the ground for efforts that eventually led to a nationwide system of apprenticeship in the pipe trades.

Apprenticeship in Plumbing. Throughout the 1914–1924 period the UA constitution contained the clause on apprenticeship that was first introduced in 1910. The clause, originally meant to apply primarily to plumbing, urged the locals to "use their best efforts and endeavor to regulate all Helpers and Apprentices until such time as local unions are otherwise advised by a convention on one or more referendum votes." As indicated previously, the clause allowed up to four apprentices per shop. The apprentices were to be registered by a joint employer-union committee, and were to remain in training for five years.[41]

During the post-nationalization decade, the UA officers viewed the apprenticeship clause not as "a hard and fast rule" but rather as "simply a declaration of policy and principle which we are aiming to put into effect." [42] Therefore, the national union made no effort to insure that the clause be observed by the locals.

In actual practice the locals' policies toward apprenticeship varied from area to area. In some cities the locals would not tolerate apprentices in unionized shops; in others the locals imposed limitations on the number of apprentices but took no interest in the actual training process; and finally, as indicated, in several cities the plumbers' locals participated with the employer associations in running programs that produced highly qualified journeymen.[43]

The nature of these joint programs may be illustrated by the example of the apprenticeship system established in Cleveland in 1922.[44] The Cleveland program was governed by the rules of a "joint agreement" between Local 55 and the Associated Plumbing Contractors of Cleveland, and was administered by a joint committee of the two organizations. The apprentices were chosen by the master plumbers but were, in effect, indentured to the Joint Apprenticeship Committee rather than to an employer. The number of apprentices allowed in any one shop depended on the number of journeymen employed; the maximum was three apprentices per shop. The term of apprenticeship lasted four years, with the pay rising from 25 per cent of a journeyman's wage, in the first year, to 50 per cent of this wage in the fourth year.

Throughout their entire term of training, apprentices were required to attend classes (four hours a week) in the local technical school. The school was well equipped, and the instruction was financed by the Cleveland Board of Education and by funds granted under the provisions of the Smith-Hughes Act.[45] The time spent by the apprentices in class work was paid for by the employers.

Under the rules of the joint agreement, the Apprenticeship Committee was to be continuously informed about the schoolwork progress made by individual apprentices. The apprentices were also responsible to the committee for any infraction of the rules of the program. Upon completion of their training, they took a special examination and, after passing it, were admitted to the membership of Local 55. Because of the preliminary weeding out of incompetent candidates, the actual record of completion of apprenticeship was very high — over 90 per cent of those accepted by the program.

The Cleveland program and the similar training systems, established in Pittsburgh, Chicago, and other cities, reflected a subtle shift in the attitudes of the unionists toward the problem of apprenticeship. In the past, regulation of apprenticeship meant to the UA locals essentially — and perhaps solely — a means of restricting entry into the trade.[46] In this view, the best apprenticeship system was therefore one that imposed the greatest restrictions on the number of apprentices. The locals that participated in the establishment of the new programs considered regulation of the number of apprentices as an important aspect of the joint agreements. But they now viewed the apprenticeship programs as also fulfilling another important goal — that of producing highly qualified craftsmen who would also be good union men and who would thus add strength to the organized sector of the pipe trades.[47]

The change in the thinking of the unionists (and this applied to both locals and the leaders) was a result of a combination of events. For one thing, the joint programs reached their most developed stage during the time when, as a result of the building boom, there were shortages of skilled workers. The danger of oversupply appeared remote, and the unionized employers had jobs for additional journeymen. Second, the worker shortage led to the founding of many plumbing schools and training programs conducted under nonunion auspices. In addition, the National Association of Master Plumbers began a movement to increase the number of apprentices, and many nonunion shops were responding favorably. It was likely that many of the workers who received training under nonunion conditions would move to the major cities where there was strong demand for construction labor. Under these circumstances it was rational for the plumbers' locals to support apprenticeship programs that were producing well-trained journeymen who would join the unions and abide by their principles and rules. Finally, the changing attitudes of the locals also reflected their secure position in relation to the employers. It is significant that the most effective and elaborate programs were developed in areas where the plumbing trade was strongly organized. There, collective bargaining was so firmly established that the unions were secure enough to participate in long-range undertakings to benefit both employers and labor organizations.[48]

In point of fact, the main result of the joint programs developed in 1914–1924 was to increase the supply of highly trained journeymen rather than to impose restrictions on entry into the plumbing trade.

Limitations on the number of apprentices in one shop did not prevent the programs from supplying what the employers considered as the required quantities of new workers. In some areas, at least, the number of journeymen trained by the apprenticeship systems appeared to be very high. In Chicago, for instance, the program set up by Local 130 and the Chicago Plumbing Contractors' Association turned out an average of 150 journeymen annually — about 10 per cent of the membership of the union in the early 1920's. Where the output of the programs fell short of local needs the fault appeared to lie with the employers who were reluctant to take on apprentices.[49] Indeed, it is reasonable to assume that the programs provided at least as many qualified journeymen as would have been produced if the apprenticeship training were run solely by the employers' association.[50]

Apprenticeship in Chicago steam fitting. The history of apprenticeship in steam fitting during 1914–1924 is, in effect, the story of only one particular program. It is, nonetheless an important story. For, as an official of the national organization of employers pointed out many years later, the very institution of apprenticeship in steam fitting traces its origin to the training program established in Chicago in 1919 as a result of the initiative of the local union of fitters (Local 597).[51]

The first step that led to this pioneering program was the merger of Local 597 — the journeymen's union — with Local 598, the union of steam fitters' helpers. In April 1915, after several months of discussions and negotiations, the two unions amalgamated, with the helpers — about 600 — becoming members of Local 597. Under the terms of the agreement, all helpers who had at least five years' experience in steam fitting automatically became journeymen; other members of Local 598 were to become journeymen after they had completed a five-year term of work as helpers. Since no new helpers were to be admitted to the union, the agreement provided, in effect, for a gradual elimination of the institution of helper in the organized sector (virtually all the major employers) of Chicago steam fitting.[52]

Since the abolition of helpers meant that their work would be taken over by higher-paid journeymen, the agreement was opposed by the employers. Local 597 was, however, ready to fight to enforce it. Under the threat of a citywide strike, the employers acceded to the gradual elimination of helpers.[53]

Once the helper was being abolished, the road was paved for the introduction of formal apprenticeship. Although for many workers the job of helper was a permanent occupation rather than a steppingstone to the position of journeymen, steam fitters normally learned their craft while working as helpers. Thus, without helpers, the future labor needs of Chicago steam fitting had to be met by another system of training.

The initiative for creating the apprenticeship program apparently came from Charles Rau, the business manager of Local 597. Rau was able to secure the cooperation of several employers and of some members of the Chicago Board of Education. The joint efforts led to an agreement between the union and the employers' association that resulted, in 1919, in the institution of a systematic program of formal apprenticeship.[54]

The Chicago apprenticeship program was conducted by a Joint Board of Arbitration composed of representatives of Local 597 and the Chicago Master Steam Fitters' Association. (Only members of the association could participate in the program.) The board determined the acceptability of applicants, made assignments of apprentices to particular employers, administered annual "progress" examinations of those in training, and gave final examinations to apprentices who had completed their terms. The apprentices were considered to be "under the jurisdiction and control" of the board, and the board had the authority "to protect their welfare and also to instruct, direct and discipline them." [55]

The apprenticeship term was fixed at five years. An employer who was assigned an apprentice had to "keep him" at work at the trade for not less than ten months in each year. As originally instituted, the program called for a minimum of eight hours of class work a year, with the board given the right to require that individuals attend special night school for eight weeks of each of the first four years of apprenticeship. However, the school requirement was soon changed to one full day every two weeks during the entire period of training. The regular classes — including mathematics, science, and mechanical drawing — were conducted in a well-equipped continuation (part-time) school (Washburn Trade School) which was financed by the Chicago Board of Education and by funds granted under the Smith–Hughes Act. Full school credits and a satisfactory school record were required before an apprentice was permitted to take his final examination. As in the previously described programs of plumbers, time spent in school was paid at the same rate as time on the job.[56]

The number of apprentices enrolled in the steam fitting program —

about 400 — was smaller than the number of helpers at the time of the merger between Locals 597 and 598. However, the program had a very low "drop-out" rate and, as already indicated, supplied what the employers viewed as "an ample number" of new journeymen.[57]

For several years the Chicago program continued to be the only systematic program of apprenticeship in the steam fitting trade. Even as late as 1928, there was only one other city — Memphis — with an organized program.[58] The major obstacle was the institution of helper. So long as steam fitting was performed by teams of a journeyman and a helper, with the job of helper considered as a permanent occupation, the trade offered little opportunity for training apprentices. Moreover, so long as journeymen could be recruited from the ranks of helpers, local employers had little interest in setting up a systematic program of training.

The institution of helper was, however, firmly established in the trade, and, even quite apart from custom and tradition, there were important reasons why it was difficult to eliminate it. If helpers were abolished, their work would have to be performed by journeymen. This would be largely true even if, after abolishing helpers, the trade introduced a system of apprenticeship. (The few apprentices kept throughout the year in a shop could not provide substitutes for all the helpers hired during the busy season, particularly if the helper–journeyman ratio on a job was one to one.) As a result, any move to do away with, or even restrict, the use of helpers was strongly opposed by employers. Although their national organization (the Heating and Piping Contractors' National Association) expressed interest in apprenticeship programs, it kept reaffirming the view "that steam fitting is a two-man trade, requiring the services of one helper for each steam fitter employed at such work." [59] The position of the local employers was equally adamant. Thus, many UA unions felt that they could not follow the Chicago example of abolishing the steam fitter's helper.[60]

In several cities, the helpers were strongly organized. In a few of these (New York, for instance), they had separate locals; in others they represented a significant proportion of the members in the local unions of steam fitters. In all these areas they were covered by contracts, and, as in Chicago prior to 1915, were considered as another "craft" group within the organized building trades of the city. In these circumstances, some UA unions — and particularly those that were exclusively helpers' organizations — felt that attempts to abolish the institution of helper would undermine what they viewed as satisfactory and well-working arrangements (both with the employers and within the work force) that had been built through collective bargaining over a period of years. Therefore, at least during the period 1914–1924, these unions generally opposed any proposals for change in the working system of steam fitting in their particular areas. In a sense then, in some of the best-organized cities, the actual structure of union organization and collective bargaining contributed to the difficulties that confronted attempts to do away with helpers.

The recognition of the difficulties that existed in other cities brings into sharper focus what was accomplished in Chicago. The Chicago apprenticeship program was created by both the union and the employers' association, and it owed its success to the efforts of the two organizations. But there should be little question that the institution of the program was made possible — and, indeed, given strong impetus — by the bold and imaginative steps taken by Local 597 to solve the issue of helpers.

The institution of apprenticeship in Chicago had an influence that extended far beyond the limits of the city's steam fitting. The steps that led to the abolition of helpers were given wide and favorable publicity in the *Journal*, and in a speech delivered by Secretary-Treasurer Burke at the Toledo (1917) convention. In 1923 the UA executive board passed a resolution specifically commending "the action of Local Union No. 597 in the establishment of the apprenticeship system, thus paving the way for other locals to use peaceful and harmonious methods to put into effect the Chicago Steam Fitters apprenticeship system or some other similar system of apprenticeship." [61] In its report to the 1924 convention the board again called the attention of the UA to the accomplishments of Local 597, and urged fitters' locals to establish programs of apprenticeship.[62] While these and other efforts of the UA officers had no immediate results, the Chicago example was eventually followed by a number of other UA locals. Thus, both through its influence on the actions of unions and employers in other cities, and through its own experience and success, the Chicago program laid a basis for the establishment of a national system of apprenticeship in the steam fitting trade.

As the preceding pages indicate, during 1914–1924 the main accomplishments in the area of apprenticeship were a result of the efforts of individual locals rather than of the UA. The UA was not, however, merely a passive observer of the progress made by the locals. Since neither one of the two national organizations of employers was ready to participate in a joint undertaking, the UA did not take any steps toward the institution of a nationwide system of apprenticeship regulation. However, the UA officers made many efforts to promote the development of apprenticeship systems in individual areas. At the urging of the officers, the UA outlawed the so-called "permit helper" system which, if used widely, would undermine any attempts to introduce systematic apprenticeship. (The permit helper was a handy man who, for a fee paid to the local union, was allowed to work alongside a plumber or a fitter.) [63]   And, as exemplified by the publicity given to the Chicago steam fitting program, the UA leaders tried continuously to make the locals conscious of the importance of instituting apprenticeship programs in their jurisdictions.

The success of the local programs had, in turn, an influence on the thinking of the leadership. In view of the experience of these programs, the national officers became more firmly convinced than ever before that it was both possible and desirable to set up "an orderly business system of apprenticeship" that would be acceptable to both union and employers. Thus, in their report to the 1924 convention, the officers indicated that the UA stood ready to take up again with the national organizations of employers the matter of instituting an apprenticeship program that would provide "sufficient mechanics of our trade to meet the growing demand that will be necessary in the progress of, and advancement of our entire American jurisdiction." [64]

JURISDICTIONAL PROBLEMS WITH OTHER ORGANIZATIONS

Most of the important problems of trade jurisdiction that confronted the UA and its locals at various times pertained to issues that arose among the pipe crafts themselves.[65] However, almost from the beginning of their national organization the UA locals were also encountering problems of jurisdiction over work assignments that involved unions of other crafts.[66] The affiliation with the AFL legitimized, in effect, the UA's claim to jurisdiction over pipe fitting. Accordingly, during the early years of nationalization, as the UA itself was growing stronger, the national officers began to take an active part in what they viewed as defense of the UA jurisdiction against encroachments by other unions.

The major jurisdictional issue during the period of nationalization (aside from the IA conflict) was the dispute with the International Brotherhood of Electrical Workers. Both the electricians and the UA gas fitters claimed jurisdiction over installations of wrought iron tubing for the conduit of electric wires. (The gas fitters argued that the tubing was essentially the same type of pipe as that used in gas installations.) Conflicts between the two unions arose in several cities, and the issue was eventually submitted to the National Building Trades Council and to the executive board of the AFL. Both the council and the AFL executive board decided in favor of the electricians. Some of the gas fitters ignored the decision, but they received no support from other trades. The matter was solved in practice by the fact that electrical contractors would normally employ members of the IBEW. The electricians also took over another job to which the gas fitters originally laid claim — the assembling, hanging, and connecting of lighting fixtures. (The gas fitters' claim originated at the time when buildings were lit by gas.) However, despite some bitter complaints from gas fitters' locals, the UA made no attempt to bring the issue before the AFL or the Building Trades Department.[67]

During 1914–1924, the UA officers devoted more time to jurisdictional disputes with unions of other crafts than in any previous period. One reason was the successful resolution of the IA conflict. This victory strengthened the UA's position as the "one general association of the pipe fitting industry," [68] and made it easier for the national officers to pursue the problem of other jurisdictional issues — some of them of several years' standing. Another was the establishment of the National Board for Jurisdictional Awards. The very nature of the board required that in the cases it handled the various building crafts be represented by their national unions.[69] Finally, some of the jurisdictional disputes of the post-nationalization period affected so many local unions that they were handled most effectively at the national level.

Virtually all the disputes of the post-nationalization decade concerned issues of jurisdiction over work. The notable exception was the problem of the railroad pipe fitters. As will be apparent from the following discussion, the dispute concerning the railroad fitters became essentially a dispute about the jurisdiction over a particular group of workers rather than about the question of work assignments.

The dispute over the railroad fitters. Since the early 1900's the UA had organized some of the pipe fitters who worked in railroad shops. As indicated in an earlier chapter, the International Association of Steam Fitters also had at one time a few locals of railroad fitters. During the nationalization period the UA made little effort to extend its organization to the railroads, and, by 1913–1914, most of the organized pipe fitters in the shops were in the locals of the Sheet Metal Workers' Alliance.* Many — indeed, probably a majority — of the Alliance men who did pipe fitting were so-called "combination men" — that is, they did both pipe fitting and sheet metal work. In addition, some of the railroad pipe fitting was done by members of the lodges of the International Association of Machinists, and, in repairing and installation of air brakes, by men organized by the Brotherhood of Railway Carmen.[70]

The affiliation of many former IA fitters and subsequent organizing efforts gave a boost to the UA unions in the railroad shops. By late 1914 Alpine could claim that the UA had 26 locals of railroad fitters, with a total membership of about 2000. As might be expected, some of these locals encountered, at one time or another, jurisdictional problems with the organizations of the Sheet Metal Workers' Alliance.[71]

In 1912 eight national unions re-established the Railway Employees' Department of the AFL. (In previous years the department existed in a different form.) At the preliminary meeting in February of that year, the railroad fitters were represented by the IA. However, the department decided to comply with the instructions of the AFL and admit the UA "as representing the pipe fitting industry." Accordingly, in November 1912, the UA attended, as a member, a Rochester, New York, meeting that became known eventually as the first biennial convention of the department.[72]

However, the UA's stay in the Railway Employees' Department was short-lived. At its second convention, held in Kansas City in April 1914, the department decided against the affiliation of the UA. Four unions voted against the UA, and four (including the UA) for it. The decisive vote was cast by Arthur O. Wharton of the machinists, the president of the department.[73] The basic reason for the decision was the UA's claim of jurisdiction over all pipe fitting. As indicated before, the members of three of the organizations affiliated with the department — the sheet metal workers, the machinists, and the carmen —

* The full name of the union was Amalgamated Sheet Metal Workers' International Alliance. In the following text the union will be referred to as "Alliance."

did pipe work of one type or another. These unions, supported in the final vote by the blacksmiths, argued that the presence of the UA in the department (and thus its stronger position in the shops) would lead to jurisdictional conflicts, and would undermine work arrangements (for instance, employment of "combination men") that had been satisfactory to both the unions and the railroads for years.

The UA protested its unseating to the AFL, and, after a hearing, the executive council of the federation declared the action of the department void.[74] This turned out to be, however, of little help to the UA. The union was granted another hearing by the department, but to no avail, and when, in 1916, it applied for readmission, the application was rejected. The UA applied again in 1918, and this time too met with a negative answer. As in 1914 the reason for these decisions was the concern of the affiliated unions that the admission of the UA would lead to jurisdictional disputes.

The position of these unions could be easily justified. In its dealings with the department, the UA always professed that it would not interfere with the rights of other organizations in the railroad shops. But in view of the UA's claim to jurisdiction over all pipe fitting, the chances of interunion disputes were high indeed. For one thing, if the UA extended its organization, there would be an increased probability of conflicts over work assignments with the other organizations — particularly with the many Alliance locals consisting of pipe fitters and "combination men." Second, there was the question of organizing the many railroad fitters and combination men who were not in any of the unions. There was little doubt that the UA could legitimately view these men as falling within its own jurisdiction. However, among the railroad unions, it was the Alliance that was considered as the union with jurisdiction over the fitters.[75] Indeed, at the time of the UA application, the constitution of the Sheet Metal Workers' Alliance specifically claimed jurisdiction over railroad shopmen who "shall include tinners, coppersmiths and pipe fitters employed in shop yards and buildings and on passenger coaches and engines of all kinds." [76] The UA could presumably go on organizing railroad fitters even if it were outside the Railway Employees' Department. But, without membership in the department, its position would be weak, since it could not participate in the many joint negotiations and agreements of the department's unions and of its systems federations.[77]

The unseating of the UA did have a negative impact on its status in the shops and roundhouses, and the union lost some of its members to the sheet metal workers. However, the UA continued its efforts to organize the railroad fitters, and met with some success. In a move that reasserted the UA's jurisdictional claim, its railroad locals established a Railroad Pipe Fitters' Association; some new UA locals were organized; and some of the existing UA unions increased their membership. As a result, the UA more or less held its own in the shops, and in 1918 had strong unions on some major U.S. lines (particularly Chicago & Northwestern and Chicago, Milwaukee, and St. Paul), and also on the railroads in Canada.[78]

As it turned out, more important than the actual organizing efforts were the discussions and negotiations that took place in 1918 between Alpine and John J. Hynes, the president of the Sheet Metal Workers' Alliance. At that time three metal trades unions — the boilermakers, the structural iron workers, and the sheet metal workers — were planning to amalgamate and form one large organization. The amalgamation could hardly be carried out, however, without the consent of the AFL and many of its affiliates. The UA was an important organization, and John Alpine was an influential figure in the AFL. (In 1918, during Gompers' absence, Alpine was the acting president of the federation.) It was reasonable to assume that so long as the railroad fitters remained in the Alliance the UA — and perhaps the federation — would oppose the amalgamation. Under these circumstances, Hynes decided to join Alpine in an agreement which, if carried out, would have transferred thousands of railroad fitters and "combination men" from the Alliance to the UA.[79]

The actual agreement, signed in Baltimore in October 1918, was formulated by representatives of the railroad locals of the two national unions. Under its terms, all fitters formerly in the Alliance would be admitted, without cost, to the UA, and the Alliance would give up any claim to jurisdiction over railroad pipe fitting. The railroad fitters were to retain considerable autonomy within the UA, and the agreement contained several provisions on their special status. In one of its clauses, the agreement implied that the transfer of the workers would have to be approved by the Railway Employee's Department, and it was apparently understood that, if the UA could not secure affiliation with the department, the agreement "would be null and void." The parties also decided that the agreement "may be submitted to all railroad pipe fitters who are now affiliated with the Amalgamated Sheet Metal Workers International Alliance." [80]

Early in 1919, the officials of the Alliance's railroad organizations submitted the Baltimore agreement "without favor or prejudice" to the decision of the locals. A few weeks later, the UA — supported now by Hynes — presented the agreement to the Railway Employees' Department, and applied, once again, for admission. In both these cases, however, the decision went against the UA and the agreement.

The Alliance's railroad locals rejected the agreement overwhelmingly because they feared that, once in the UA, they would lose their autonomy; that the UA could not participate in the joint agreements of the six shop unions; and that establishment of UA locals would disrupt existing work relations in the shops. The department decided to postpone its decision on the UA application until its next convention. However, when the convention met, in April 1920, it rejected the UA application without discussion. (The application was protested by numerous resolutions from the Alliance's locals of fitters, and, in a committee meeting, was also strongly opposed by the machinists.) [81]

The executive board of the Sheet Metal Workers' Alliance had previously approved the Baltimore agreement. However, in view of the completely negative reaction of the railroad locals, Hynes and his fellow officers decided not to take any further steps to carry it out. The UA reacted, in turn, by bringing up the matter at the 1920 (Montreal) convention of the AFL. The federation's convention then decided that the Baltimore agreement should be carried out in the immediate future.[82]

Although the original reason for the agreement no longer existed (the amalgamation of the three national unions never materialized), the Alliance decided to follow AFL instructions. Accordingly, in September 1920, the union requested its railroad locals to transfer all fitters to the UA unions, and indicated that it would no longer accept any per capita tax from pipe fitters. This resulted in a strong reaction from the Alliance's unions. A few locals decided to abide by the instructions of the parent organization. However, most of them (with over 85 per cent of the union's membership on the railroads) refused to transfer any of their members to the UA and, indeed, left the national union and formed an organization of their own — International Association of Railroad Metal Workers. About the same time, the machinists asked their railroad lodges to start taking in pipe fitters from the former locals of the Alliance.[83]

The new developments persuaded the leaders of the Alliance that their original decision could not be carried out without serious difficulties. Since the new International Association consisted of locals with both fitters and metal workers, it posed a danger of dual unionism not only to the UA but also to the Alliance. Moreover, it appeared that if any of the AFL unions benefited from the original move, it would be the machinists rather than the UA. In these circumstances, Hynes decided to change the union's policy. In December 1920 after a consultation with the Railway Employees' Department, the Alliance invited the railroad locals back into its organization. The locals accepted and rejoined the union as a railroad branch of the sheet metal workers.[84]

From the viewpoint of the UA, Hynes' move constituted a repudiation of the Baltimore agreement. Accordingly, the union brought up the matter before the executive council of the AFL. The council decided that "the railroad fitters properly came under the jurisdiction of the UA," and ordered the Alliance to turn them over. The council also indicated that the "situation arose because of the UA having been denied representation in the Railway Employees Department" and declared that the UA was justified in its demand for affiliation with the department. These decisions were later reaffirmed by the 1921 (Denver) convention of the federation.[85]

The decision of the AFL led to new efforts to settle the problem of railroad fitters. Almost immediately after the federation's convention, Hynes and the representatives of the railroad branch of the Alliance began preliminary discussions with the UA. These efforts were renewed when the Alliance's convention instructed its officers to continue negotiations "to the end that an amicable understanding will be arrived at between those two organizations, as per action of the American Federation of Labor." [86]

In February 1922 the negotiators agreed upon a plan that was expected to provide a solution. It consisted of two agreements — one temporary and one permanent — with the latter to take effect after the temporary one had been carried out. The permanent agreement consisted principally of the provisions of the old Baltimore agreement. However, the parties recognized that, in order to carry it out, it would first be necessary to institute separation of work along craft lines — that is, to separate pipe fitting from sheet metal work, and presumably eliminate "combination men." Since this required some reorganization of the shop work, it had to be done with the cooperation of the road managements. Therefore, while efforts were being made to secure such cooperation, the locals were to observe the temporary agreement. According to this, on roads where there were UA unions, the Alliance locals were to transfer all full-time pipe fitters to the UA; if there were no UA unions, the Alliance locals were to send a per capita tax for every full-time fitter among their members to the UA. The Alliance locals were also obligated "to immediately start a campaign of educa-tion . . . having for its purpose the seating of the United Association in the various System Federations and the Railway Employees Depart-ment." [87]

Since the temporary agreement had no definite time limit, the 1922 plan reflected some major concessions on the part of the UA. But, even this compromise program encountered serious opposition. In March 1922 the two agreements were submitted to the railroad membership of the Alliance for a referendum, and were rejected by a nine to one vote. A few weeks later, the convention of the Railway Employees' Department took up a new UA application for readmission, and re-jected it unanimously.[88]

In spite of these setbacks, Coefield made attempts to continue negotiations with the Alliance, but these were interrupted, in July 1922, by the great strike of the railroads shopmen.[89] The strike lasted for several months and ended in the defeat of the unions. The poststrike conditions on the railroads were not propitious to any program of union and shop work reorganization.[90] In these circumstances, and in view of the hostile attitude of the railroad unions, the UA, in effect, gave up further attempts to extend its organization to the railroad fitters. The result was that eventually most of the UA railroad locals in the United States were disbanded, and their members taken over by the unions of the Sheet Metal Workers' Alliance. Only in Canada did the UA retain its strength among the railroad pipe fitters.[91]

In 1921 the Sheet Metal Workers' Alliance estimated that it had in its railroad locals about 16,000 members who could be classified as pipe fitters. (They were either full-time fitters or "combination men.")[92] The UA's failure to extend its organization to these men represented a major setback — indeed, the only major setback — in the union's efforts to exercise jurisdiction over all pipe fitting. The reasons for this lay in a combination of factors — the absence of strict craft division of labor between pipe fitting and other metal work in the railroad shops; the historical experience of the UA; and the inability of the UA to gain admission to the Railway Employees' Department.

(a) The absence of strict division of labor — along craft lines — between pipe fitting and other metal work, and the presence of large numbers of "combination men" constituted a major obstacle to UA attempts to establish itself in the railroad shops. To quote one of the leaders of the Alliance's railroad locals:

If the conditions were the same as they are in the building trade, if we simply had a bunch of pipe fitters in our organization that should belong to the plumbers, they would have been turned over long ago.[93]

The wide use of iron pipes was brought to the railroad shops by the introduction of air equipment on locomotives and of heating systems in passenger cars. However the work on these pipes was performed by men who had originally worked with copper and copper pipes, and who frequently alternated — particularly in smaller shops and roundhouses — between pipe fitting, sheet metal work, and copper work. It was this development that gave rise to the institution of "combination men." As already indicated, the "combination men" probably represented a majority of the members of Alliance locals.

(b) At the time of the spread of iron pipe work in the railroad shops, the UA was engaged in the conflict with the International Association of Steam Fitters. As a result, the union could devote no effort to organizing men who did pipe fitting on railroads — whether "combination men" or full time fitters.[94] The organizing opportunity was taken by the Sheet Metal Workers' Alliance which adjusted its organization and jurisdiction to the special conditions of the railroad shops. But, once the Alliance unions were firmly established in the shops, the UA could claim its organizing rights only by stressing the concept of strict craft jurisdiction (over pipe fitting). For reasons indicated, this concept was not well suited to the actual work conditions on the railroads. The result was that the UA encountered strong opposition to its efforts to take the fitters out of Alliance locals.

(c) The railroad locals of the Alliance realized that, without affiliation with the Railway Employees' Department, the UA could not offer any effective union protection. The unseating of the UA from the department and its inability to gain readmission were also a result of the lateness of the union's organizing efforts on the railroads. As already indicated, by 1914 at least three of the railroad unions had good reason to be concerned about the possibility of jurisdictional conflicts with the UA. An additional factor — especially in 1919–1920 when the UA had the support of the leaders of the Alliance — was the particularly hostile attitude of the machinists. Throughout 1914–1924, the machinists were involved in a jurisdictional dispute with the UA, and this naturally influenced their view of the union.

Disputes over work assignments. Organization of railroad fitters appeared to offer an opportunity for a significant increase in the actual extent of UA jurisdiction and membership, and, accordingly, it was treated as an important problem by the leadership of the national union. But to most of the UA members, the question of the union's position on the railroads was a side issue — one very much removed from the area of their immediate employment. To these members — and to their locals — much more important were the questions of jurisdiction over work assignments in construction, and the conflicts that they had in this connection with the local organizations of the other national unions.

The UA's experience in jurisdictional disputes with other national unions (outside the IA) was not as full as that of some other building trades unions. Nevertheless, during the post nationalization decade, the union and its locals did have several contests with other organizations. Some of these were settled on a local level, either through inter-union agreement or arbitration; [95] others were eventually settled on the national level by a variety of means — agreements between the national organizations, verdicts of the AFL, decisions of the National Board for Jurisdictional Awards. The following paragraphs give a brief outline of some of the more important disputes of the 1914–1924 period.

The sheet metal workers. The dispute between the UA steam fitters and the sheet metal workers arose in connection with the installation of air coolers, air washers, and blowers (fans). By 1916 conflicts occurred in several cities, and Alpine recognized that the issue would best be settled through an agreement between the two national unions.[96] Actual agreement was not reached, however, until September 1918 — when Alpine and John Hynes, the Alliance's president, were engaged in negotiations concerning the railroad fitters.

The agreement was a compromise which explicitly recognized the established jurisdictions of the two national organizations. All sheet metal work, when used on air washers, fans or blowers, or on their housing, was recognized as the work of the members of the Alliance;

all pipe fitting in connection with the installations was given to the steam fitters.[97]

In spite of the 1918 agreement, some additional conflicts arose, and in 1920 the issue was submitted to the newly formed National Board for Jurisdictional Awards, where it became the subject of the board's first award. In a decision that was accepted by both unions, the board simply confirmed, without any change, the provisions of the original agreement.[98]

The iron workers. The dispute with the iron workers went back at least as far as 1913. The UA claimed jurisdiction over the installation of iron pipe railings and iron pipe guards for enclosures and staircases. The reason was that these installations generally involved the same type of pipe fitting or joining as that in plumbing and steam fitting (in some of the demarcation agreements these installations were classified as the work of either plumbers or fitters). The iron workers, however, argued that, unless the pipes of the railings were also used for the conduit of fluids and gasses, the work belonged to them. Both unions recorded their claims with the Building Trades Department, and the dispute dragged out for years until, in 1920, it was submitted to the National Board for Jurisdictional Awards.

The board decided that pipe railing consisting of standard-sized cut and threaded pipe, not used in connection with ornamental or structural work, was the work of the plumbers and the steam fitters. The original award was later (in September 1920) supplemented by a special interpretation which emphasized the method of joining the railing pipes. According to this, the pipe railings to be installed by the iron workers had to have "a preponderance of slip-joints." Judging from the absence of complaints on the part of UA unions, the decision of the board, essentially favorable to the UA, was observed in practice by the locals of both organizations.[99]

The boiler makers. The dispute with the International Brotherhood of Boiler Makers concerned the issue of whether the boilermakers or the steam fitters should install the so-called "economizers" on boilers. (An "economizer" is an apparatus which performs as a feed-water heater, receiving water from the boiler feed pumps, and delivering it at higher temperatures to the steam-generating sections.) In 1913 the Chicago Joint Conference Board — a local agency set up to settle jurisdictional conflicts — awarded the work to the steam fitters. The issue came up again in 1923 during the work on an electric utility plant in Chicago. The unions submitted the dispute to the Building Trades Council which decided in favor of the UA. The boiler makers then turned to the executive council of the AFL.[100]

The executive council referred the issue to the executive boards of the two unions "for the purpose of making an effort to reach an adjustment." A joint meeting of the representatives of these bodies produced no agreement, and the council was thus obliged to render a decision. The decision awarded the installation of "economizers" to the UA steam fitters.[101]

The steam engineers. As in the preceding case, the dispute with the International Union of Steam and Operating Engineers pertained to very specific work assignment — the maintaining of temporary (low-pressure) heat while the heating system was being completed and the building was still under construction. Both the UA steam fitters and the steam engineers claimed jurisdiction over this work, and the dispute was thus submitted to the National Board for Jurisdictional Awards.

In March 1920, the board made a compromise decision. According to the board, the jurisdiction over maintaining heat rested with the steam fitters until the time of the initial test of the heating system. Immediately after the completion of the test, the work was to be taken over by a stationary (steam) engineer.[102]

The decision was unsatisfactory to both the UA and the steam engineers. The fitters felt that, according to the award, their work was completed too soon; the steam engineers wanted to operate the heating system from the time it was ready to function. As a result, the case was brought up again, and, in August 1923 — more than three years after its original award — the board made a new decision. This time the ruling was more satisfactory to the UA. The steam fitters were given jurisdiction over the maintaining of temporary heat "until the general test has been made and the work accepted by the owner or his agent." [103]

The steam engineers were naturally dissatisfied, and their president, Arthur Huddell, asked the board for a rehearing. Prior to that, the UA and several steam fitters' locals agreed to the proposals of employer associations for reducing the costs of work in maintaining temporary heat. The employers, who were on the side of the steam fitters anyhow, gave, in turn, strong support to the UA at the board's rehearing. Perhaps partly as a result of this support, the rehearing resulted in what

Coefield termed as "quite a victory for the United Association" — that is, a reaffirmation of the 1923 decision.[104]

The machinists. Jurisdictional disputes between UA locals and the lodges of the International Association of Machinists occurred first in 1906, but became more frequent after 1910. During the years of mobilization, war, and the postwar boom, disputes between the UA and the machinists were taking place in many areas of the country — from Boston to San Francisco. From the viewpoint of the UA, the reason was the insistence of the machinists on claiming jurisdiction over joining, fitting, and installations of certain types of pipes — particularly flange pipes. (Another pipe claimed by the IAM was large pipe — from two to five inches in diameter, and bolted by machinery.) Many of the conflicts over work on these pipes took place in navy yards and shipyards. (During 1915–1920 many UA members did marine pipe fitting and plumbing work.) Other disputes occurred, however, in the installation of refrigeration equipment and in other construction work requiring installation of machinery and piping systems (breweries, for instance).[105]

Some UA unions made efforts to settle their disputes locally and in a few cases actually succeeded. But the efforts to settle the basic jurisdictional issue on a national level turned into, what became for years, a series of frustrated attempts.[106]

The UA first brought up the dispute before the AFL during the 1913 convention. Since the two national unions could not agree on a settlement, the federation's executive council made a decision of its own, and, in February 1914, awarded the disputed pipe fitting to the UA. At the next (1914) convention of the federation the machinists asked for a reopening of the case. The convention ordered that a three-man committee investigate the issue and submit evidence to the executive council which would then decide whether to reopen the case. Nothing positive was accomplished, however, during the following year because the two unions could not agree on a third — presumably impartial — member of the investigating committee. The 1915 convention of the AFL decided that Gompers appoint the third member. However every one of the men he selected was too busy to devote time to the dispute, and, as a result, no new evidence was presented to the council, and the case was not reopened.[107]

Since the executive council made no new decision, the original one was still valid. The machinists ignored the 1914 award, however, and generally held on to the pipe work they originally claimed. This caused the UA to turn to direct negotiations with the leaders of the IAM. A joint meeting was arranged, but when it took place (in September 1919) no agreement was reached.[108] The reason apparently was that the Machinists would not give up their claims to the pipe fitting in the shipyards.

In 1920 the UA turned once again to the AFL convention, and asked the federation to direct the IAM to cease infringing on its jurisdiction. This led to another series of efforts to settle the dispute. A number of conferences between the UA, the machinists, and the AFL executive council took place in 1920, 1921, and 1922, with no resulting agreement. Further efforts were abandoned during the railroad shopmen's strike in which the IAM was deeply involved.[109]

The end of the dispute did not come until November 1925. By that time, employment in shipyards was only a fraction of that in 1919, and only a relatively small group of IAM members did marine work. This undoubtedly made it easier for the machinists' officers to enter into an agreement acceptable to the UA. Under its terms, "jurisdiction over pipe fitting of all description and sizes, without regard to the mode or means in the making of joints or connections" was recognized as belonging to the UA. The machinists retained jurisdiction over work on machinery "of all description," and over certain specific work such as assembling mechanical oiling devices. (All oil piping, however, was under UA jurisdiction.) In effect then the agreement between the two national unions confirmed the basic jurisdictional claims of the United Association.

Some of the IAM lodges whose members worked in the shipyards protested the terms of the 1925 accord. However, during the 1920's and the early 1930's, the agreement was generally observed and worked well.[110]

Summary. The cases outlined above pertain to some of the more important disputes, and they cannot thus fully reflect the variety of jurisdictional problems encountered by the UA in 1914–1924. (In addition to these disputes, the union also had jurisdictional problems with compressed air workers — later merged with hod carriers — bricklayers, painters, carpenters, and other organizations.) The cases illustrate, however, the basic principle of the jurisdiction that has been vested in and protected by the UA — the right to claim all work pertaining to fitting, joining, and installation of pipes and pipe fittings "of all description and sizes."

As suggested by the preceding description, the UA was, by and large, very successful in protecting its jurisdiction over pipe fitting. The major setback was, of course, the failure to organize the railroad fitters. Yet, from the viewpoint of the long-run development of the union, this setback was much less important than it appeared to be back in 1920–1921. Railroad employment reached its peak in 1920 and has been falling, more or less continuously, ever since. The UA thus lost a battle in a declining industry. At the same time, however, the union retained jurisdiction over pipe fitting in the expanding sectors of the economy — in construction of industrial plants, of public utilities, of petroleum facilities, and of residential buildings.

Chapter 9

The Union in Perspective

By the middle 1920's the United Association reached a plateau in its development as a national union of the pipe trade. What lay ahead after a few more years of prosperity was the ordeal of the Great Depression of the 1930's. A new period of expansion in membership did not begin until about 1940.

The UA of the 1920's was very different from the union that was undergoing major reforms during the years of nationalization, and, in many ways, also different from the UA of 1914. In spite of the many changes that over a period of years affected every aspect of its activity — changes in government, membership, and leaders — the UA of the mid-twenties also retained some of the basic features that characterized the national union from the time of its founding.

(a) The UA of the twenties was led and administered by professional union leaders — men who spent a large part or sometimes most of their lives managing union affairs, and who during their tenure of office had acquired considerable knowledge of the problems of union organization, and of the economics and technology of the pipe trades. As described earlier, the development of professional union leadership in the UA began during the period of nationalization. The trend toward increasing stability of leadership and its professionalization continued in subsequent years, and by the time of the mid-1920's most of the UA leaders and organizers had held positions in the national union for at least fifteen years, with some — including Secretary-Treasurer Thomas Burke — for over two decades.

The UA governmental system made the national leaders ultimately answerable to the conventions of the organization. But the system also gave the officers considerable freedom to shape and execute policies. Under these circumstances, the professional nature of UA leadership imparted a quality of continuity to the union's policies and a quality of stability to its government.

(b) In spite of the many changes that, over a period of years, strengthened the position of the national union and its officers, the

United Association retained its essentially democratic charter. To be sure, the process of UA government bore little resemblance to the democracy of the town-meeting type of government, and the UA officers were much more than mere executors of the decisions made by their constituents. But the policies originated by the UA leaders could not be pursued for any length of time unless they were broadly consistent with the preferences of the locals to begin with, or unless the national leaders were able to persuade the locals that these policies would benefit the union and its members.

One reason was that the UA conventions — well attended by delegates of the locals — continued to perform their functions as a union parliament and a court of last appeal. The national officers were normally able to win the support of the majority of convention delegates for past or future policies. But the approval was by no means assured. In cases where the UA policies ran counter to strong preferences of the locals — as in the situation of the sprinkler fitters' contract in 1921 — the leaders were forced to yield to the decisions of the convention. Another reason was, as past history indicated, that widespread dissatisfaction with UA policies could lead to campaigns by individual locals or groups of locals that would mobilize opposition to the national leadership even during interconvention periods. The possibility of such campaigns — and the fact that under the UA constitution they could lead to a calling of a special convention — provided another assurance that the policies of the officers would be basically consistent with the preferences of the majority of the membership.

(c) The characteristics of the UA government emphasized above reflected to a large extent the characteristics and nature of the union membership.

Because of the skilled nature of their crafts, the UA members represented a highly literate segment of the labor movement — a characteristic reflected in the emphasis placed by the UA on publishing of a union journal.[1] (The *UA Journal* provided a great deal of information about problems and policies and carried in each issue reports by the president and the general organizers.) Moreover, by the time of the postwar organization period, many of the UA members, particularly the local officers, had had rich experience with the institution of unionism — in local union government and through participation in national conventions. And finally, perhaps because of their close contact with, and sometimes experience in, small business enterprises, UA members and their local leaders normally took a pragmatic and businesslike view of the problems of managing the national union.

The relatively sophisticated unionists — attached to the traditions of their craft and their locals, and frequently well informed about the problems of the UA — would not tolerate any attempts, if such were ever made, to transform the UA into an autocratic organization.[2] Yet, at the same time, the members seemed to agree with one of their officers that the UA "should not be a sentimental association" and that it was "founded on business principles."[3] Accordingly, they were willing to leave the management of the organization to the experienced leaders who would normally exercise a considerable amount of executive power. The result was that the UA government, while ultimately responsive to the preferences of the members, was also both stable and professionally run.[4]

(d) In the 1920's, UA unions in most major cities and in hundreds of smaller areas had firmly established and frequently friendly bargaining relationships with local employers. In many of the larger cities collective bargaining constituted, in fact, an integral aspect of conducing business enterprises in the pipe trades, and the contracts between local employers and unions had a long tradition. In addition, UA locals and the national officers had firmly established bargaining relationships with several large contractors who conducted business over wide areas of the country, and with the major manufacturers and installers of sprinkler fitting systems.

As indicated in Chapter 3, there were several factors that facilitated acceptance of collective bargaining by the employers: many employers had started as journeymen and were former UA members; the union-enforced wage scale provided a minimum cost basis for firms bidding for contracts in a given area; the unions would join forces with the employers to ban installations of certain devices (for example, "anti-syphon traps") or to lobby for enactment of state and city laws regulating the trade; and in some areas the contracts with employers' associations would make it more difficult for new firms to enter the pipe trade. These factors continued to contribute to the development of stable collective bargaining relationships between UA locals and employers even in the post-nationalization years.[5] But the most important reason for the development of what in the UA viewpoint were satisfactory relationships with employers was the growth of the organizational strength of the UA and its locals. As the locals were increasing their membership among journeymen, they became the best, and in many areas the only, sources from which employers could get first-class mechanics in the pipe trades (in some cities, Chicago, for instance, UA locals had been in this position for years). The leaders of UA locals and the national officers had had long experience in dealing with employers, and they took full advantage of the growing numerical strength of the UA. As a result, during the period of the construction boom of the 1920's UA locals were firmly established throughout the country as the bargaining representatives of the pipe trades.

(e) The UA was also firmly established as the national organization with exclusive jurisdiction over the pipe crafts and over any work pertaining to fitting, joining, and installation of pipes and pipe fittings. (Railroad pipe fitting, of course, constituted an exception.) The UA's jurisdiction over all types of pipe fitting was recognized by the AFL, by other national unions, and by the employers. And as indicated earlier, the UA was, in fact, generally successful in protecting its jurisdiction from encroachment by other organizations.

The basic reason for the UA's success in maintaining its jurisdiction was that the union had been able to bring about the affiliation of the IA steam fitters. First, as a result of the affiliation the UA could count among its members almost all the organized workers in the pipe trades. Second, the affiliation eliminated the danger of work assignment disputes that would undoubtedly have undermined the UA's exclusive jurisdiction over pipe fitting. Third, the drawn-out conflict with the IA eventually resulted in an unequivocal reaffirmation — by the AFL and the Building Trades Department — of the original jurisdiction of the national union.

To be sure, the UA did have several jurisdictional disputes with other unions after 1914. But these disputes had to do with very specific work assignments — frequently those on the very fringe of UA jurisdiction. The basic position of the UA as *the* union with a claim over pipe fitting was not really questioned by other unions and, so far as organized labor was concerned, the UA had within its legitimate jurisdiction not only plumbing, steam fitting, gas fitting, and sprinkler fitting, but also the expanding areas of pipe fitting installations in chemical, oil, refrigeration, public utilities, and other industries.[6]

(f) Another characteristic of the UA was its strong commitment to the policy of instituting programs of regulation and training of apprentices. The concern about regulation of apprenticeship was one of the factors that led to the founding of the national union, and it continued unabated throughout the years of UA's growth. Originally, the UA's apprenticeship policies were concerned only with plumbing — the craft where the traditional system of indentured apprenticeship broke down prior to the rise of national organizations. However, during the Alpine administration the union began to concern itself also with the problem of apprenticeship in steam fitting, and by the mid-1920's the UA was firmly committed to the view that the institution of steam fitter's helper should be abolished, and that, like plumbing, the steam fitting trade should have joint union — employer programs of regulation and training of apprentices.

The continuing concern with apprenticeship resulted in some very substantial achievements. For reasons explained earlier, the UA was unable to institute a nationwide program of apprenticeship. However, in several cities plumbers' unions and local associations of employers jointly established highly effective apprenticeship systems. Equally important, the steam fitters' local in Chicago abolished the helpers and instituted a union–employer program which, as the UA leaders pointed out, could serve as a model for other locals to follow. By the time of the Great Depression, the UA had thus not only a long tradition of commitment to a policy of regulating and training apprentices but also a great deal of actual experience with programs that successfully trained future journeymen for both plumbing and steam fitting, and that could provide a base for developing a national program of apprenticeship in all the pipe trades.

The UA emerged from the period of the Great Depression in a strong financial position and with a relatively small loss of membership. By 1940, as the economic situation improved, the union began a period of remarkable growth and expansion — a period that brought the UA to its present position as one of the strongest organizations in the labor movement.[7]

The experience of the UA during the depressed thirties and the subsequent period of its rapid growth deserves careful study. But there is little doubt that the high viability of the union — its ability to preserve a relatively strong position during the depression and to grow rapidly in the years after 1940 — derived largely from the basic nature of the organization as it was formed during the years of the nationalization and post-nationalization decades.

To be sure, the technological and economic changes that have taken place since the 1920's have been favorable to the UA. The growth of refrigeration and air conditioning, of chemical, oil, public utility and other industries, and the rise of the atomic energy industry and aero-space installations have created new demands for pipe fitting and have expanded the area of UA jurisdiction. But the development of the UA since the 1920's could hardly be viewed as a mere by-product of a favorable technological environment. A major part of the explanation has to be sought in the characteristics of the national union that were described in the preceding paragraphs: its government that was both effective and ultimately responsive to the membership; well-established relations with employers; full control of jurisdiction over pipe fitting; and strong commitment to the policy of training future journeymen for the trade. In developing a national union with these characteristics, the leaders, the locals, and the members of the UA had provided, by the time of the 1920's, a solid base for the future growth of their organization.

Notes

Abbreviations Frequently Used

Journal refers to the United Association *Journal* (the official publication of the UA) whose title changed over a period of years. For example, *Journal* (1894) was called *Plumbers, Gas Fitters and Steam Fitters Journal.* Its present title is *UA Journal.*

Constitution (UA) indicates the constitution of the United Association in the year indicated in parentheses.

Proceedings, UA refers to the national convention of the United Association in the cited year.

Proceedings, AFL pertains to the national convention of the AFL in the cited year.

Proceedings, Building Trades Department is in reference to the national convention of the building trades department of the AFL in the year in parentheses.

Chapter 1

1. The U.S. Census listed all the pipe fitters under one classification. In the 1880 Census this classification was described as "plumbers and gas fitters." Many of the steam fitters were undoubtedly included in this classification; others may have been classified as "mechanics." From 1890 on, the pipe crafts were described as "plumbers, gas fitters and steam fitters." The total number of craftsmen in the pipe trades (including self-employed but excluding apprentices and helpers) given by the Census data in 1880–1910 was: 1880–19,383; 1890–56,607; 1900–92,216; 1910–148,304. Bureau of the Census, *Occupations of the Twelfth Census* (Washington, 1904); *Thirteenth Census of the United States, 1910,* Population (Washington, 1914), vol. IV.

2. This estimate is based on the number of plumbers, steam fitters, and gas fitters organized in the New York area in 1886. Many plumbers worked in very small shops that escaped unionization, and thus the actual percentage of plumbers among the three crafts may be understated. See *Proceedings, Third Annual Convention of the IAPSG,* Chicago, 1886, pp. 15–16.

3. This is based on the membership of the national union of the fitters — the National Association of Steam and Hot Water Fitters and that of the United Association submitted to the Industrial Commission of 1900. The assumption is that the United Association had 500 steam fitters among its members.

4. The following sketch of historical development and the nature of plumbing functions is based on these sources: L. S. Nielsen, *Standard Plumbing Engineering Design* (New York, 1963), ch. 1; H. A. J. Lamb, "Sanitation, A Historical Survey," *Architect's Journal,* v. 85; F. P. Stearns, "The Development of Water Supplies and Water Supply Engineering," American Society of Civil Engineers, *Transactions,* 1906, vol. LVI; R. S. Kirby and P. G. Laurson, *The Early Years of Modern Civil Engineering* (New Haven, 1932), p. 212; J. Garrett, "Making

Cast Iron Pipe," *Journal of the New England Water Works Association*, September 1896; W. Goetting, "Revising Some Plumbing Traditions," *Metal Worker, Plumber and Steam Fitter*, November 10, 1916; E. B. Phelps, *Public Health Engineering*, New York, 1948; W. Champness, *A Short History of the Worshipful Company of Plumbers* (Washington, 1955); W. T. "Some Common Facts About Plumbing", *Architectural Record*, July-September, 1891; *Industrial Chicago — The Building Interests* (Chicago, 1891), pp. 32–53; W. L. Badger, "Some Phases of the History of Chemical Engineering," *The Journal of Engineering Education*, April 1932. In addition to these sources I relied on the information provided by Norman F. Piron, Assistant Director, Training Department for Apprentices and Journeymen, United Association, and on a series of his articles published for the apprentices under a general title "Plumbing — Applied Science."

5. As late as 1890 some local unions of plumbers and gas fitters also included tinsmiths in their membership. See for example Bureau of Statistics of Labor of the State of New York, *Eighth Annual Report*, part 1, Albany, 1891, p. 164.

6. Even in 1889 a leading English text on plumbing included instructions for making lead pipe by hand. P. J. Davis, *Standard Practical Plumbing* (2nd ed. rev.: London, 1889), pp. 49–50.

7. E. W. Bemis, "Relation of Trade Unions to Apprentices," *Quarterly Journal of Economics*, October 1891, p. 89.

8. The description of steam and hot water fitting is based on: W. J. Baldwin, *Steam Heating for Buildings* (New York, 1883); R. C. Carpenter, *Heating and Ventilating Buildings* (New York, 1900); W. S. Munroe, *Steam Heating and Ventilation* (New York, 1902); "Modern Sanitary Engineering," Harper's Magazine, April 1884; New York Steam Corporation, *Fifty Years of New York Steam Service* (New York, 1932); *Industrial Chicago — The Building Interests* (Chicago, 1891), pp. 335–338; R. M. Starbuck, *Questions and Answers on Steam and Hot Water Heating* (Hartford, 1912); Witt Carrier, R. E. Charne, W. A. Grant, *Modern Air Conditioning, Heating and Ventilating* (New York, 1948). I have also been aided by interviews with Joseph P. Corcoran, Director of Training Department for Apprentices and Journeymen, United Association.

9. A. M. Schlesinger, *The Rise of the City* (New York, 1933), p. 140; also *Industrial Chicago*, p. 238.

10. This paragraph is based on O. E. Anderson, Jr., *Refrigeration in America* (Princeton, 1953), pp. 86–96.

11. The description of gas fitting is based on these sources: W. P. Gerhard, *Gas Lighting and Gas Fitting* (New York, 1894); W. T. O'Dea, *The Social History of Lighting* (London, 1958); A. Dunbar, *The Gas Fitters Question Book* (Boston, 1900); Industrial Chicago, pp. 141, 270–277; W. P. Gerhard, *The American Practice of Gas Piping and Gas Lighting in Buildings* (New York, 1908).

12. *Proceedings, Third Annual Convention of the IAPSG*, p. 133.

13. J. H. Ashworth, *The Helper and American Trade Unions* (Baltimore, 1815), pp. 16–18.

14. For a typical example of the usage of the two terms as synonymous see "Without a Helper," *Journal*, April 1894, p. 18.

15. *Constitution, UA* (1897), p. 25.

16. In the three censuses between 1880 and 1900 all the "gainful workers" who were classified as "plumbers, gas fitters or steam fitters" were put under the

rubric of "Building Trades." The 1910 Census indicated that over 80 per cent of the pipe fitters were employed in the construction industry. In 1930 — a year of depression and high unemployment — the construction industry was less important as a source of jobs, but even then 70 per cent of those classified in the pipe crafts were actually employed in construction. (See sources cited in note 1 and also Bureau of the Census, *Fifteenth Census of the United States, 1930, Population*, Vol. V, Washington 1933.) Although in the 1880–1900 Censuses all the pipe fitting journeymen were listed under "Building Trades" it is reasonable to assume that some plumbers and steam fitters also worked in other industries (railroad shops, for example). However, their number was probably small. By 1910 many pipe fitters were employed outside of construction — particularly in railroad shops and in manufacturing establishments. Indeed, already in 1909 the UA had a local (Local Union 128) composed of pipe fitters employed by the General Electric plant in Schenectady.

17. The census data indicate that the 1880–1900 period was one of very rapid growth in the plumbing and heating industries in construction. These data pertain to the number of workers in the various building crafts. Between 1880 and 1900 the median increase in the number of five major crafts — carpenters, masons, painters, plasterers, and roofers — was 62 per cent; the increase in the number of plumbers and fitters was over 300 per cent. (See the data in Bureau of the Census, *Occupations of the Twelfth Census*, Washington, 1904.)

18. In the 1929 census of construction the data for establishments doing less than $25,000.00 worth of annual business were provided for only two categories: a) heating and piping, and b) plumbing and heating combined. In heating and piping 38.7 per cent of establishments had value of business of $25,000 or more; in the category of plumbing and heating combined (including only plumbing) only 18.7 per cent did annual business of $25,000 or more. (Bureau of the Census, *Fifteenth Census of the United States, 1930. Construction Industry*, Washington 1933, Tables 1 and 12.)

19. Ashworth, *The Helper and American Trade Unions*, p. 57.

20. *Journal*, December 1894, p. 3; December 1898, p. 10; November 1902, p. 4; February 1903, p. 12; September 1912, p. 10.

21. *Report of the Industrial Commission*, vol. VII, Washington, 1901, p. 953.

22. Computed from Bureau of the Census, *Construction Industry*, Table 6.

23. For description of conditions of entry into plumbing see L. P. Mutter and K. R. Davis, *Establishing and Operating a Heating and Plumbing Contracting Business* (Washington, 1946); also Research Department of Engineering Publications, Inc., *The Plumbing and Heating Market* (Chicago, 1928).

24. Competitive pressures that focused on plumbing and steam heating firms were probably further increased by the fact that plumbing and heating appear to have represented a fairly substantial part of the total cost of structures. There are no data that would permit estimating the cost of these installations as a share of total cost of building prior to the 1930's. Estimates pertaining to the 1930's and 1940's suggest that plumbing amounted to perhaps 6–9 per cent of the total construction cost (excluding land) of buildings. For heating the equivalent, percentage varied from 2 to 7.5. It should be noted, however, that the relative shares of plumbing and heating have varied over time, depending on many factors — technology, cost of materials, and labor, and the nature of structures to be built. For estimates in housebuilding see S. J. Maisel, *Housebuilding in Transition* (Berkeley, 1953), p. 372; "Labor and Material Costs in Small-House Construction," *Monthly Labor Review*, May 1939, p. 1059. More

general estimates may be obtained from the data in the 1939 Census of Construction. These indicate considerable variations in the share of plumbing and heating in total cost of construction, depending on the type of structure. For all new structures combined the data indicated that plumbing costs were 8.4 per cent and heating costs were 6.3 per cent of total construction costs. See Bureau of the Census, *Census of Business, 1939, Volume IV, Construction 1939*, Washington, 1943, Table 4a. Other estimates may be found also in Department of Commerce, Bureau of Foreign and Domestic Commerce, *The Construction Industry* (Washington, April 1936), pp. 31–33.

25. *Industrial Commission*, vol. VII, pp. 965–968; vol. VIII, p. 443. *Journal*, February 1901, p. 5; December 1901, p. 12. As described in Chapters 3 and 6, these attempts were, at times, helped by the so-called "exclusive agreements" signed by the local association of contractors and local unions.

26. Computed from data in Table 5b in Bureau of the Census, *Construction, 1939*. See also J. C. Humphrey, *The Plumbing Contracting Industry*, National Recovery Administration (Washington, September 1935), p. 17.

27. Mutter and Davis, *Establishing and Operating a Heating and Plumbing Contracting Business*, pp. 14, 129.

28. R. E. Montgomery, *Industrial Relations in the Chicago Building Trades* (Chicago, 1927), pp. 193, 205–206; *Proceedings*, UA (1899), pp. 12, 31, 36–38, 51–52; *Proceedings*, UA (1900), p. 38; Department of Labour (Canada), *Investigation into the Amalgamated Builders' Council and Related Organizations* (Ottawa, 1930), pp. 7–13.

29. "The Convention in Detail," *The Hydraulic and Sanitary Plumber* (New York, July 5, 1883), p. 244; *Industrial Chicago*, p. 100.

30. *Industrial Chicago*, p. 253; *Industrial Commission*, vol. VII, pp. 953–55; Joint Executive Committee, the Master Steam and Hot Water Fitters' Association, *Circular No. 1*, February 1890, pp. 5–65; *Official Bulletin of the National Association of the Master Steam and Hot Water Fitters*, July 1897, p. 219.

31. R. Lubove, *The Progressives and the Slums* (Pittsburgh, 1962), p. 142.

32. *Journal*, November 1892, p. 5. In the 1892–1900 period the *Journal* frequently reproduced plumbing codes of various cities.

33. "The Convention in Detail," p. 244.

34. *Journal*, January 1893, p. 2; W. Haber and H. M. Levinson, *Labor Relations and Productivity in the Building Trades* (Ann Arbor, 1959), p. 180.

35. Raising of minimum requirements for installation of plumbing may be considered as equivalent to an increase in minimum price of a "unit of plumbing." If the demand for plumbing is inelastic, the total revenue received by the local plumbers as a group will increase. An alternative formulation of the problem may be in terms of "tie-in" sales analysis. For example, a certain design of plumbing may be considered as one product and additional venting as a product tied to it. Some writers have, in fact, claimed that many plumbing codes impose unduly high standards of quality and quantity on builders and home-owners. See G. C. Whipple, "Reducing the Cost of Housing by Eliminating Unnecessary Plumbing Code Requirements," in National Housing Association, *Housing Problems in America, Proceedings of the Ninth National Conference on Housing*, Philadelphia, December 5, 6 and 7 (New York, 1923), pp. 74–75; G. C. Shaw, "Unnecessary Plumbing Code Requirements," pp. 311–314; Haber and Levinson, *Labor Relations and Productivity in the Building Trades*, pp. 180–181.

36. In 1881 New York City passed a law requiring registration of master

plumbers. However, no examination was specified. A law requiring examination was not passed until 1896. Massachusetts appears to be the first state to have required licensing preceded by examinations for both masters and journeymen plumbers. It passed such a law in 1893. Illinois passed a plumbing licensing law in 1897. During the 1890's several municipalities in various states passed licensing laws. Gordon Atkins, *Health, Housing and Poverty in New York City, 1865–1898* (Ann Arbor, 1947), pp. 119, 290; *Journal*, December 1892, p. 6; February 1893, p. 8; May 1893, p. 6; July 1893, p. 5; November 1893, p. 5; July 1896.

37. *Proceedings*, UA (1893), pp. 8–9; *Journal*, January 1893, p. 2; August 1908, p. 15; October 1909, p. 8.

38. For an explicit statement by an UA organizer that introduction of licensing examinations will eventually bring the end of the scab plumbers, and will eliminate potential strike breakers, see *Journal*, October 1909, p. 9. The contractors sometimes opposed licensing of journeymen (but not of master plumbers) because they feared that it would bring about shortage of workers. *Journal*, April 1910, pp. 12–13. See also W. Gellhorn, *Individual Freedom and Governmental Restraints* (Baton Rouge, 1956), p. 202, fn. 57.

39. C. D. Edwards, "Legal Requirements That Building Contractors Be Licensed," *Law and Contemporary Problems*, Winter 1947, p. 77.

40. For an example of such law see *Journal*, December 1892, p. 6. Also Edwards, "Legal Requirements That Building Contractors Be Licensed," p. 82.

Chapter 2

1. John R. Commons *et al., History of Labour in the United States* (New York, 1918), pp. 390, 475, 480.

2. Royal E. Montgomery, *Industrial Relations in the History of Chicago Building Trades* (Chicago, 1927), p. 14; Commons *et al., Labour in the United States*, pp. 610, 622.

3. John Hamill, unpub. ms., p. 5; James O.Hagen, unpub. ms., p. 1 (These two manuscripts contain reminiscences of two early officers of the union. They are in the library of the United Association.) "How the Plumbers and Fitters Organized a National Body," *Journal*, October 1895, p. 2; Ira B. Cross, *A History of Labor Movement in California* (Berkeley, 1933), p. 31.

4. One such man was James Crotty, a prominent leader of the New York plumbers. For his speech mentioning the experience of the previous failures see *Proceedings, Third Annual Convention of the IAPSG*, Chicago, 1886, p. 56.

5. The 1880's were actually characterized by general prosperity and expansion of economic activity. But this prosperity was interrupted by the 1884–1885 secession.

6. The information on organizations in these cities is in Hamill and in *Proceedings, Third Annual Convention of the IAPSG*. See also Cross, *A History of Labor Movement in California*, p. 144.

7. *Report of the Preliminary Convention, NTA 85*, Brooklyn, 1886, p. 8; *Proceedings, Third Annual Convention of the IAPSG*, p. 33; *Report of the Industrial Commission*, vol. VIII, Washington, 1901, p. 198.

8. The Steam Fitter, May 1907, p. 19; John Mangan, *History of the Steam Fitters' Protective Association of Chicago* (Chicago, 1930), p. 11.

9. Commons *et al., History of Labour in the United States,* vol. II, pp. 344 and 381.

10. M. Reder, *Labor in a Growing Economy* (New York, 1957), p. 41.

11. *Proceedings, Third Annual Convention of the IAPSG,* pp. 50–51, 91.

12. Cross, *A History of Labor Movement in California,* p. 173.

13. *The Steam Fitter,* May 1907, p. 17; Mangan, *History of the Steam Fitters' Protective Association of Chicago,* p. 13.

14. *Proceedings, Third Annual Convention of the IAPSG,* p. 47.

15. Norman J. Ware, *The Labor Movement in the United States, 1860–1890* (New York, 1964), pp. 174–186.

16. *Proceedings, Third Annual Convention of the IAPSG,* p. 47.

17. For evidence of union concern about apprentices, see State of New York, *Fourth Annual Report of the Bureau of Statistics of Labor for the year 1886* (Albany, 1887), pp. 156–158; *Report of the Preliminary Convention, NTA 85,* p. 17. The concern about strike help was evidenced in the fact that the New York unionists were helping unions in other cities such as Washington and Milwaukee.

18. As indicated in the text the name of this organization was changed in 1885 to International Association of Journeymen Plumbers, Steam Fitters and Gas Fitters. The following paragraphs — dealing with the history of the International Association of Journeymen Plumbers, Steam Fitters, and Gas Fitters, and of the National Trade Assembly 85 (Knights of Labor) — are based largely on the following sources: *Proceedings, Third Annual Convention of the IAPSG; Proceedings, Fourth Annual Convention of the IAPSG,* Milwaukee, September 1887; *Report of the Preliminary Convention, NTA 85.* The first of these sources contains a lengthy excerpt from the second (Cincinnati) convention of the IAPSG.

19. *Proceedings, Third Annual Convention of the IAPSG,* p. 130.

20. Excerpt from the Second Annual Convention of the IAPSG reproduced in *Proceedings, Third Annual Convention of the IAPSG,* pp. 31, 35, 42.

21. The excerpt from the proceedings of the 1885 convention reproduced in the *Proceedings, Third Annual Convention of the IAPSG,* does not cover the decisions to change the name of the organization. But other documents and the discussions during the 1886 IAPSG convention clearly indicate that the new name of the union dates back to the 1885 convention. The earliest available document containing the new name is a letter dated June 16, 1886, written by Patrick Coyle to T. V. Powderly of the Knights. This letter and other relevant evidence are in *Proceedings, Third Annual Convention of the IAPSG,* pp. 8, 9, 49, 50, 57.

22. Because of its origin as a secret society the Knights of Labor was attacked by some Catholic clergy as an organization whose objects were opposed to the views of the Catholic Church. Although other Catholic clergymen — notably Cardinal Gibbons — defended the Knights, the criticisms voiced by many churchmen had some negative influence on the Knights' ability to recruit members among the Catholic workers. For a discussion of this issue, see Ware, *The Labor Movement in the United States,* pp. 73–102.

23. *Proceedings, Third Annual Convention of the IAPSG,* p. 86.

24. *Report of the Preliminary Convention, NTA 85,* p. 8.

25. *The Rasp, The Journeymen Plumbers, Gas Fitters and Steam Fitters Paper,* October 1888, p. 5.

26. The description of the strike is based on material in *Fourth Annual*

Report of the Bureau of Statistics of Labor of the State of New York, pp. 114–116, 476–480; and *Fifth Annual Report of the Bureau of Statistics of Labor of the State of New York for the Year 1887* (Albany, 1888), pp. 198–204.

27. *Fourth Annual Report*, p. 477.

28. *Fifth Annual Report*, pp. 201–204, 547–550; *Proceedings, Fourth Annual Convention of the IAPSG*, pp. 20–21, 199–201.

29. *The Rasp*, November 1888, p. 5.

30. *The Steam Fitter*, May 1907, p. 19.

31. Hamill ms.

32. *Proceedings, Fourth Annual Convention of the IAPSG*, p. 78.

33. *Constitution of the IAPSG*, 1886, p. 18.

34. Commons *et al.*, vol. II, *History of Labor in the United States*, pp. 430–38.

35. *Constitution of the IAPSG*, p. 5.

36. Albert Shaw, "Cooperation in the Northwest" in *History of Cooperation in the United States*, John Hopkins University Studies in Historical and Political Science (Baltimore, 1888), p. 320.

37. *Proceedings, Third Annual Convention of the IAPSG*, pp. 149–153; Shaw, "Cooperation in the Northwest," pp. 153, 320, 324.

38. *Proceedings, Fourth Annual Convention of the IAPSG*, pp. 42, 50–51.

39. *Proceedings, UA* (1891), p. 113.

40. *The Rasp*, October 1888, p. 6.

41. Circular of the UA, December 2, 1889.

42. P. Quinlan to R. A. O'Brien, April 25, 1889.

43. Hamill ms.

44. *Proceedings, UA* (1904), p. 60.

45. See, for instance, *Journal*, November 1895, p. 5.

46. Hamill ms.

47. *Proceedings, Third Annual Convention of the IAPSG*, p. 124.

48. *Proceedings, Fourth Annual Convention of the IAPSG*, pp. 20–21.

49. J. H. Ashworth, *The Helper and American Trade Unions* (Baltimore, 1915), pp. 56–58.

50. *Journal*, May 1894, p. 14; July 1896, p. 6.

51. *Proceedings, Third Annual Convention of the IAPSG*, pp. 142–143; *Journal*, October 1892, pp. 2–3; August 1893, p. 2.

52. *Fourth Annual Report* (New York), pp. 115–116. Paul H. Douglas, *American Apprenticeship and Industrial Education* (New York, 1921), p. 74.

53. *Journal*, September 1894, p. 2; *Proceedings, UA* (1893), p. 25.

54. For reprints of some of this correspondence see *Journal*, August 1962, pp. 3–5.

55. Quinlan to O'Brien. The contact between Quinlan and O'Brien was first suggested by Philip Grace, the editor of *The Rasp* (a plumbers' newspaper) and a member of the Brooklyn local of NTA 85.

56. *Preliminary Convention, Held in Brooklyn, July 29, 1889, The Call*.

57. James O'Hagen ms.; *The Call for the General Convention to be Held in Washington, D.C., In October 1889*.

58. *Minutes of the General Convention (1889)*. The following account is based on these minutes and on a circular sent by P. Quinlan to various local unions.

59. *Proceedings, UA* (1890).

60. Mangan, *History of the Steam Fitters' Protective Association of Chicago*, p. 18.

Chapter 3

1. *Constitution, UA* (1891), p. 5.
2. *Proceedings, UA* (1897), p. 25.
3. Rendig Fels, *American Business Cycles, 1865–1897* (Chapel Hill, 1959), pp. 209–219.
4. *Proceedings, UA* (1897), pp. 25, 27; *Journal*, October 1892, p. 6; March 1894, p. 12; December 1894, p. 8.
5. 1890 figure estimated on the basis of financial return for the third quarter; 1891 figure is the 1892 membership less about 200. See *Journal*, p. 6; 1893 from *Proceedings, UA* (1893), p. 2; 1894 membership is the estimate used by the UA in planning death benefits in 1894 (*Journal*, February 1895, pp. 1–2); figures for 1896 and 1897 from *Proceedings, UA* (1897), p. 23.
6. *Proceedings, UA* (1897), pp. 3–7, 55.
7. *Constitution, UA*, 1891, 1893, 1897.
8. Interestingly enough, the old NTA 85 Constitution did provide for representation of individual crafts on the executive board. This precedent was originally ignored by the founders of the UA.
9. This account is based on the constitutions of the UA for the period, and on convention proceedings.
10. *Proceedings, UA* (1893), p. 16.
11. *Constitution, UA* (1893), p. 10.
12. *Proceedings, UA* (1893), p. 3.
13. For a brief biography of Counahan see *Journal*, May 1894, p. 3.
14. For reports of such ad hoc organizers see *Journal*, April 1895, p. 1; July 1895, p. 2; December 1895, p. 2.
15. See for instance *Constitution, UA* (1891), p. 10; (1897), pp. 11–14.
16. *Proceedings, UA* (1897), p. 27.
17. *Proceedings, UA* (1897), p. 88; *Journal*, November 1895, p. 6.
18. *Journal*, November 1894, p. 4; July 1895, p. 4; October 1895, p. 3; November 1895, p. 7; *Proceedings, UA* (1897), pp. 43, 45, 47, 49, 96, 97.
19. *Journal*, June 1895, p. 4.
20. *Proceedings, UA* (1890), p. 86; *Constitution, UA* (1891), pp. 14–15, 17.
21. *Constitution, UA* (1891), p. 14.
22. *Journal*, April 1893, pp. 3–4.
23. *Constitution, UA* (1897), pp. 17–19.
24. *Journal*, January 1893, p. 5.
25. *Proceedings, UA* (1897), p. 89.
26. *Agreement between the Association of Master Plumbers of the City of New York and the Amalgamated Society of Journeymen Plumbers and Gas Fitters of the City of New York*, February 10, 1896.
27. *Journal*, June 1896, p. 3; *Proceedings, UA* (1897), p. 27.
28. *Journal*, August 1896, p. 2.
29. *Proceedings, UA* (1897), p. 27.
30. *Journal*, December 1895, p. 1.
31. *Proceedings, UA* (1893), p. 6.
32. *Journal*, March 1893, p. 2; January 1893, p. 5.
33. *Proceedings, UA* (1893), p. 19; (1897), p. 84.
34. *Constitution, UA* (1897), p. 38.
35. *Proceedings, UA* (1897), pp. 66–67.

36. For examples of social contacts between employers and journeymen, see *Journal*, March 1893, pp. 3, 4; July 1896, p. 6. It was characteristic of the relations between the employers and the union that the *Plumber's Trade Journal*, a paper edited for the employers collected funds to help out the family of the sick president of the UA, Patrick Quinlan (*Journal*, January 1893, p. 4).

37. *Journal*, October 1892, p. 8; *Proceedings, UA* (1891), p. 128.

38. This was most conspicuously revealed in a survey conducted by the UA, *Proceedings, UA* (1897), pp. 63, 78.

39. *Proceedings, UA* (1890), p. 82; (1891), p. 127; (1897), p. 55.

40. "The Convention in Detail," *The Hydraulic and Sanitary Plumber*, New York, July 5, 1883, p. 232; *Journal*, July 1896, p. 6.

41. *Proceedings, UA* (1893), p. 25; *Journal*, December 1892, p. 5.

42. *Journal*, March 1893, pp. 4–5; July 1895, p. 4.

43. *Proceedings, UA* (1893), p. 24; *Constitution, UA* (1897), pp. 24–25.

44. *Proceedings, UA* (1897), p. 78.

45. *Journal*, May 1893, p. 3; July 1896, p. 5; August 1896, p. 2.

46. *Proceedings, UA* (1897), pp. 74–76, 91–96.

Appendix to Chapter 3

1. Quinlan never recovered and died in January 1893.

2. John A. Lee apparently was very successful as an acting president during Quinlan's illness. However, because of a desire to become a city plumbing inspector, he declined to run for the office of the president in 1892 and became a member of the executive board.

3. Richard A. O'Brien became a city inspector of plumbing.

Chapter 4

1. *Constitution, UA* (1906), p. 6.

2. In 1913 the UA membership was almost 8 times that of 1898; the membership of all American unions in 1913 was about $5\frac{1}{2}$ times that of total American membership in 1898. (See Leo Troy, "Trades Union Membership, 1897–1962" *Review of Economics and Statistics*, February 1965, p. 93.)

3. *Proceedings, UA* (1898), p. 9.

4. Alvin H. Hansen, *Business Cycles and National Income* (New York, 1951), pp. 44–46; Miles L. Colean and Robinson Newcomb, *Stabilizing Construction: The Record and Potential* (New York, 1952), p. 239.

5. *Proceedings, UA* (1898), p. 21; (1893), p. 16; (1900), p. 17; (1901), p. 31; (1904), p. 76.

6. Between 1898 and 1913, money wages of plumbers increased by about 55 per cent and real wages by 29 per cent. Moreover, most of the increase in real wages (about 23 per cent) took place during the years prior to 1907 (Computed from money wage data for selected cities in Bureau of Labor Statistics, *History of Wages in the United States from Colonial Times to 1928*, Bulletin No. 499 (Washington, 1929), pp. 209–210; and from cost of living index in Albert Rees, *Real Wages in Manufacturing, 1890–1914* (Princeton, 1961), p. 117.)

7. *Proceedings, UA* (1898), pp. 54–55; *Constitution, UA* (1898), p. 16; *Journal*, November 1898, p. 21.

8. *Proceedings, UA* (1899), pp. 9, 15.

9. *Proceedings, UA* (1900), p. 30; *Journal*, February 1901, p. 8.

10. *Proceedings, UA* (1899), p. 15.

11. *Proceedings, UA* (1898), p. 50; *Constitution, UA* (1898), p. 14.

12. *Proceedings, UA* (1899), pp. 25, 26, 59–61; *Journal*, March 1900, p. 10.

13. *Proceedings, UA* (1900), pp. 21, 35–36, 59–61; (1901), pp. 24, 31, 50, 55–56, 73–74, 77.

14. *Constitution, UA* (1899), p. 11.

15. *Journal*, October 1901, pp. 3, 5.

16. *Proceedings, UA* (1901), pp. 77–78.

17. *Journal*, February 1902, p. 6; April 1902, p. 5.

18. *Journal*, December 1901, p. 9; June 1902, p. 9; July 1902, p. 6; *Proceedings, UA* (1902), pp. 36–40.

19. *Proceedings, UA* (1902), pp. 36–40, 47–94, 50–53, 99–100, 102–103, 105, 108.

20. *Journal*, December 1902, pp. 4–6.

21. *Journal*, March 1903, pp. 3, 7; *Proceedings, UA* (1904), p. 45; *Journal*, January 1903, p. 7.

22. *Journal*, June 1903, pp. 3, 10–11, 14.

23. *Constitution, UA* (1901), p. 6.

24. *Journal*, June 1903, pp. 5–7.

25. *Proceedings, UA* (1904), pp. 29, 43, 87–88, 94, 105–114.

26. *Journal*, November 1919, p. 3.

27. *Journal*, July 1906, pp. 12–14; *Proceedings, UA* (1906), pp. 106–107; 53, 95.

28. *Journal*, July 1906, p. 14; *Proceedings, UA* (1906), pp. 44–46, 90–93.

29. The constitution of the UA did permit the appointment of organizers under special circumstances, but these were not met in this particular case. *Proceedings, UA* (1906), pp. 89–90. See also *Constitution, UA* (1904), pp. 26–27.

30. *Proceedings, UA* (1906), pp. 86–90.

31. *Journal*, July 1906, pp. 12–14, 16; June 1906, pp. 1, 3, 12; January 1906, pp. 3; February 1906, p. 3; September 1906, pp. 12–13.

32. *Proceedings, UA* (1906), pp. 83, 95, 110–116.

33. Particularly good examples of this talent are provided by Alpine's actions during the conflict with the IA. See especially the description to the UA tactics in Chicago and in New York in Chapter 5.

34. *The New York Times*, April 22, 1947, p. 27 (Alpine's obituary); *Journal*, January 1908, p. 8; *Proceedings, UA* (1904), pp. 89, 124; *Journal*, July 1906, p. 8; December 1908, p. 6.

35. For example, in 1908 a provision was introduced that any applicant for sick benefits had to submit a certificate from a physician. Another example is provided by the introduction of monthly dues stamps in 1910. This change reduced the administrative burden both on the local and the national levels. *Journal*, March 1909, p. 6; *Proceedings, UA* (1910), p. 68.

36. *Proceedings, UA* (1908), pp. 8, 106–108; (1910), pp. 106–107.

37. *Journal*, November 1911, p. 38; May 1912, p. 32.

38. *Proceedings, UA* (1913), pp. 108, 184–185; (1908), pp. 47, 105–106; (1910), pp. 124–128.

39. *Constitution, UA* (1913), pp. 14, 15, 17–18; *Proceedings, UA* (1910), p. 82.

40. *Journal*, April 1906, p. 6; *Proceedings, UA* (1910), p. 73; *Journal*, September 1910, p. 61; *Proceedings, UA* (1913), p. 75.

41. *Journal*, September 1910, p. 38, 70; *Proceedings, UA* (1910), p. 98.

42. *Journal*, September 1910, p. 38; *Proceedings, UA* (1913), p. 75; (1910), pp. 142–43.

43. The estimates of yearly earnings of an average journeyman were made as follows: Hourly wage data for Chicago are in Bureau of Labor Statistics, *History of Wages*, p. 211. These data also indicate that in Chicago the plumbers working in construction had in 1910 an eight-hour day. The number of days per year worked by plumbers in construction is given (for 1920) by Federated American Engineering Societies, *Waste in Industry*, p. 64 and cited in William Haber, *Industrial Relations in the Building Industry* (Cambridge, Mass.: Harvard University Press, 1930), p. 98. The daily wages in Chicago in 1910 were $5.52. Thomas Burke estimated that in that year an average member of the UA made $4.90. Thus, compared with the average earnings of plumbers, the salaries of the officers would be still more attractive.

44. Lloyd Ulman, *The Rise of the National Union* (Cambridge, 1955), p. 222.

45. T. W. Glocker, The Government of American Trade Unions (Baltimore, 1913), p. 184.

46. Characteristic of this businesslike approach have been the deliberations of the convention delegates pertaining to the expansion of the organizing staff. The arguments frequently were in terms of comparing the additional costs of new organizers with the additional revenue that would be brought to the UA from the increased organizing activities. See, for instance, *Proceedings, UA* (1904), p. 75.

47. See, for instance, Clark Kerr, "Unions and Union Leaders of Their Own Choosing," reprinted in G. F. Bloom, H. R. Northrup, R. L. Rowan, *Readings in Labor Economics* (Homewood, 1963), p. 283.

48. *Constitution, UA* (1897), p. 11.

49. *Proceedings, UA* (1900), p. 55; *Constitution, UA* (1900), p. 13.

50. *Constitution, UA* (1906), p. 12.

51. Merrick used Alpine as special organizer when the latter was vice-president. Alpine used several vice-presidents, particularly J. Valilla. And some vice-presidents eventually became full-time and fully paid officers. See, for instance, *Journal*, February 1914, p. 13.

52. *Proceedings, UA* (1898), p. 48; (1902), p. 43–44; (1910), pp. 112–115.

53. *Constitution, UA* (1906), p. 54 and constitution revised in later years.

54. *Journal*, January 1915, p. 14.

55. *Proceedings, UA* (1898), p. 44. Ulman, *The Rise of the National Trade Union*, pp. 116–122.

56. *Proceedings, UA* (1898), pp. 16–17, 43, 56; (1899), pp. 47, 54–55; (1900), p. 46.

57. *Journal*, July 1899, p. 7.

58. *Proceedings, UA* (1899), p. 57.

59. *Proceedings, UA* (1900), p. 21, 54; *Constitution, UA* (1900), pp. 21–23.

60. *Constitution, UA* (1904), p. 30.

61. *Proceedings, UA* (1908), p. 97; (1910), p. 92; (1913), p. 93.

62. *Proceedings, UA* (1910), pp. 82, 92, 112; (1913), pp. 102–104, 106, 128.

63. See, for instance, *Journal*, November 1910, pp. 44–45.

64. *Proceedings, UA* (1899), p. 54.

65. *Constitution, UA* (1891), p. 15.

66. *Proceedings, UA* (1902), p. 32–33; (1900), p. 51; (1901), pp. 30, 61.

67. *Constitution, UA* (1913), pp. 40–44, 50.

68. *Proceedings, UA* (1904), p. 76; (1913), p. 79.

69. Haber, *Industrial Relations in the Building Industry*, pp. 360–61; *Journal*, October 1904, p. 8.

70. *Journal*, October 1904, p. 8; February 1899, p. 9; March 1899, p. 6; April 1899, p. 6; May 1899, p. 12; August 1899, p. 5.

71. *Proceedings, UA* (1901), pp. 39, 45–47, 70–71, 75.

72. *Journal*, December 1899, p. 7; January 1901, p. 10; *Proceedings, AFL* (1901), pp. 90, 250; *Proceedings, UA* (1900), pp. 22, 39, 64; (1901), pp. 45–47, 54.

73. *Journal*, January 1902, pp. 1, 4; March 1902, pp. 3, 6; April 1902, p. 4; *Proceedings, UA* (1902), pp. 31–32.

74. *Proceedings, UA* (1901), pp. 19, 34; *Journal*, January 1902, p. 1; *Proceedings, UA* (1902), pp. 31–32.

75. *Journal*, April 1902, p. 4.

76. *Proceedings, UA* (1902), pp. 31–32, 47–53, 101–03.

77. *Journal*, December 1902, pp. 4–6; July 1903, p. 12; February 1904, p. 7; May 1904, p. 7; April 1904, pp. 5, 8, 10; May 1904, pp. 1, 4.

78. Haber, *Industrial Relations in the Building Industry*, pp. 346–62.

79. *Journal*, June 1904, p. 6.

80. *Journal*, August 1904, pp. 6, 7, 11; *Proceedings, UA* (1904), pp. 29–30, 47–48.

81. *Journal*, October 1904, pp. 3, 8; December 1904, pp. 10, 12; January 1905, p. 7; July 1904, p. 7; January 1905, p. 8; March 1905, p. 11; May 1905, pp. 4, 7–8; July 1905, p. 12; September 1905, p. 13; June 1906, pp. 4–5; July 1906, pp. 13–18; September 1906, p. 6, 7–8; August 1906, pp. 7–8, 10.

82. *Journal*, September 1906, pp. 7–8; *Proceedings, UA* (1906), pp. 26, 30–32.

83. *Journal*, January 1907, p. 10.

84. *Journal*, September 1907, p. 13; December 1907, pp. 9, 10, 14, 17; January 1908, pp. 7–9; *Proceedings, UA* (1908), pp. 44, 110.

85. *Journal*, December 1913, pp. 12–13; February 1914, p. 13.

Chapter 5

1. *Proceedings, UA* (1897), p. 67; *Journal*, February 1903, p. 4; January 1911, p. 16.

2. Nathaniel R. Whitney, *Jurisdiction in American Building Trades Unions*, (Baltimore, 1914), p. 172.

3. *Journal*, March 1904, p. 5; December 1906, p. 8; September 1909, p. 12; *The Steam Fitter*, February 1911, p. 21.

4. *Journal*, May 1901, p. 16; *Proceedings, UA* (1900), p. 44.

5. *Proceedings, UA* (1900), p. 44; *Journal*, November 1904, p. 1.

6. Journal, April 1903, p. 3.

7. Ross F. Tucker, *The Decisions of the General Arbitration Board of the*

New York Building Trades Affecting Jurisdiction of Trades (New York, 1910), pp. 14, 23–25; Whitney, *Jurisdiction in American Building Trades Unions*, p. 140; John Mangan, *History of the Steam Fitters' Protective Association in Chicago* (Chicago, 1930), pp. 26–34; *Proceedings, UA* (1899), pp. 47–48; *Proceedings, UA* (1904), p. 117; *Proceedings, UA* (1901), pp. 72–76; *Journal*, August 1903, p. 7.

8. *Journal*, March 1904, p. 9; August 1903, p. 7; *Proceedings, UA* (1906), p. 102; *Journal*, December 1907, p. 8; *Proceedings, UA* (1904), p. 60; *The Steam Fitter*, April 1911, p. 19.

9. *Proceedings, UA* (1906), pp. 72–75, 109.

10. *Constitution, UA* (1908), p. 32.

11. *Proceedings, UA* (1904), p. 100.

12. *The Steam Fitter*, November 1909, p. 15; April 1910, p. 1; *Proceedings, UA* (1904), p. 63; (1908), p. 73; *Journal*, February 1906, p. 12.

13. *The Steam Fitter*, January 1913, p. 7.

14. *The Steam Fitter*, March 1903, pp. 12–13; *Proceedings, Fourteenth Annual Convention of the Master Steam and Hot Water Association*, Atlantic City, June 12–14, 1902, p. 74.

15. *The Steam Fitter*, October 1908, p. 11; May 1909, p. 4; October 1912, p. 2; February 1903, pp. 2–3.

16. This is tellingly expressed throughout the slim volume of John Mangan's reminiscences. Mangan, *History of the Steam Fitters' Protective Association in Chicago.*

17. *Proceedings, UA* (1898), p. 64.

18. *Proceedings of the Eleventh Annual Convention of the National Association of Steam and Hot Water Fitters and Helpers of America*, Toledo, Nov. 14–17, 1898, pp. 14, 28.

19. *Proceedings, AFL* (1898), pp. 140–141.

20. *Proceedings, AFL* (1898), p. 141.

21. *The Steam Fitter*, March 1903, p. 4.

22. *Proceedings, AFL* (1899), p. 57; Philip Taft, *The A.F. of L. in the Time of Gompers* (New York, 1957), p. 208.

23. Whitney, *Jurisdiction in American Building Trades Unions*, pp. 16–17; *Proceedings, AFL* (1899), p. 57.

24. *Proceedings, AFL* (1900), p. 97.

25. *Journal*, July 1901, p. 4.

26. *Journal*, March 1901, p. 6; *Proceedings, UA* (1901), p. 71; *Journal*, March 1902, pp. 9, 16.

27. *Proceedings, UA* (1899), pp. 12, 59; (1900), p. 44.

28. *Proceedings, AFL* (1901), p. 161.

29. *Journal*, February 1902, p. 4; May 1902, pp. 3–5.

30. As indicated before, the matter will be considered in the following chapter.

31. *Proceedings, UA* (1902), p. 79.

32. *Journal*, October 1902, pp. 6–8.

33. *Proceedings, AFL* (1902), pp. 55, 97, 98, 131, 133, 198, 199, 209.

34. *Journal*, January 1903, p. 1.

35. *Journal*, February 1903, pp. 4–5; March 1903, p. 9; Mangan, *History of the Steam Fitters' Protective Association in Chicago*, pp. 139–141.

36. Mangan, *History of the Steam Fitters' Protective Association in Chicago*, pp. 141–43; *The Steam Fitter*, March 1903, p. 17.

37. *Journal*, May 1903, p. 8.

38. *Journal*, July 1903, p. 3; *Proceedings, AFL* (1903), pp. 84, 121, 250.

39. *Journal*, January 1904, p. 6.

40. *The Steam Fitter*, July 1907, p. 19; November 1906, p. 4.

41. *Journal*, March 1904, p. 5; *The Steam Fitter*, April 1904, p. 3.

42. Taft, *The A.F. of L. in the Time of Gompers*, p. 208; *Proceedings, AFL* (1904), pp. 67, 134.

43. *Proceedings, UA* (1901), p. 42; Taft, p. 208.

44. Mangan, *History of the Steam Fitters' Protective Association in Chicago*, pp. 26–34; *Proceedings, UA* (1904), p. 119; *Proceedings*, UA (1906), p. 72; Whitney, *Jurisdiction in American Building Trades*, p. 140.

45. *Proceedings, AFL* (1905), pp. 119, 195–196.

46. *Proceedings, AFL*, pp. 203–204; *Journal*, June 1906, p. 10.

47. *Journal*, June 1906, p. 10.

48. *Proceedings, UA* (1906), p. 29; Taft, pp. 208–209.

49. *Proceedings, AFL* (1906), p. 218; (1907), pp. 145–46, 248–249, 269.

50. *The Steam Fitter*, March 1908, pp. 5–8.

51. *Proceedings, AFL* (1908), pp. 77, 243.

52. *Proceedings, Building Trades Department* (1908), pp. 105–107.

53. *Journal*, March 1909, pp. 27–50; November 1909, p. 4.

54. *Journal*, March 1909, p. 5; *Proceedings, UA* (1910), p. 93.

55. *Journal*, March 1909, pp. 27–28; *The Steam Fitter*, March 1909, p. 6.

56. *Journal*, August 1909, p. 7.

57. *Proceedings, Building Trades Department* (1909), *pp.* 30–33, 91–97.

58. *The Steam Fitter*, January 1910, pp. 6–8.

59. *Journal*, November 1909, p. 3; January 1910, pp. 5–6; September 1910, p. 55.

60. *The Steam Fitter*, January 1911, pp. 7–9; *Journal*, January 1911, pp. 9–10.

61. *The Steam Fitter*, January 1907, p. 20.

62. *Proceedings, Building Trades Department* (1908), p. 105.

63. *The Steam Fitter*, January 1913, p. 12.

64. Taft, *The A.F. of L. in the Time of Gompers*, p. 208.

65. *Journal*, September 1910, p. 58; August 1913, p. 58.

66. *Journal*, March 1912, p. 12; April 1912, p. 16; June 1912, p. 12; November 1912, p. 12; March 1913, p. 24; *Proceedings, UA* (1913), p. 84.

67. *Journal*, February 1911, p. 20; November 1912, p. 12; July 1913, p. 21.

68. *Proceedings, Building Trades Department* (1911), pp. 58–63, p. 62; *Journal*, July 1911, pp. 18, 35–37.

69. *Proceedings, AFL* (1911), p. 112, 335–41.

70. *Journal*, February 1912, pp. 9–10; *Proceedings, AFL* (1912), p. 111.

71. *Proceedings, AFL* (1912), pp. 112–113; *The Steam Fitter*, March 1912, pp. 5–7; June 1912, pp. 3–7.

72. *Proceedings, AFL* (1912), p. 96; pp. 180–82; pp. 189–90; pp. 339–41; *The Steam Fitter*, January 1913, pp. 4–29.

73. Mangan, *History of the Steam Fitters' Association in Chicago*, p. 44.

74. *Journal*, June 1913, p. 17; May 1911, p. 10; July 1911, p. 18; August 1911, p. 27; January 1913, p. 12; June 1913, p. 10.

75. R. E. Montgomery, *Industrial Relations in the Chicago Building Trades* (Chicago, 1927), p. 69.

76. Mangan, *History of the Steam Fitters' Association in Chicago*, p. 92;

Journal, March 1913, p. 17; *Proceedings, UA* (1913), p. 155; Montgomery, *op. cit.*, p. 21, pp. 29–30, 34–35, 217–18.

77. *Proceedings, UA* (1913), p. 154; Montgomery, *Industrial Relations in the Chicago Building Trades*, p. 54.

78. *Proceedings, Building Trades Department* (1911), p. 37; *Proceedings, UA* (1913), pp. 153–54, 159; *The Steam Fitter*, March 1911, p. 19.

79. *Journal*, April 1911, pp. 9, 11; *The Steam Fitter*, May 1911, p. 3; *Journal*, June 1911, p. 10.

80. *The Steam Fitter*, May 1911, pp. 2–4; August 1911, pp. 4–6; *The Chicago Daily Tribune*, March 9, 1911, p. 8; March 24, pp. 1–2; April 8, p. 1; May 10, p. 1; May 23, pp. 1–2; May 24, p. 1; June 5, pp. 1–2.

81. *Journal*, August 1911, p. 9; July 1911, p. 12; December 1911, p. 36; *Proceedings, Building Trades Department* (1911), p. 38; *The Chicago Daily Tribune*, May 30, 1911, p. 1; June 24, p. 4; July 20, p. 1.

82. *Journal*, October 1911, pp. 9–11, 13; *The Steam Fitter*, November 1911, p. 12; *Proceedings, Building Trades Department* (1911), p. 37; *The Chicago Daily Tribune*, July 15, 1911, p. 3.

83. *Journal*, October 1911, p. 9; August 1912, p. 14.

84. Mangan, *History of the Steam Fitters' Association in Chicago*, pp. 45, 93, 103–105; *Journal*, March 1913, pp. 14–15, 17; *Proceedings, UA* (1913), p. 155.

85. *Proceedings, UA* (1913), pp. 153–54; *Journal*, February 1914, p. 13.

86. *Journal*, May 1912, p. 11; June 1912, pp. 12, 14, 22; July 1912, p. 13; August 1912, p. 23; July, 1913, p. 21; *Proceedings, Building Trades Department* (1911), pp. 38–41; *Journal*, April 1912, p. 13; June 1912, p. 17; July 1912, p. 15; November 1912, p. 12; February 1913, p. 14; *The Steam Fitter*, October 1912, p. 2; *Proceedings, Building Trades Department* (1912), pp. 32–39.

87. *Proceedings, UA* (1913), pp. 80, 84.

88. *Proceedings, UA*, p. 84; *Journal*, April 1914, p. 11; Whitney, *Jurisdiction in American Building Trades*, p. 154. See also Tucker, *The Decisions of the General Arbitration Board*, pp. 14, 23–25.

89. *Proceedings, UA* (1913), p. 84; *Journal*, June 1913, p. 14.

90. *Journal*, June 1913, pp. 14, 37; July 1913, p. 12; August 1913, p. 13; December 1913, p. 11; May 1914, p. 10; April 1914, pp. 11–12; May 1914, pp. 9–14.

91. *Journal*, October 1914, p. 13. The word "virtually" is used advisedly. As a later chapter will indicate, the United Association eventually failed to organize the railroad fitters.

92. *Constitution, UA* (1902), p. 13; *Constitution, UA* (1904), p. 22; (1908), p. 16; (1913), p. 16.

93. *Proceedings, UA* (1913), p. 134; *Constitution, UA* (1913), p. 29.

94. *Proceedings, UA* (1913), pp. 163–65; *Constitution, UA* (1913), p. 34.

95. *Proceedings, UA* (1913), p. 164.

Chapter 6

1. John V. Morris, *Fires and Firefighters* (Boston, 1955), pp. 270–71; *Journal*, July 1902, pp. 12–13.

2. Morris, *Fires and Firefighters*, pp. 268–271; Pennsylvania State Uni-

versity, *Introduction to Automatic Sprinklers,* A correspondence course Study Guide, pp. 5–7.

3. *Proceedings, UA* (1906), pp. 30–31.

4. *Proceedings, UA* (1901), p. 37; *Journal,* July 1902, p. 13.

5. *Proceedings, UA* (1899), p. 72; *Proceedings, AFL* (1898), p. vi; *List of Organizations Affiliated with American Federation of Labor,* June 11, 1900, Washington.

6. *Proceedings, AFL* (1898), pp. 76, 136, 146.

7. *Proceedings, UA* (1899), p. 73.

8. *Proceedings, AFL* (1899), p. 131.

9. *Proceedings, UA* (1901), p. 36; *Proceedings, AFL* (1901), p. 103.

10. *Proceedings, UA* (1901), pp. 35–37, 82–83.

11. *Journal,* August 1901, p. 1; *Proceedings, UA* (1901), pp. 36–37; 82–84.

12. *Proceedings, AFL* (1901), pp. 103, 247; (1902), pp. 97, 147, 198; *Constitution, UA* (1904), p. 6.

13. *Proceedings, UA* (1902), p. 46; (1906), pp. 30–31, 84; (1910), pp. 128–29; (1913), pp. 76, 112–113.

14. *Journal,* December 1913, p. 11; December 1914, p. 13; January 1915, p. 12; May 1915, p. 12; August 1913, p. 60.

15. *Proceedings, UA* (1900), p. 15; (1901), p. 25; (1906), p. 80.

16. *Journal,* July 1904, pp. 13–14.

17. *Journal,* April 1899, p. 4; *Proceedings, UA* (1899), p. 31; (1900) pp. 15, 47.

18. *Proceedings, UA* (1898), pp. 46–47; *Proceedings, UA* (1899), p. 62; *Constitution, UA* (1899), p. 27.

19. *Proceedings, UA* (1904), p. 120; *Constitution, UA* (1904), p. 37; *Proceedings, UA* (1910), p. 92; *Constitution, UA* (1910), pp. 31–32.

20. *Proceedings, UA* (1901), pp. 57, 61.

21. *Proceedings, UA* (1908), p. 56; *Journal,* August 1913, pp. 60, 65–66.

22. *Proceedings, UA* (1913), p. 135; *Constitution, UA* (1913), pp. 35–36.

23. *Reports of the Industrial Commission* (Washington, 1901), vol. XVII, p. 389; vol. VII, p. 965; *Journal,* September 1899, p. 7; April 1899, p. 13; May 1899, pp. 13–14; June 1899, p. 13; August 1899, pp. 11, 17; June 1900, p. 8.

24. *Proceedings, UA* (1901), p. 51.

25. *Industrial Commission,* vol. VII, p. 968; vol. VIII, p. 442; *Proceedings, UA* (1901), p. 65; *Journal,* October 1901, p. 4.

26. *Industrial Commission,* vol. VII, p. 965, 968; Royal E. Montgomery, *Industrial Relations in the Chicago Building Trades* (Chicago, 1927), p. 191; *Journal,* October 1901, pp. 7, 10; December 1901, p. 12.

27. *Proceedings, UA* (1901), p. 66.

28. *Industrial Commission,* vol. VII, pp. 969–70; *Proceedings, UA* (1899), pp. 12, 31, 33–45; *Journal,* April 1899, p. 13.

29. *Proceedings, UA* (1899), p. 12.

30. *Proceedings, UA* (1899), p. 48; *Constitution, UA* (1899), p. 30.

31. *Proceedings, UA* (1900), pp. 16, 38–39, 47–50; Montgomery, *Industrial Relations In The Chicago Building Trades,* p. 22.

32. *Proceedings,* UA (1900), pp. 16, 50–51; (1901), pp. 51, 65–66.

33. *Journal,* March 1901, p. 4; April 1901, p. 3–4.

34. *Proceedings, UA* (1913), pp. 173–174.

35. *Journal,* August 1913, p. 66; *Proceedings, UA* (1913), p. 173.

Chapter 7

1. The following outline of the changing economic environment in 1914–1924 is based on the following sources: V. W. Lanfear, *Business Fluctuations and the American Labor Movement* (New York, 1924); T. Wilson, *Fluctuations in Income and Employment* (New York, 1948); R. A. Gordon, *Cyclical Experience in the Interwar Period: The Investment Boom of the Twenties* (Berkeley, 1952); D. Hamberg, *Business Cycles* (New York, 1951).

2. As compared with the preceding year, the volume of new construction rose by 10 per cent in 1921, by 39 per cent in 1922, by 11 per cent in 1923, and by 21 per cent in 1924. See U.S. Department of Commerce, *Historical Statistics of the United States* (Washington, 1960), p. 381.

3. One of these sources is Leon Wolman's study of union growth. Wolman's figures of UA membership for the years 1915–1923 are based on correspondence with UA headquarters. Although these figures are much larger than the figures from official UA sources, they do show the same direction in the year-to-year changes. For 1920, Wolman's figures are 15,000 larger than for 1919 (75,000 as against 60,000 in 1919). A second source is the UA officers' report to the 1921 national convention. While reporting the 1921 membership figure, the UA officers stressed the record number of withdrawals — 14,000 — of which 6,000 took place recently under the impact of the 1920–1921 depression. When combined with a very large number of expulsions and suspensions, these figures suggest that prior to the depression UA membership must have been about 60,000. See Leon Wolman, *Growth of American Trade Unions, 1880–1923*, p. 110; *Proceedings, UA* (1921), p. 69. The membership figures apparently furnished by the UA to the AFL offices are completely worthless since for every year between 1915 and 1921 the membership is given as 32,000.

4. Leo Troy, "Trade Union Membership, 1897–1962," *Review of Economics and Statistics*, February 1965, p. 93.

5. *Proceedings, UA* (1924), p. 69.

6. Troy, "Trade Union Membership, 1897–1962," p. 93.

7. Lanfear, *Business Fluctuations in Income and Employment*, pp. 86–127; Selig Perlman and Philip Taft, *History of Labor in the United States, 1896–1932* (New York, 1932), pp. 489–524.

8. *Journal*, May 1915, p. 12; July 1915, pp. 12–13; February 1916, p. 11; October 1916, p. 9.

9. *Journal*, June 1917, p. 9; Waldo G. Leland and Newton D. Mereness, *Introduction to the American Official Sources for the Economic and Social History of the World War* (New Haven, 1926), p. 321.

10. Perlman and Taft, *History of Labor in the United States, 1896–1932*, pp. 403–404; Alexander M. Bing, *War-Time Strikes and Their Adjustment* (New York, 1921), pp. 14–19, 297–98; Louis B. Wehle, "Labor Problems in the United States During the War," *Quarterly Journal of Economics*, February 1918, p. 367.

11. Bing, *War-Time Strikes and Their Adjustment*, pp. 126–32, 311–13; *Journal*, June 1918, p. 22.

12. *Journal*, March 1917, p. 13; July 1917, p. 8; November 1917, p. 7; October 1918, p. 11.

13. *Proceedings, UA* (1917), pp. 79, 99, 111–128; 129–135; 165–175.

14. *Journal*, May 1919, p. 26; July 1919, p. 28; August 1919, pp. 28–29;

September 1919, pp. 26–29; October 1919, pp. 30–34; December 1919, p. 25; April 1920, p. 4.

15. *Proceedings, AFL* (1919), pp. 423–24; Journal, November 1919, pp. 2, 37; *New York Times*, April 22, 1947, p. 27.

16. *Journal*, November 1919, pp. 19, 38.

17. *Journal*, March 1940, pp. 2–3; *New York Times*, February 9, 1940, p. 19; *Journal*, January 1912, p. 36; *Proceedings, UA* (1913), p. 185.

18. *Proceedings, UA* (1917), pp. 131, 169; (1921), pp. 189–191.

19. *Journal*, August 1917, p. 11.

20. *Journal*, January 1921, p. 18; *Proceedings, UA* (1921), pp. 70–71. For monthly statistics of price changes in 1915–1920 see Paul H. Douglas, *Real Wages in the United States* (Cambridge, 1930), p. 57.

21. The available data on wages of the pipefitting workers (and all building trades workers) refer only to union negotiated minimum rates. Since they do not indicate bonuses, overtime, and wages paid above the union minimum — all undoubtedly present in a tight labor market of the period — the statistics understate the actual rise of pipefitting and other building trades wages. But the lag of wage changes behind the cost-of-living increases is so great that there is no question that the real wages of the construction workers fell during the 1915–1919 period. Douglas' calculations, based on union minimum rates, indicate that, between 1915 and 1919, hourly rates of all building trades rose by 38 per cent while the cost of living rose twice as much — by 76.5 per cent. The data on union minimum rates indicate that in the same period the rates of the plumbers rose by 39.6 per cent and those of the steam fitters by about 30 per cent. See Douglas, *Real Wages in the United States*, pp. 57, 135; U.S. Department of Labor, Bureau of Labor Statistics, *Union Wages and Hours: Building Trades*, Bulletin No. 1487, Washington, June 1966. Other sources also indicate that building rates lagged behind the cost-of-living increases. See Lanfear, *Business Fluctuations and the American Labor Movement*, p. 34; Bing, *War-Time Strikes and Their Adjustment*, p. 219.

22. Between May 1919 and May 1920, the cost of living rose by 21 per cent but the minimum union rates rose by 32 per cent for the steam fitters and by 23 per cent for the plumbers. Again these data unquestionably understate the rise of the actual hourly earnings (as distinct from minimum rates).

23. *Proceedings, UA* (1921), p. 69.

24. Wilson, *Fluctuations in Income and Employment*, p. 106; *Proceedings, UA* (1921), pp. 69–71; W. Haber, *Industrial Relations in the Building Industry* (Cambridge, 1930), p. 387–399; 409–19; *Journal*, April 1920, p. 9; February 1921, p. 2; March 1921, pp. 4, 5, 14; June 1921, p. 11; *Proceedings, UA* (1924), p. 63.

25. *Proceedings, UA* (1921), pp. 68, 70–71, 91–92, 106, 130–136, 153, 155–156, 159–160.

26. *Journal*, September 1922, p. 29; *Proceedings, UA* (1924), pp. 67–69.

27. S. Lebergott, *Manpower in Economic Growth* (New York, 1964), p. 514; Douglas, *Real Wages in the United States*, p. 57. The fitters' rates rose 17 per cent and those of the plumbers 12 per cent. Since this was a period of prosperity and high demand for labor, these figures — for minimum rates — understate the increase of the actual hourly earnings, B.L.S., *Union Wages and Hours, Proceedings, UA* (1924), p. 69.

28. *Journal*, February 1916, p. 33; May 1916, pp. 32–33; August 1917, p. 10; *Proceedings, UA* (1921), p. 69; (1924), p. 68; (1917), pp. 148–49.

29. *Journal*, August 1917, p. 12; *Proceedings, UA* (1917), p. 81.

30. *Constitution, UA* (1921), pp. 21–22. Early in 1920 the Executive Board submitted the issue of holding a convention that year to a referendum. Again it was indicated that a special assessment was necessary. Although the proposal for the 1920 convention was defeated, the vote was very close and there were some questions about voting procedures in some locals. Hence the provision that made possible calling special conventions had a particular meaning; *Journal* 1920, p. 25; May 1920, p. 24; June 1920, p. 23.

31. *Proceedings, UA* (1924), pp. 100–101, 140–143; (1921), p. 173.

32. *Journal*, August 1917, p. 23; October 1918, p. 11.

33. *Constitution, UA* (1921), pp. 8, 16, 40; *Proceedings, UA* (1924), p. 119; *Constitution, UA* (1924), p. 54.

34. *Proceedings, UA* (1921), p. 167.

35. *Constitution, UA* (1921), p. 51.

36. *Journal*, November 1919, p. 40; *Proceedings, UA* (1921), pp. 75–76, 86.

37. *Constitution, UA* (1921), p. 40.

38. *Proceedings, UA* (1924), pp. 72–73, 105–107; 133–38; (1928), pp. 86–93.

Chapter 8

1. *Journal*, June 1918, p. 9; *Proceedings, UA* (1917), pp. 152–53; (1921), p. 90; John Mangan, *History of the Steam Fitters' Protective Association of Chicago* (Chicago, 1930), pp. 102–103.

2. Mangan, *History of the Steam Fitters' Protective Association of Chicago*, pp. 94, 98; *Journal*, February 1918, p. 14; *Proceedings, UA* (1921), p. 143; Haber, *Industrial Relations in the Building Industry*, p. 165; *Proceedings, UA* (1928), p. 71.

3. Mangan, *History of the Steam Fitters' Protective Association*, pp. 82, 98; *Proceedings, UA* (1917), p. 152; (1928), p. 154.

4. For example, the Chicago agreement — a prototype for other agreements — stated that among the steam fitter's duties was "all pipe work in power plants that is now recognized as steam fitter's work," Mangan, *History of the Steam Fitters' Protective Association,* p. 105.

5. *Journal*, August 1917, p. 15; September 1918, p. 7; *Proceedings, UA* (1917), p. 154.

6. In his evaluation of the 1917 convention Alpine observed: "It is a fact that not one jurisdiction question between the Plumber and the Steam Fitter arose on the floor of this convention and men were fraternizing with all the zest of good fellowship who but a short time ago were engaged in the struggle that disturbed the entire labor movement of North America and threatened the very existence of the Building Trades Movement." *Journal*, September 1917, p. 6.

7. *Journal*, August 1917, p. 12; *Proceedings, UA* (1917), p. 82; (1924), p. 72; (1921), p. 144.

8. Mangan, *History of the Steam Fitters' Association,* pp. 90–91, 92–99; *Proceedings, UA* (1924), p. 162; (1928), pp. 151, 153.

9. R. M. Montgomery, *Industrial Relations in the Chicago Building Trades* (Chicago, 1927), p. 130; Mangan, *History of the Steam Fitters' Association,* p. 98.

10. *Proceedings, UA* (1921), p. 142; Mangan, *History of the Steam Fitters' Association*, p. 100.

11. *Proceedings, UA* (1921), pp. 146–147, 175–178.

12. The UA officers claimed that "millions of dollars' worth of work" was getting away from UA jurisdiction "because of wasted energy and time fighting among ourselves." *Proceedings, UA* (1921), p. 67.

13. *Journal*, December 1920, p. 20; February 1921, p. 4.

14. *Proceedings, UA* (1921), pp. 67; 89–90, 141–142; 144–146; 179–181.

15. *Constitution, UA* (1921), p. 43.

16. *Proceedings, UA* (1924), p. 72; *Journal*, September 1922, p. 29, 32, 34; July 1923, p. 17. *The New York Times* (1922), April 22, p. 1; May 12, p. 3; Haber, *Industrial Relations in the Building Industry*, p. 165.

17. *Proceedings, UA* (1928), p. 152; (1924), pp. 154–165.

18. For a detailed analysis of the Landis award and its aftermath see Montgomery, *Industrial Relations in the Chicago Business Trades*, pp. 233–309. The gas fitters had a special objection to the Landis ruling that penalized the unions that prohibited the employers to work with tools. Montgomery, *Industrial Relations in the Chicago Building Trades*, pp. 253–254, 267; *Proceedings, UA* (1924), pp. 154–155, 159, 161. For the UA view of the Landis award see *Journal*, May 1922, p. 2.

19. *Proceedings, UA* (1924), pp. 155, 159–160, 163.

20. *Proceedings, UA* (1924), p. 157; *Journal*, October 1923, pp. 26, 27.

21. *Proceedings, UA* (1924), p. 159.

22. *Journal*, October 1923, p. 28.

23. *Proceedings, UA* (1924), pp. 72–73, 146–47.

24. *Proceedings, UA*, p. 151; *Constitution, UA* (1924), pp. 43, 154, 159, 160, 165.

25. The account of the settling of the Chicago conflict is based on the following: *Proceedings, UA* (1928), pp. 150–155; *Journal*, July 1929, pp. 5–8; Mangan, *History of the Steam Fitters' Protective Association*, pp. 75–117.

26. Mangan, *History of the Steam Fitters' Protective Association*, pp. 55–56; 201–202; *Proceedings, UA* (1934), pp. 143–44 (1924), p. 73. John T. Dunlop, "Jurisdictional Disputes," *Proceedings of New York University Second Annual Conference on Labor*. See also Montgomery, *Industrial Relations in the Chicago Building Trades*, pp. 119–144; Haber, *Industrial Relations in the Building Industry*, pp. 152–196.

27. *Journal*, May 1915, pp. 10–11, 15; August 1917, p. 9.

28. *Proceedings, UA* (1917), p. 164; *Journal*, December 1915, p. 12; August 1916, p. 49; October 1916, p. 8; August 1917, p. 9.

29. Journal, June 1916, p. 9; March 1917, p. 10; June 1916, p. 9; November 1919, p. 32; January 1920, p. 7; *Proceedings, UA* (1924), p. 79; *Journal*, December 1921, p. 20.

30. *Journal*, August 1919, p. 8; February 1920, p. 4; *Proceedings, UA* (1917), p. 164.

31. The UA officers never specified the number of road men covered by the agreement but indicated that they were a majority of the Local 669 membership. On the basis of balloting in a 1920 referendum, it appears that there were about 400 fitters in the auxiliaries (there were also about 400 in the six locals with separate charters). Leonard indicated that Local 669 would be the largest local union in the UA. A reasonable guess is that Local 669 had about 1,000 road fitters as members.

32. *Proceedings, UA* (1928), p. 167; (1921), pp. 140–141; (1938), p. 134.

33. *Proceedings, UA* (1917), pp. 70–72, 137, 142, 146, 155, 165; *Journal,* August 1917, p. 9; July 1919, p. 9.

34. *Journal,* October 1919, p. 6; November 1919, p. 7; August 1919, p. 8; January 1920, p. 7; February 1920, p. 4.

35. *Proceedings, UA* (1921), pp. 140, 183.

36. *Journal,* February 1922, p. 9; May 1922, p. 8; June 1922, p. 8; *Proceedings, UA* (1924), p. 79.

37. *Proceedings, UA* (1924), p. 79; *Journal,* March 1923, p. 10; April 1923, p. 10.

38. *Proceedings, UA* (1924), p. 149.

39. In 1917, Alpine specifically indicated that standardization of the sprinkler fitters' wages was one of the aims of the agreement. But he realized that this aim had to be accomplished in steps rather than in one move. *Journal,* August 1917, p. 9.

40. R. M. Montgomery, *Industrial Relations in the Chicago Building Trades,* (Chicago, 1927), p. 176.

41. *Constitution, UA* (1924).

42. *Proceedings, UA* (1921), p. 125.

43. *Proceedings, UA* (1917), p. 139; *Proceedings, UA* (1921), p. 125; Bureau of Labor Statistics, *Apprenticeship in Building Construction,* Bulletin No. 459, Washington 1928, pp. 18–19, 25, 31, 70, 75; *Proceedings, UA* (1928), p. 120; Montgomery, *Industrial Relations in the Chicago Building Trades,* p. 165.

44. The description of the Cleveland apprenticeship system is based on B.L.S. No. 459, pp. 45–54 and on the text of a booklet *Joint Apprenticeship Agreement between Associated Plumbing Contractors of Cleveland and Journeymen Plumbers Union, Local 55,* Adopted July 6th 1922 (Cleveland, n.d.).

45. All the best programs derived some benefit from this Federal law. The Smith-Hughes Act provided federal grants to be matched by the states. The funds were to be spent on salaries of teachers of vocational and trade subjects and on preparing teachers. For an analysis of the law, see Paul H. Douglas, *American Apprenticeship and Industrial Education* (New York, 1921), pp. 293–306.

46. This view has also been reflected in the UA constitutional provision of the nationalization period. Between 1904 and 1910 the constitution stated: "It is the opinion of the United Association that Local Unions throughout our jurisdiction should use their best endeavors to abolish all Helpers and Apprentices so far as possible." *Constitution, UA* (1908), p. 33.

47. *Proceedings, UA* (1924), pp. 74, 145; (1928), pp. 120, 72–73.

48. *Proceedings, UA* (1924), p. 74; B.L.S. No. 459, pp. 12–13; Haber, *Industrial Relations in the Building Industry* (Cambridge, 1930).

49. B.L.S. No. 459, pp. 37, 51; M. Conyngton, "Apprenticeship in the Building Trades in Washington, D.C.," *Monthly Labor Review,* January 1925, p. 4.

50. Sumner H. Slichter, *Union Policies and Industrial Management* (Washington, 1941), pp. 32–33.

51. *Proceedings, UA* (1945), p. 69.

52. John Mangan, *History of the Steam Fitters' Protective Association of Chicago,* p. 45; *Journal,* May 1915, p. 11.

53. *Proceedings, UA* (1917), p. 141; Mangan, *History of Steam Fitters' Protective Association,* p. 46, 141.

54. *Proceedings, UA* (1945), p. 69; Mangan, *History of the Steam Fitters' Protective Association*, p. 46. The Chicago fitters had some experience with formal training of journeymen since even prior to the institution of the apprenticeship system Local 597 sponsored night school work for its members. *Proceedings, UA* (1917), p. 162.

55. *Apprentice Rules of the Chicago Master Steam Fitters' Association and the Steam Fitters' Protective Association*, compiled by the Joint Board of Arbitration, October, 1919, pp. 1–4; B.L.S. No. 459, pp. 35–36.

56. Apprentice Rules, pp. 2–3; Montgomery, *Industrial Relations in the Chicago Building Trades*, p. 36.

57. B.L.S. No. 459, *op. cit.*, p. 36. Under a supplementary agreement signed in later years the union agreed to furnish "the required number of apprentices in the steam-fitting trade, with a view of taking care of the shortage that might be created through the growth of the trade, disability, or incapacitation through old age and death," Montgomery, *Industrial Relations in the Chicago Building Trades*, p. 175.

58. B.L.S. No. 459, pp. 60–61.

59. *Declaration of Principles*, adopted at the Thirty-First Annual Convention of the Heating and Piping Contractors National Association, held at Cleveland, Ohio, May 24, 27, 1920; *Proceedings, UA* (1924), p. 129.

60. *Proceedings, UA* (1917), pp. 140–141; (1924), p. 150.

61. *Journal*, October 1923, p. 32.

62. *Proceedings, UA* (1924), p. 74.

63. *Journal*, July 1923, p. 3; October 1923, p. 32; *Proceedings, UA* (1924), pp. 75, 145; *Constitution, UA* (1924), pp. 45–46.

64. *Proceedings, UA* (1924), p. 74.

65. For example, in 1904–1909, the New York plumbers and steam fitters were involved in eight disputes that resulted in arbitration awards. Six of these concerned issues that arose between the two pipe crafts. Ross F. Tucker, *The Decisions of the General Arbitration Board of the New York Building Trades Affecting Jurisdiction of Trade* (New York, 1910). For similar evidence, see Nathaniel R. Whitney, *Jurisdiction in American Building Trades* (Baltimore, 1914) and Montgomery, *Industrial Relations in the Chicago Building Trades*, pp. 128–131.

66. In 1893, the Denver plumbers were involved in a jurisdictional conflict with the local union of drain-layers (laborers). *Journal*, September 1893, p. 3.

67. *Proceedings, UA* (1900), p. 45; (1901), p. 71; *Journal*, December 1901, p. 11; March 1902, p. 4; August 1902, p. 13; *American Federationist*, November 1902, p. 845; *Proceedings, UA* (1904), pp. 81, 89–90; *Journal*, August 1908, p. 14; *Proceedings, UA* (1910), pp. 101, 137; (1913), pp. 167–68.

68. *Proceedings, UA* (1912), p. 339.

69. W. Haber, *Industrial Relations in the Building Industry* (Cambridge, 1930), pp. 180–81.

70. *Proceedings, UA* (1913), pp. 77, 114–15; *Proceedings, Railway Employees Department* (1914), pp. 144–46, 154; *Proceedings, Twentieth General Convention of the Amalgamated Sheet Metal Workers International Alliance*, August 1 to 5, 1921, St. Paul, Minnesota, pp. 130–132.

71. *Proceedings, AFL* (1914), p. 452; *Journal*, December 1914, p. 36; *Proceedings, Railway Employees Department* (1914), p. 143.

72. *Minutes of (Preliminary) Meeting of the Railroad Employees Department of the A.F. of L.*, held at Chicago, January 4, 1912; *Minutes of First*

Meeting of the Railway Employees Department, Rochester, New York, November 9, 1912, p. 1; Selig Perlman and Philip Taft, *History of Labor in the United States, 1896–1932* (New York, 1935), pp. 369–373.

73. *Proceedings, Railway Employees Department* (1914), pp. 143–154.

74. *Journal*, December 1914, p. 36; *Proceedings, Railway Employees Department* (1916), pp. 71–73.

75. *Proceedings, Railway Employees Department* (1918), pp. 216–217.

76. *Constitution of the Amalgamated Sheet Metal Workers' International Alliance.* Revised and Amended at Convention Held in Boston, Massachusetts, August 5 to 9, 1918, p. 7.

77. *Journal*, December 1914, p. 36.

78. *Journal*, December 1914, p. 36; November 1915, p. 15; June 1916, p. 16; August 1917, pp. 10, 35; *Proceedings, UA* (1917), pp. 137–38; *Journal*, February 1918, p. 15; *Proceedings, Railway Employees Department* (1918), p. 216.

79. *Proceedings, Twentieth General Convention of the ASMWIA*, pp. 33–34.

80. *Proceedings, Twentieth General Convention of the ASMWIA*, pp. 34–36; *Journal*, May 1920, pp. 22–24; *Proceedings, Railway Employees Department* (1920), pp. 124–25.

81. *Proceedings, Twentieth General Convention of the ASMWIA*, pp. 53–54; *Proceedings, Railway Employees Department* (1920), pp. 293–94, 170, 184–85, 215, 222, 224; *Journal*, May 1920, pp. 21–22.

82. *Proceedings, AFL* (1920), p. 459; *Journal*, August 1920, p. 18; *Proceedings, Twentieth General Convention of the ASMWIA*, p. 54.

83. *Proceedings, Twentieth General Convention of the ASMWIA*, pp. 54–56; *Journal*, October 1920, p. 5; *Proceedings, AFL* (1921), p. 135.

84. *Proceedings, Twentieth General Convention of the ASMWIA*, pp. 38, 55–58; *Journal*, October 1920, p. 5; December 1920, p. 12; *Proceedings, UA* (1921), p. 174.

85. *Journal*, January 1921, p. 4; April 1921, p. 4; July 1921, p. 38; *Proceedings, AFL* (1921), pp. 135, 468–69.

86. *Proceedings, Twentieth General Convention of the ASMWIA*, pp. 127, 132, 139; *Journal*, December 1921, p. 8; January 1922, p. 9.

87. *Journal*, March 1922, pp. 32–37.

88. *Proceedings, Railway Employees Department* (1922), pp. 163–64, 530; *Journal*, June 1922, pp. 8, 19.

89. *Journal*, January 1923, p. 10; February 1923, p. 11.

90. Perlman and Taft, *History of Labor in the United States*, pp. 519–23; *Proceedings*, (1921), p. 70.

91. *Proceedings, UA* (1928), p. 106; (1938), p. 183.

92. *Proceedings, UA* (1921), pp. 66, 183–84. The figure of 16,000 was probably an optimistic estimate. In the 1922 referendum the total vote of the Alliance's locals was about 6,200. The original estimate may have referred to 1920 when the railroad employment was at its peak.

93. *Proceedings, Twentieth General Convention of the ASMWIA*, pp. 128–131.

94. *Proceedings, UA* (1913), p. 77.

95. Montgomery, *Industrial Relations in the Chicago Building Trades*, p. 130; *Journal*, April 1917, p. 8; August 1917, p. 10; February 1923, p. 12; *Proceedings, UA* (1924), p. 71.

96. *Journal*, June 1916, p. 10.

97. *Proceedings, Twentieth General Convention of the ASMWIA*, pp. 28–29.

98. Haber, *Industrial Relations in the Building Industry*, p. 182; *Agreements and Decisions Rendered Affecting the Building Industry*, April 1, 1965, pp. 81–82.

99. *Proceedings, UA* (1913), p. 168; Mangan, *History of the Steam Fitters' Protective Association*, p. 105; *Journal*, April 1920, p. 23; August 1921, p. 6; *Agreements and Decisions*, p. 84; Haber, *Industrial Relations in the Building Industry*, p. 182.

100. Montgomery, *Industrial Relations in the Chicago Building Trades*, p. 130; *Journal*, June 1923, p. 10; *Mechanical Engineers' Handbook*, Theodore Baumeister, ed., New York, 1958, pp. 9–40.

101. *Journal*, March 1924, p. 9; September 1924, p. 8; *Proceedings, AFL* (1924), pp. 83–84; *Proceedings, UA* (1924), p. 71.

102. *Agreements and Decisions*, p. 83; *Journal*, April 1920, p. 22.

103. *Journal*, September 1923, p. 8; *Agreements and Decisions*, p. 83.

104. *Journal*, December 1923, p. 6; March 1924, pp. 9–10; *Proceedings, UA* (1924), p. 71.

105. *Journal*, December 1906, p. 6; *Proceedings, UA* (1910), p. 137; (1913), p. 83; *Journal*, May 1917, p. 10; June 1917, p. 14; *Proceedings, UA* (1917), pp. 87–88; *Journal*, August 1917, p. 10; *Proceedings*, AFL (1913), pp. 188, 341–42.

106. *Proceedings, UA* (1917), p. 88; (1924), p. 71.

107. *Proceedings, AFL* (1913), pp. 188, 341–42; *Journal*, March 1914, p. 9; *Proceedings, AFL* (1914), pp. 303, 417; *Proceedings, AFL* (1915), pp. 130, 418; (1916), p. 128.

108. *Journal*, August 1919, p. 34; November 1919, p. 36; Mark Perlman, *The Machinists* (Cambridge: Harvard University Press, 1961), p. 243.

109. *Proceedings, AFL* (1920), pp. 293, 376–77; *Journal*, August 1920, p. 18; September 1920, p. 4; November 1920, p. 4; *Proceedings, AFL* (1921), pp. 140, 468; *Journal*, July 1921, p. 38; *Proceedings, AFL* (1922), pp. 133, 479; *Proceedings, UA* (1924), pp. 70–71.

110. Perlman, *The Machinists*, pp. 61, 243; *Proceedings, UA* (1938), pp. 110–11.

Chapter 9

1. Even prior to the founding of the UA the unionized pipe crafts had a paper that reported on the problems of the crafts and their organizations. This was *The Rasp, The Journeymen Plumbers, Gas Fitters and Steam Fitters Paper*, published in the late 1880's in Brooklyn by Philip Grace, an outstanding member of the Brooklyn assembly of NTA 85. At the second (1890) convention of the UA the delegates recognized as the organ of the union a paper called *The American Plumber*, published in Boston by Philip P. Connealy, one of the founders of the UA. The convention then allocated $60 for the support of the paper. This arrangement was not continued, however, in the following year, and a new effort was made in 1892 when the fourth (Minneapolis) convention authorized the Secretary to publish a paper for the UA. The first issue of the *United Association Journal* appeared on October 15, 1892. The paper was published through August 1896 when its publication was suspended under the impact of the depressed financial conditions of the UA. *The Journal* was started

again in September 1898 and has been published continuously ever since. *Proceedings, UA* (1890), p. 97; (1893), p. 2; (1897), p. 27; *Journal,* September 1898, p. 1.

2. The delegates to UA conventions were normally careful to make sure that the new laws would not reduce the power of the national convention as the court of last appeal. For instance, in 1924, the Committee on Laws recommended that a presidential order to consolidate two locals should be "final and conclusive, and not appealable." After a long debate — notable for an eloquent speech delivered against the proposal by George Meany — the convention defeated the Committee's recommendation. *Proceedings, UA* (1924), pp. 105–107.

3. *Proceedings, UA* (1924), p. 103. For similar expressions of businesslike attitude toward the problem of UA government see *Proceedings, UA* (1917) p. 122; (1921), pp. 99, 170, 135.

4. Another reason for the democratic nature of the UA may be found in the fact that the union was a multi-craft organization, with each craft deeply conscious of its own traditions and interests. The steam fitters, the sprinkler fitters (in the auxiliaries) and, at times, the gas fitters may be thus viewed as "structured subgroups" which retained basic loyalty to the UA but also had a separate existence, and could become (in convention caucuses or even especially organized meetings) relatively autonomous centers of power within the UA. The existence of such subgroups is viewed by some sociologists as making a major contribution to the preservation of pluralism and democracy within a larger organization. See "Union Democracy and Secondary Organization" by S. M. Lipset, M. A. Trow and J. S. Coleman in *American Social Pattern,* William Petersen, ed. (Garden City: New York, 1956, pp. 179–180 and *passim*).

5. "The master plumbers today throughout the United States and Canada are made up more or less of our ex-members" stated one of the delegates to the 1921 convention of the UA. *Proceedings, UA* (1921) p. 110. This was true to a lesser extent in steam fitting, but in that trade some prominent employers were former journeymen and union members. *Proceedings, UA* (1942), p. 68. For examples of various types of union actions helpful to the employers, see State of New York, *Intermediate Report of the Joint Legislative Committee on Housing,* Legislative Document (1922) No. 60, Albany 1922, pp. 101, 106; *Journal,* May 1924, p. 11; Royal E. Montgomery, *Industrial Relations in the Chicago Building Trades* (Chicago, 1927), p. 206.

6. UA jurisdiction over pipe fitting was also well established in Canada. By the end of 1924, the UA had 37 local unions there. The membership consisted of all the pipe trades — plumbers, steam fitters, gas fitters, sprinkler fitters, railroad fitters, and others. Some of the Canadian locals had been affiliated with the UA since the early 1890's (Local Union 46 Toronto). However, throughout the period covered by this study, the Canadian unions had to face many special problems related to the economic and legal conditions of their country, and, as a result, they played only a limited role in influencing the major policies of the UA.

7. In June 1938 at the trough of the 1937–1938 recession — and after a period of many years of depression — the UA had 47,450 members in good standing and an additional 6,536 members who were less than one year behind in their dues. If these members are counted — as they probably should be in view of the time to which the count refers — total UA membership was slightly

larger than that reported during the prosperous year of the 1924 convention. In June 1938, the UA also had over a million dollars in its treasury. This condition existed despite the fact that during the depressed years the union expended on it various benefits and on its organizational activity several hundred thousand dollars more than it was able to collect from the locals, and despite the fact that it had not imposed any national assessment since 1922. The main explanation was that prior to the economic depression the union had about $1,800,000 in its various funds, and that these funds were conservatively managed. *Proceedings, UA* (1938) pp. 40, 45, 58; (1928), p. 77. For the record of the dramatic rise in membership after 1940, see *Proceedings, UA* (1942), p. 32.

INDEX

Alliance. *See* Sheet Metal Workers' Alliance

Alpine, John, 79, 81, 83, 85–86, 150–155 *passim*, 195, 230, n6; presidency of 84, 86–87 *passim*, 88, 94, 149–150; and railroad fitters, 195; and sheet metal workers, 200; and sprinkler fitters, 138, 153; and steam fitters' helpers, 140; and war effort work, 149–150

Amalgamated Sheet Metal Workers' International Alliance. *See* Sheet Metal Workers' Alliance

Amalgamated Society of Journeymen Plumbers and Gas Fitters of the City of New York, 48–49, 59, 101–103

American Federation of Labor: and affiliation of UA, 58–59; and railroad pipe fitters, 193–200 *passim*; and UA-IA conflict, 114–127 *passim*

    Building Trades Department: and Chicago interunion dispute, 130; Pittsburgh agreement and UA-IA conflict, 122–127 *passim*

American Plumber, 235–236, nl

Appeals, Committee on, 94. *See also* Conventions, as courts of last appeal

Apprentices and helpers, gas fitters and "fixture hangers," 9

    In the plumbing craft, 9–10; problem of regulation of, concern of unions, 22, 36–37; conditions of, in Chicago and New York, 57; considered a national issue, 22, 37–38, 55, 138–140, 209–210; difficulties and failure of UA to deal with, 55–57, 138–140 *passim*; local policies and changes in provisions for, 139, 184–185; New York strike (1886) over, 29; joint programs of training (Cleveland and Chicago), 185–187 *passim*

    In steam (and hot water) fitting, 8–9; attitude change of UA on, 139–140; abolition of, in Chicago, 184, 187–188, 190; difficulties in elimination of, 189–191; helpers' locals, 131, 189; joint programs of training (Chicago and Memphis), 187–191

Atlantic City, New Jersey, conventions: (1924) 159–160, 163, 172–173, 191, 236, n2, (1928) 173–174

Baltimore agreement, 195–196, 197

Benefits: early provisions for, 45–46; need for integrated system of, 69–70, 71–72, 92; paid to locals, 155; reforms (1902–1906) in, 72–74, 75–77 *passim*, 83; suspension of payments for, 154–157 *passim*

Birmingham, Alabama, convention of 1904, 77–79, 82, 97, 137, 139

Boiler makers' dispute, 201–202

Boston, Massachusetts: problem of initiation fees in, 95; and UA-IA conflict, 126, 131. *See also* Conventions Boston (1913)

Brass pipe, 5, 7

Brotherhood of Railway Carmen, 193–194 *passim*

Buffalo, New York: convention of 1901, 69–70, 71, 74, 99, 137, 144–145; plumbers' strike (1895), 45–46

Building trades. *See* Construction industries

Burke, Thomas, 71, 75, 181; in the New York conflict, 106–107; elected organizer, 79, 84, 88; elected secretary-treasurer, 88, 151, 154, 155, 190, 206; on traveling members, 98

Canada, 42, 179, 198, 236, n6; Toronto convention of 1906, 82, 83–84, 88

Chicago, Illinois: apprentice regulations (early), 57; early locals in, 19–21 *passim*; joint NTA 85–IAPSG convention in, 26–28; interunion dispute (1911), 128–131; locals, and UA management, 80, 81, 82; Marshall Field building, 125; official headquarters of UA, 50; Pipe Trades Council, 130–131; output of plumbers' joint program of apprenticeship, 187; plumbers' union chartered as Local 130, 49–50, 82; plumbers fight "materials clauses," 144; sprinkler fitters' affiliation with

WERTHEIM PUBLICATIONS IN INDUSTRIAL RELATIONS

PUBLISHED BY HARVARD UNIVERSITY PRESS

Daniel L. Horowitz, *The Italian Labor Movement*, 1963

Adolf Sturmthal, *Workers Councils: A Study of Workplace Organization on Both Sides of the Iron Curtain*, 1964

Vernon H. Jensen, *Hiring of Dock Workers and Employment Practices in the Ports of New York, Liverpool, London, Rotterdam, and Marseilles*, 1964

John L. Blackman, Jr., *Presidential Seizures in Labor Disputes*, 1967

Mary Lee Ingbar and Lester D. Taylor, *Hospital Costs in Massachusetts: An Econometric Survey*, 1968

STUDIES IN LABOR-MANAGEMENT HISTORY

Lloyd Ulman, *The Rise of the National Trade Union: The Development and Significance of Its Structure, Governing Institutions, and Economic Policies*, 1955

Joseph P. Goldberg, *The Maritime Story: A Study in Labor-Management Relations, 1957*, 1958

Walter Galenson, *The CIO Challenge to the AFL: A History of the American Labor Movement, 1935–1941*, 1960

Morris A. Horowitz, *The New York Hotel Industry: A Labor Relations Study*, 1960

Mark Perlman, *The Machinists: A New Study in Trade Unionism*, 1961

Fred C. Munson, *Labor Relations in the Lithographic Industry*, 1963

Garth L. Mangum, *The Operating Engineers: The Economic History of a Trade Union*, 1964

David Brody, *The Butcher Workmen: A Study of Unionization*, 1964

F. Ray Marshall, *Labor in the South*, 1967

Philip Taft, *Labor Politics American Style: The California State Federation of Labor*, 1968

Martin Segal, *The Rise of the United Association: National Unionism in the Pipe Trades, 1884–1924*, 1969

PUBLISHED BY MC GRAW-HILL

Robert J. Alexander, *Labor Relations in Argentina, Brazil, and Chile*, 1961

Carl M. Stevens, *Strategy and Collective Bargaining Negotiations*, 1963

John T. Dunlop and Vasilii P. Diatchenko, *Labor Productivity*, 1964

James G. Scoville, *The Job Content of the U.S. Economy, 1940–1970*, 1969

John T. Dunlop and Nikolay P. Fedorenko, *Planning and Markets: Modern Trends in Various Economic Systems*, 1969